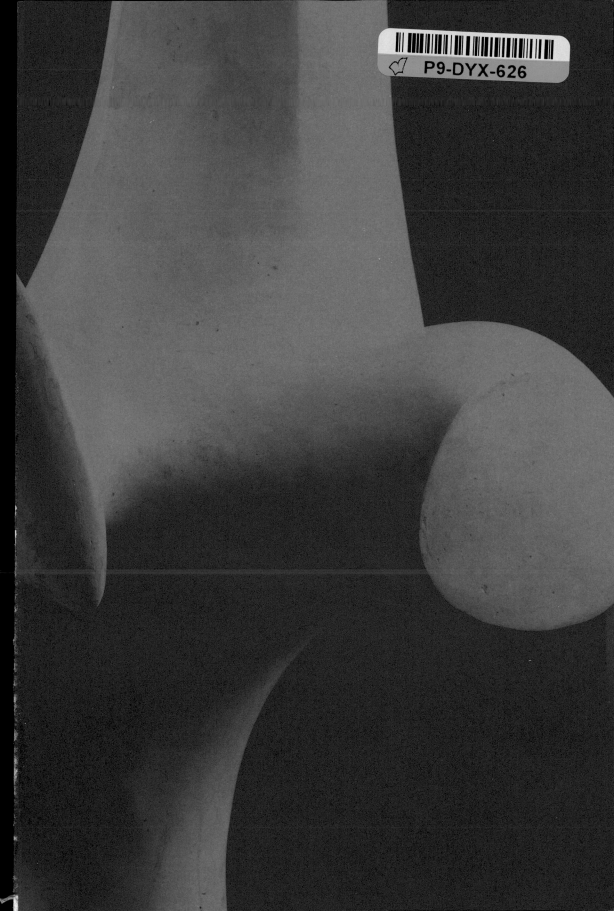

Art Gallery of Ontario
Musée des beaux-arts de l'Ontario
Toronto

Art Gallery of Ontario

Selected Works

The Art Gallery of Ontario is generously funded by the Ontario Ministry of Culture and Communications. Additional financial support is received from the Municipality of Metropolitan Toronto (Cultural Affairs Division), Communications Canada and The Canada Council.

The Art Gallery of Ontario gratefully acknowledges the financial support of the Government of Ontario through the Ministry of Culture and Communications for this publication.

This book illustrates 350 of the thousands of works in the AGO's permanent collection. For reasons of space and conservation requirements, it cannot always be guaranteed that an object illustrated will be on display.

Editor's Note

All dimensions for works of art are given in centimetres. For two-dimensional works, height precedes width; for works of three dimensions, measurements are given as height by width by depth or length.

The numbers that follow the credit line are accession numbers, assigned by the AGO to each work that enters the permanent collection.

Nationality for all artists is given as country of birth except for artists of Canadian historical works, whose nationality is given as Canadian.

Printed in Canada

Graphic design by Bruce Mau

Canadian Cataloguing in Publication Data
Art Gallery of Ontario
        Art Gallery of Ontario : selected works
Issued also in French under title: Musée des beaux-arts de l'Ontario : oeuvres choisies
ISBN 0-919777-79-1

1. Art Gallery of Ontario – Catalogs. 2. Art, European – Ontario – Toronto – Catalogs. 3. Art, Canadian – Ontario – Toronto – Catalogs. I. Title.
N910.T6A55 1990   708.11'3541   C90-093015-2

ISBN 0-919777-77-5

Contents

Acknowledgements

This illustrated handbook is one of the most effective means available to the Art Gallery of Ontario to fulfill its responsibility to the public to make the collections more accessible. It also provides a way of meeting our obligation to donors to make the collections better known. Finally, this book presents the Gallery and its holdings to a wider audience as an important centre of study, research, pleasure and contemplation, thus assisting us in our efforts to realize our mission of bringing art and people together.

A project of this magnitude necessarily involves the help and support of many people. The selection of the works from the permanent collection was done judiciously by the curators at the Art Gallery of Ontario. We are grateful to David McTavish, former curator of European painting and sculpture, for supervising the project and for his excellent entries on our Old Masters. Catherine Van Baren, senior editor at the AGO, coordinated all aspects of the project from start to finish and completed the editing. We thank her especially for her perseverance and her dedication to this project.

The professional staff of the Art Gallery of Ontario's Curatorial Division made this book possible by contributing their expert knowledge, their time and their support to this important project. Roald Nasgaard, deputy director and chief curator, is to be thanked for completing the supervision of this project and for writing several of the international contemporary entries. Christina Ritchie, assistant curator of international contemporary art, researched and wrote the bulk of the entries in this area.

Katharine Lochnan, curator of prints and drawings, Dennis Reid, curator of Canadian historical art, and Philip Monk, curator of contemporary Canadian art, ably supervised the research and writing of the entries in their respective areas. Alan Wilkinson, curator of twentieth century art, contributed entries on Henry Moore and early Modern European sculpture and painting. Michèle Thériault, assistant curator of contemporary Canadian art, and Michael Parke-Taylor, assistant curator of prints and drawings, completed several entries in their respective areas. Barbara Fischer, former assistant curator of contemporary art, contributed to the contemporary Canadian entries. Maia-Mari Sutnik, coordinator of Photographic Services at the AGO, wrote on the photographic works in the collection. The entries on Inuit art were supplied by Curator Norman Zepp, who wishes to acknowledge the contribution of Jean Blodgett, whose writings in the Klamer collection catalogue provided the basis for those entries.

The AGO owes a special debt to the following people, who researched and wrote entries on a freelance basis: Brenda Rix, former assistant curator of prints and drawings, who completed the majority of the print and drawing entries; Kim Sloan, who contributed the entries on British watercolours; Ann Cameron, who conducted research for some of the Old Master entries; Megan Duffin, who assisted in the research for the European sculpture entries; Phileen Tattersall and Alina Payne, who researched a number of the European paintings; and both Karen Finlay, former assistant curator of European painting and sculpture, and David Wistow, education officer/writer at the AGO, for the entry on Augustus John. Robert Stacey and Tom Smart did excellent work in writing the Canadian historical entries. Marie Maltais is to be thanked for several entries in the contemporary Canadian area, while Anna Hudson contributed many of the contemporary Canadian entries and several entries on Modern European painting.

All the curators at the AGO and freelance writer/curator Robert Stacey are to be acknowledged for their contribution to the introduction.

The staff of the AGO's Photographic Services department reliably met the enormous demands of coordinating and completing all of the photography of the works included in this book. We are grateful to Faye Van Horne for coordinating the photography of so many works and to Karen Heffernan and Felicia Cukier for their assistance. Carlo Catenazzi is to be acknowledged for expertly photographing the works; he was ably assisted by William Wilson, Brenda Dereniuk and Sean Weaver. Maia-Mari Sutnik is to be thanked for obtaining permission to reproduce many of the works.

The staff of the Technical Services and Conservation departments are also acknowledged for their efforts in examining, measuring, repairing and transporting the works of art included in the book. The Registration department, especially Sandi McKessock, provided all the information contained in the captions. Wendy Hebditch accurately and expertly input onto computer and proofread the entire manuscript. Terry Hicks and Magda Kryt assisted in the copy editing and proofreading. Mara Meikle, assistant to the chief curator, lent a helping hand in coordinating various aspects of this project. Elizabeth Addison, marketing and communications director, and Noni Regan, art support director, are also to be thanked for providing their professional advice throughout all stages of the project.

We are especially grateful to Margaret Machell, former archivist at the AGO, for reading the introductory essay and making helpful suggestions and for her significant research on the Gallery's history.

Alan Terakawa, head of the Publications and Design department, contributed his expertise and considerable effort in the production of this book. Micheline Sainte-Marie and Jacques Goulet at Les textes au point in Montreal, in consultation with Professor Émile Seutin, completed an excellent translation of the manuscript into Canada's other official language. The Gallery thanks Bruce Mau for the fine design of this publication. We also acknowledge the special efforts of all those who were involved in the production of a book in which we can all take enormous pride.

William J. Withrow
Director, Art Gallery of Ontario

Figure 1: Group-of-Seven artist Arthur Lismer conduct-
ing a children's outdoor sketching class in Grange Park
in 1934. He had begun running the art school three
years earlier. Now known as the Anne Tanenbaum Gallery
School, the centre is still run by professional artists
today, with approximately 1000 students of all ages
enrolled in more than 60 courses a year.

Introduction

All art museums are products of their particular circumstances of location and creation. Like the communities alongside which it develops, every major gallery is unique in its own way, yet all galleries are the same in at least one regard. However universal the aspirations of the collectors, curators and directors whose individual tastes are reflected in the holdings by which an art institution comes to be known, the specifics of place and time, economics and history, race and nationality determine the character of the building and its contents, and can never fully be erased. Nor should we want them to be, for it is these shaping factors that give galleries and museums their identities, setting each on its own, the better to find its own role in the evolving larger culture of which it is a part.

In his introduction to the previous handbook of the Art Gallery of Ontario, published in 1974 to coincide with the opening of the first stage of a major renovation and rebuilding program, then Chief Curator Richard Wattenmaker observed that

> Each museum contains a unique cross-section of the cultural heritage of past and/or present civilizations, and the individual works interrelate in special ways that cannot be duplicated precisely by any other collection. There is a distinct randomness to the formation of museum collections which ebbs and flows according to the tastes and finances of each generation which guides it, with no single institution able to have the ideal selection of works from any

period or tradition. Once a gallery reaches a certain level of consistency, its collection tends to take on a unified interrelatedness which is the result of both the process of natural selection, geography and a conscious intention to augment strengths or emphases which have become manifest in the course of time.

Thus, in the AGO of today, we can still detect traces not only of the conservatism and thrift of the founders and the sometimes vexed relationships between the Gallery and its various constituencies, but also the daring and initiative of certain idealists who stared down the nay-sayers and set a lasting example of far-sighted generosity to their successors. Even the radical changes of the past few decades can be seen as the inevitable outcome of decisions made and conditions faced by the representatives of *fin-de-siècle* Toronto who defied the formidable odds against their collective project. As the Gallery prepares for another turning of the century, a look back at its earliest beginnings is in order.

Origins and Beginnings

The origins of the Art Gallery of Ontario date back to well before its formal inauguration as the Art Museum of Toronto in 1900. The need felt by the leading citizens and artists of the burgeoning provincial capital for a public facility dedicated to the collecting and exhibiting of art both historical and contemporary, foreign and Canadian, had been recognized over a half-century before by the Chief Superintendent of Education, Dr. Egerton Ryerson. The Educational Museum of Upper Canada, which opened in the Normal School at St. James Square, Toronto, in 1857 (the same year, incidentally, that saw the establishment of the globally imitated Educational Museum in South Kensington, London), was established "with a view to encourage the Fine Arts in Canada." It originally housed the results of Ryerson's two

European collecting tours, undertaken in 1855 and 1856, during which
he acquired over 200 paintings and engravings (most of them copies
of Old Masters) and nearly 1,000 plaster casts of antique statuary.

By 1875 the museum's mandate to display "objects of taste" for
educative purposes had expanded to include the collecting of works
by living Canadian artists. Thanks to the lobbying efforts of the
Ontario Society of Artists, the Ontario Ministry of Education entered
a new agreement with the OSA in 1895, which led to the formation
of "a Canadian Art Gallery in the Education Department," otherwise
known as the Provincial Art Gallery. The Education Department's
tripartite program of annual purchases from OSA exhibitions continued until 1914, by which time another institution better suited to
such activities – the Art Museum of Toronto – had initiated its own
collecting policy and was well on its way to becoming a force in the
Canadian art world second only to the National Gallery of Canada.
If the NGC can trace its roots to the founding of the Royal Canadian
Academy in Ottawa in 1880, the present AGO, for its part, is an out-
growth of the OSA, which held its first exhibition in Toronto in 1872.

The inadequacy of the OSA's own quarters at 165 King St. W.,
and of the space provided for the yearly shows mounted by the society
at the Provincial Art Gallery from 1897 to 1912, combined with the
desire for a more arm's-length arrangement with the Ontario government, brought together artists and patrons during the early spring of
1900 to consider the formation of an Art Museum Association. The
convenor of the Art Museum Committee, struck in March 1900, was
the painter and teacher G.A. Reid, then president of the OSA; another
artist, Robert F. Gagen, was appointed secretary, and Byron E. (later
Sir Edmund) Walker was elected chairman. Leading the "subscribers"
at the first meeting of this council were citizens with such Social
Register names as Walker, Flavelle, Cox, Mackenzie, Massey and
Nicholls – names that, along with Osler and Ellis, would figure with

Figure 2: The Grange, later to become the Art Museum of Toronto's first permanent home, was built between 1817 and 1820 by D'Arcy Boulton, Jr. This view was probably painted in the mid-1870s, when the house was occupied by Goldwin Smith and his wife Harriette, widow of William Henry Boulton (who was D'Arcy's second son).

Henri Perré (Canadian, 1828-90) *The Grange*; watercolour on paper, 31.8 x 53.3 cm. AGO, Goldwin Smith Collection.

those of the principal early benefactors of the Gallery. Other founder-members included such prominent critics and connoisseurs of the day as E.F.B. Johnston and Prof. James Mavor.

Collecting the Buildings

The Art Museum Committee identified as its first and most pressing objective the locating of a central site for the proposed new structure. It was frustrated in this design, unfortunately, by the lack of an available or affordable property on which to build. Without a permanent facility, active collecting had to be postponed.

Confronted with the need to house the pictures, statuary and *objets d'art* that private benefactions were beginning to bring in, the Museum in 1909 opted for the loan of temporary quarters in the Toronto Public Library, at College and St. George streets. Also in 1909, William Cruikshank, a veteran painter and teacher, donated a book of his own pen-and-ink sketches – effectively the future AGO's first Canadian acquisition.

The deed by Mrs. Goldwin Smith of The Grange, along with six acres of land, allowed the realization of plans dating back to 1902, when Edmund Walker had outlined to Harriette and Goldwin Smith his idea of using the Grange land as the site for the nascent Art Museum of Toronto. The conditions of Mrs. Smith's will and an agreement entered into with the City of Toronto in 1911 affirmed that the grounds of this historic property would be used as a public park, that the house would be restored as a memorial to the Smiths, and that the mayor and city council would approve a moderate grant permitting the commencement of construction of a gallery building immediately to the north of The Grange. The latter, meanwhile, was occupied by the Central Ontario School of Art and Industrial Design, incorporated as the Ontario College of Art in 1912. (The relationship of the two institutions would long be an intimate one, thanks not only to their physical proximity, which continued when the OCA moved to its G.A. Reid-designed new quarters to the east of The Grange in 1921, but also to the 1912 decision to appoint two members of the Museum to the College's council.)

Built between 1817 and 1820 by D'Arcy Boulton, Jr., The Grange is Toronto's oldest remaining brick dwelling (fig. 2). Having been altered in the 1840s to reflect the growing prestige of its owners, the classically proportioned English-style manor was restored between 1967 and 1973 to represent a gentleman's house of the period 1837-40. It was during the 1830s and 1840s that The Grange came into its own as the hub of Toronto's social and cultural circles. This status was subsequently enhanced by the occupancy of Goldwin Smith and his wife Harriette (*née* Dixon) – the widow of D'Arcy Boulton, Jr.'s second son, William Henry – in the year of their marriage, 1875 (figs. 10, 11). Though Smith advocated Canada's commercial union with the U.S., he also strongly supported the nationalist aspirations of the "Confederation School" of Canadian painters and their juniors in the OSA. His art collection, which consisted mostly of copies but which included two authenticated Guardi *capricci*, formed one of the bases of the future Gallery's permanent collection. Hence the appropriateness of Edmund Walker's appeal to the Smiths for the dedication of their home to the cause of a public art museum for Toronto. Their legacy is commemorated in the seal of the Art Gallery of Toronto, which also incorporates the arms of the Boultons and the Dixons.

In April 1911 a committee was appointed to consider plans for the erection of the first section of the proposed art museum, and the following November the City of Toronto agreed to contribute $5,000 per annum toward its upkeep. Following the appointment of E.R. Grieg as curator, secretary and treasurer of the museum in 1912, The Grange was formally opened in June 1913, but the onset of WWI in

Figure 3: Darling and Pearson's original concept (which was never built) for the proposed Art Gallery of Toronto, drawn by S.H. Maw in 1914. The building was to have been a two-storey structure (running the length of Dundas Street from McCaul to Beverley streets), with interconnected galleries grouped around three court-yards: a central sculpture court, flanked by Italian and English gardens. An art school was to have occupied the left wing of the Gallery. The back of The Grange is visible at the upper centre of this bird's-eye view.

Over, Figure 4: Joint exhibition of the Royal Canadian Academy and the Ontario Society of Artists, held in the three galleries in the first wing of the new Art Gallery of Toronto, April 1918.

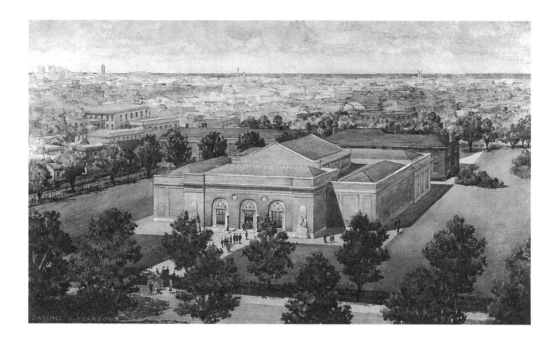

Figure 5: S.H. Maw's bird's-eye view in watercolour of Darling and Pearson's concept for the 1924 addition, which opened on January 29, 1926. Besides the central sculpture courtyard, the building featured galleries on three sides, an entrance hallway, cloakrooms, and a print gallery on the second floor. Two additional galleries were built in 1935.

1914 interrupted plans for the erection of new galleries (fig. 3). The situation became desperate when the Toronto Public Library Board informed its tenant that the rooms it occupied were needed for storage space, and that it would have to vacate the premises. Spurred on by this crisis, the architect selected to draw up plans for the proposed building, Frank Darling, in 1916 submitted drawings and estimates for the small section of the new gallery approved for construction, the cost of which was not to exceed $75,000.

Work got underway with surprising alacrity, and on April 4, 1918, the first wing of the projected complex, consisting of three rooms running along the north side of The Grange, was opened to the public. This event was accompanied by a change in curatorial policy: whereas, before, artists were permitted exhibitions, the cost to be borne by the exhibitors, now these solo shows were to be "especially of a retrospective character," and current works of living artists were to be exhibited in groups of at least three. Nonetheless, professional artists from the start figured prominently on the board and on the acquisition and exhibition committees of the museum.

Nineteen-eighteen also witnessed the adopting of the new name of the Art Gallery of Toronto, to avoid confusion with the Royal Ontario Museum, formally established in 1912 as part of the University of Toronto. In 1965 a further name change, to the Art Gallery of Ontario, was made to reflect the broadening of the Gallery's mandate to serve the entire province.

The growth of the collections and the success of appeals to the beneficence of civic-minded members of Toronto's élite after WWI necessitated further expansion, which the architectural firm of Darling and Pearson was engaged to carry out in 1925. The concept called for the flanking of a central court for the exhibiting of sculpture with two sets of rectangular galleries, and a new entrance on Dundas Street (fig. 5). This reorientation onto the busy thoroughfare and

the realignment of the Gallery along Dundas between McCaul and
Beverley streets affirmed the AGT's acceptance of its public responsibility, even though it continued to rely on private benefactors not only
for collection-building but for capital projects.

Each phase of the new program was to bear the name of the
donor who made it possible or whose contributions deserved com-
memoration: the Walker Sculpture Court, dedicated to the memory of
the late Sir Edmund Walker (fig. 7), and the Fudger Memorial Galleries, financed by Mr. H.H. Fudger as a memorial for his son, were
both officially opened in January 1926. In 1933 the two galleries to the
east of the sculpture court were renamed the Leonard Gallery and
Rotunda in honour of another benefactor, Reuben Wells Leonard,
whose gift of $10,000 enabled the Gallery to acquire twenty-nine
Canadian paintings, and from whose estate in 1930 the Gallery had
received a memorial fund that allowed it to add to the European
collection. Outstanding among the gifts of the Reuben Wells Leonard
Estate is Nicolas Poussin's *Venus, Mother of Aeneas*, of c.1635.

By the early 1930s, the lingering effects of the Depression required
the search for other sources of support, with state and civic funding
being solicited to augment a dwindling supply of private largesse.
Grants of $7,500 each from the City of Toronto and the Provincial and
Dominion governments, matched by an equivalent sum from the
T. Eaton Company, permitted the erection in 1933 of the Margaret
Eaton and Wood Memorial galleries, the latter of which was named
after philanthropists, E.R. and Frank P. Wood. Darling, Pearson and
Cleveland acted as architects on these two additions, both of which
were demolished in the early 1970s to make way for the linking of the
modern expansion projects known as Stage I and Stage II.

This ambitious undertaking was conceived in 1968 by the
Toronto architect John C. Parkin to allow for three successive building stages. The first of these, completed in 1974, wrapped around

the original structure and provided the Gallery with a modern physical plant featuring new offices, art storage, workshops, a restaurant, and exhibition space – including the rededicated Margaret Eaton and F.P. Wood galleries and the large Zacks Wing (so named in recognition of a major gift made to the Stage I capital campaign by Sam and Ayala Zacks). What captured the public imagination, however, was the Henry Moore Sculpture Centre (fig. 9), designed to house the large collection of original plasters, bronzes, prints and drawings donated by the artist. This facility placed the AGO at the forefront of international centres dedicated to the exhibition and study of 20th-century sculpture.

Stage II, again carried out by Parkin Partnership, Architects and Planners, opened in 1977. Carrying the Gallery westward toward Beverley Street, it provided much-needed space for the Canadian Historical, Canadian Contemporary, and Print and Drawing collections, and homes for the E.P. Taylor Reference Library and Audio-Visual Centre, and the world-renowned Gallery School, established in 1931 by Arthur Lismer and in 1989 renamed the Anne Tanenbaum Gallery School (fig. 1).

Although Stage II allowed the Gallery to accept and mount major touring exhibitions, which in turn raised its profile both at home and abroad, the 1968 concept called for the completion of a further stage to meet long-term space and storage requirements. This had to be postponed for economic reasons, and planning for Stage III did not resume until 1982. The program called for the provision of fifty percent more art-display space, including a gallery of Inuit art, contemporary galleries, an indoor sculpture court, a new print and drawing centre, a new library, new storage vaults, and expanded facilities for technical workshops, offices, conservation studios, and retail operations.

The winner of the Stage III architectural competition, held in

1987, was the internationally respected firm of Barton Myers Associates (fig. 6). After clearing several serious obstacles, construction of Stage III finally commenced in the fall of 1989 and is scheduled for completion in 1992.

Building the Collections

Any public gallery is ultimately the sum of its holdings, and although the modern art museum is as much a community centre as an exhibiting and collecting institution, its principal objective still is to acquire, conserve, display and elucidate individual works of human creation. While all galleries are to a greater or lesser extent expressions of the curators who ensure that these functions are carried out, they are also the barometers of the cultural climates in which they either flourish or languish. Especially in their formative phases, they are dependent for their very existence not only on what the private sector considers worthy of esteem, but on what is available for it to select from, to cherish — and to donate.

Turn-of-the-century Toronto has been described as reactionary if not philistine in its tastes and its politics, but lately this gloomy picture has been subject to reassessment. Certainly the city's collectors were fewer and less adventuresome than those of Montreal, but in many ways the ground on which the seeds of Toronto's visual culture were strewn proved to be more fertile than that of the rival city, as subsequent history has demonstrated.

The enlightened amateurism and administrative improvisation typical of all Canadian art institutions during the first decades of existence had both its good and its bad points. However much they may have complained about being ignored in favour of deceased foreign artists, Toronto painters, sculptors and printmakers were able to influence the decision-making process by sitting on boards and

Figure 6: Model of the Stage III expansion, design by Barton Myers Associates. As Myers's "design philosophy" statement explains: "The expansion attempts to revalue the historical layers of the building and to make a coherent composition of the elements of the existing building in combination with the new components. The result is clear and composite, a reinforcement and an enhancement of the Art Gallery of Ontario, and a strong statement of the contemporary values of the institution."

committees, by electing their numbers to prominent positions within the management structure, and by virtue of their professional societies' access to annual slots in the Art Gallery of Toronto's exhibition schedule. The relatively small and united art community also benefitted from close social (and sometimes business) contacts among themselves, and with Gallery staff, and the collectors who so largely controlled the agenda. With few commercial galleries in which to show and sell their work, local artists had to maintain friendly relations with the only public gallery at their disposal — and vice versa, since the Gallery needed a source of art to build its collection. The success of the Group of Seven in becoming Canada's national landscape school cannot be dissociated, for instance, from the support shown to its members by the Gallery not only at the time of its first exhibition, held at the AGT in May 1920, but long before and after.

The pattern established in the 1910s and 1920s continued throughout the next two decades. The successor to the first curator E.R. Grieg (1912-28), Fred Haines (1928-32), was a painter and teacher, and his replacement, Martin Baldwin (1932-47), was by profession an architect. The Gallery hired its first fine-arts-trained curator only in 1948, when Sidney Key, an expert on British painting, succeeded Baldwin, who was appointed director. Baldwin served in that capacity until 1961, when he was replaced by William Withrow — who would hold this position for the next thirty years. After 1948, as elsewhere throughout the art world, all curators in all departments would be academically accredited specialists in their respective fields.

This increasing reliance on curatorial expertise in the areas of collecting and organizing exhibitions had the inevitable effect of diminishing the roles of professional (and amateur) artists in controlling the policies and operations of the Gallery. A compelling factor in this transition was the steady, sometimes dramatic climb in salesroom and auction prices for artworks, particularly those by Old Masters.

By mid-century, the big private collections from which the AGT drew
the core of its permanent holdings had all passed into public hands or
been dispersed, and many of the treasures accepted into the Gallery
on trust or on *prima facie* evidence were undergoing critical scrutiny
as to authorship and provenance. No longer could the advice and
opinions of donors, dealers and artists automatically be relied upon to
verify the authenticity or value of gifts and purchases. With greater
accountability to the public and to posterity came a certain loss of
innocence and of fellowship with the Toronto art community out of
which, after all, the Gallery had evolved.

Until the appointment of Sidney Key (who served until 1954),
the Executive Committee and Council were responsible for all acquisitions. The bulk of these came from the exhibitions of the professional art associations – the RCA, the OSA, the Canadian Art Club, and
subsequently such societies as the Canadian Society of Graphic Art
and the Canadian Society of Painters in Watercolour – to which the
Gallery had first choice and from each of which were usually purchased
one or two works. Since artists who belonged to these groups were
advantageously positioned on the Executive Committee, which recommended acquisitions to the Council, a degree of cronyism was involved
in the shaping of the Gallery's Canadian Collection. But the system
worked surprisingly well until the 1960s – a fact to which the manifest
strengths of this collection, second only to that of the National Gallery of Canada, provide ample testimony. Balancing conservative and
advanced views, these juries-of-peers more often than not ensured that
the Gallery bought the best, or at least the most representative, artworks of the era. Also weighing in favour of this aspect of collecting
was the relative inexpensiveness of contemporary Canadian pictures and
sculptures, and the occasional availability of special acquisition funds.

Not until 1951 were the Canadian and Non-Canadian Collection
committees struck, to be followed, in 1953, by the American Fund,

renamed the Canadian-American Committee in 1960, and the Contemporary Collection Committee, in 1962. Only in 1969-70 was the committee structure further altered to reflect the growth of the collections in the areas of contemporary Canadian art and European Old Masters. The next two decades saw the hiving-off or creation of several new committees and departments: the Henry Moore Committee, in 1973; the Canadian Historical Collection Committee, in 1974; the Print and Drawing Collection Committee, in 1977; and the Contemporary Canadian Committee, in 1982. In 1988 the Inuit Collection Committee was formed.

When the Art Gallery of Toronto became the Art Gallery of Ontario in 1965, it expanded its mandate to include special exhibitions that travelled to communities across the province, and a visiting artists' program. Originally, the Extension Services department was affiliated with the Education Branch, but was absorbed into the Curatorial Division in 1981.

European Art Before 1965

The European Collection, perhaps more than any other aspect of the Gallery, mirrors in its genesis and metamorphoses the nature of the Toronto collecting community, its prejudices and passions, its frugality, its resistance to change, and its occasional willingness to take real risks. By contrast, its more numerous, more cosmopolitan, and generally wealthier Montreal counterpart had begun, by 1900, to acquire canvases by the French Impressionists and Post-Impressionists; such, after all, was the milieu from which the first modern Canadian painter, J.W. Morrice, had emerged. The connoisseurs of the anglophone and anglophile government, business and communications capital of Ontario favoured, on the other hand, the 18th-and 19th-century British portrait, genre and landscape painters, in addition to the more contemporary Barbizon, Hague and Glasgow schools. Little wonder, then, that examples of such work should have figured so prominently among the gifts and bequests offered to the fledgling gallery by the magnates and local gentry, who also tended to serve on its acquisitions and exhibition committees.

It was not until 1906 that the Museum purchased its first canvas, E.R. Hornel's *The Captive Butterfly*, from its first loan exhibition, *Pictures by Glasgow Painters*, held at the OSA Gallery. This acquisition, undoubtedly reflecting the influence of the expatriate Scots political economist and writer James Mavor, set a pattern for the privileging of British art that would not be broken until the 1950s. Five years later, again in what the committee no doubt considered a bold step, a work by another contemporary European painter was selected for purchase by subscription: Henri Le Sidaner's *Le pavillon, crépuscule, Lago Maggiore*. Both the Canadian and European collections benefitted from the decision made in 1912 to augment with annual purchases the "C.N.E. Art Loan Collection" loaned to the AGT by the Canadian National Exhibition. In order to attract the attention of potential donors by offering a public showcase for their possessions, the Gallery mounted the first of a series of loan exhibitions in 1909 that displayed artworks from private collections alongside pictures borrowed from other North American museums. By this means, potential benefactors could be subtly cajoled into doing for Toronto what the art patrons of Cleveland, Toledo, Boston and New York had done for their own cities. Among the first such exemplary figures were Senator George Cox, whose collection of Barbizon landscapes, a feature of the loan exhibition of 1909, was acquired as a donation from his son and daughter-in-law in 1926; Chester Massey, whose gift of 1916 consisted of Constable's early *Coming Storm*, a portrait by Henner, and a landscape by Corot; Mrs. W.M. Boultbee, who presented Boudin's *Trouville Harbour*, in 1919; and Sir Edmund Osler, who bequeathed his most important pictures in 1924, including a pair of portraits by Raeburn.

The opening of the new building in the winter of 1926, and the mounting of the inaugural exhibition, gave a new momentum to the Gallery's collecting activities. Some of the resulting acquisitions came through happy accidents, others through concerted campaigns, and still others through outside interventions. One such was that of C.T. Currelly, director of the Royal Ontario Museum, who secured for the AGT eleven pictures from the collection of Old Masters paintings – including representative views of Venice by Canaletto and Luca Carlevaris – formed by the English connoisseur, Dr. Ludwig Mond, the bulk of which collection had gone to the National Gallery, London. To take advantage of similar possibilities, the Gallery decided to retain as advisor the British painter, illustrator, designer and collector Charles Ricketts, who evidently saw no conflict in performing the same services for the National Gallery of Canada. Ricketts recom- mended the purchase of a half-length portrait by the 16th-century Italian master, Paris Bordone, and in 1928 successfully bid on Toronto's behalf for Rubens's c.1638 oil sketch, *The Elevation of the Cross*, from the sale of the celebrated Holford Collection of London.

The opening of the Walker Sculpture Court in 1926 can be seen as laying the foundations for the Henry Moore Sculpture Centre in 1974. It gave impetus to the serious exposition and collecting of sculp- ture by the Gallery, as evidenced by the acquisition of two works by Paul Manship, a bust by Jacob Epstein, and of several major pieces by Rodin. In the latter instance, one can detect the lingering influence on the acquisitions committee of James Mavor, who met the great Frenchman in 1900.

The pursuit of more contemporary French artists, in particular such Impressionists as Monet, Sisley and Pissarro, was deferred because of the scarcity of examples of their canvases in private hands, but these

Figure 7: The Walker Court, c.1950, showing sculptures by (among others) Auguste Rodin, Paul Manship and Ivan Mestrovic.

painters began to be included in loan exhibitions in the 1920s and 1930s and to enter the permanent collection in the 1940s and 1950s. Here the efforts of the Women's and Junior Women's (later the Volunteers') committees in fund-raising played a crucial role, for otherwise the Gallery could never have competed with foreign museums and individuals for such increasingly expensive pictures. No less valuable was the advice given by Dr. Harold Tovell and his wife Ruth Massey Tovell, who by the 1920s were in contact with the French avant-garde artist Raymond Duchamp-Villon (whose powerful portrait bust, *Baudelaire*, was donated by the Tovells' sons in their memory in 1962), and who were able to recommend purchases and to make important donations.

The focus of collecting remained, however, on earlier painting and sculptures; to acquire desirable examples of these the Gallery had to continue to depend on private benefactors. Of the latter, none proved more generous than Frank P. Wood, who more than any other individual shaped the European Collection from the 1920s to the 1930s. He did so not only through such gifts as fine portraits by Hals and Rembrandt, van Dyck's *Daedalus and Icarus*, Gainsborough's *The Harvest Waggon*, Sargent's *Portrait of Dr. Joseph Joachim*, and bronzes by Bourdelle, but through the donation of funds that allowed for the purchase of two canvases by Pissarro in 1933, and the Gallery's second Sisley, in 1934. Also in 1934, Wood — whose own preference was for the art of the 17th and 18th centuries — was involved in the purchasing of two canvases by Renoir and one each by Bonnard and Morrice. It was on Wood's advice that the first Impressionist painting to enter the collection, Monet's *Vétheuil in Summertime*, was bought by the Gallery in 1929. Finally, the Frank P. Wood Endowment allowed the purchase in 1956 of a magnificent Degas oil on canvas, *Woman in Bath*, of around 1892.

Few such triumphs could be counted in the 1950s; the gift by general subscription of Tintoretto's enormous *Christ Washing His*

Disciples' Feet, in 1959, and the bequest by W. Redelmeier of several 17th-century Dutch masters being perhaps the most noteworthy exceptions. The 1960s began auspiciously for the Gallery with the acquisition of a major altarpiece by Eustache Le Sueur, which had languished since early in the century in a Toronto boys' school. The decade witnessed a series of donations from Toronto collectors such as Gerald and Aileen Larkin, J.J. Vaughan, John Paris Bickell and Mrs. R.Y. Eaton, which helped to strengthen previously weak areas.

The identifying of these weaknesses and the devising of strategies to correct them increasingly fell to the curators and assistant curators who put their stamp on the Gallery during this transitional period. Curator Jean Sutherland Boggs (1962-64), who went on to become the director of the National Gallery of Canada, successfully recommended the purchase of a superb still life by Chardin and *The Fanatics of Tangier* by Delacroix in the first year of her tenure, which was also marked by the gift of Claude's enchanting *Coast View with the Embarkation of Carlo and Ubaldo*. Gaps in the 18th-and 19th-century holdings were filled with a pair of Roman *capricci* by Giovanni Paolo Panini and an early portrait by Jean-François Millet, while the last work to be recommended by Ricketts's successor as advisor, Anthony Blunt, Henry Fuseli's huge *Lear Banishing Cordelia*, provided the Gallery with a prime example of British early Romantic art. In 1964 Boggs organized the extremely popular *Picasso and Man* exhibition, from which the Gallery purchased the artist's *Seated Woman* of 1926-27.

Boggs's successor, David S. Brooke (1965-68), helped to build up the AGO's small collection of Italian Baroque paintings with Mattia Preti's large *St. Paul the Hermit*, and went on to organize the 1968 Tissot exhibition, from which the Gallery purchased *The Milliner's Shop* with the assistance of the Corporations' Subscription Fund. Concentration on the late 19th century continued with Chief Curator

Mario Amaya (1968-72), whose range of interests can be gauged from his acquisition of a large Renaissance altarpiece by Bartolommeo di Giovanni, and his coordinating the Toronto showing of the international exhibition, *The Sacred and Profane in Symbolist Art*, in 1969.

Richard Wattenmaker, the chief curator from 1972 to 1978, contributed to the strengthening of the French 18th-century section by recommending the purchase of Boucher's *Les Sabots*, but most tellingly revealed his curatorial hand with the *Puvis de Chavannes and the Modern Tradition* exhibition of 1975, from which *The Bathers* was bought. His successor, Roald Nasgaard, after buttressing the Gallery's representation of the earlier French schools with Simon Marmion's *The Mass of St. Gregory*, focused on another neglected field by mounting *The Mystic North: Symbolist Landscape Painting in Northern Europe and North America, 1890-1940* in 1984.

Toronto became a world centre for the study of small-scale bronzes by sculptors such as Foggini and Soldani-Benzi in 1982, when Margaret and Ian Ross offered to the Gallery their renowned collection of fifty Florentine Baroque sculptures as a joint gift and purchase. Earlier, the Rosses had donated a smaller collection of works of this school to the Royal Ontario Museum. Then, after a period of relative inactivity in the collecting of European paintings, the AGO received significant gifts from Joey and Toby Tanenbaum and Professor and Mrs. Gilbert Bagnani, among others, during David McTavish's term as the AGO's first curator of the European Painting and Sculpture Collection (1986-89). The Gallery was afforded an opportunity to buy its first French Neoclassical painting, Nicolas-André Monsiau's *Zeuxis Choosing His Models*, by a timely gift from the Volunteer Committee Fund in 1988. To oversee the continuing growth and deepening of the European Collection, the Gallery hired Janet Brooke as McTavish's replacement as curator of the department in 1989.

The Gallery's holdings in European art of the period 1900-60 were added to only disparately during the 1930s and 1940s. Collecting in this area was characterized first by single, isolated acquisitions (such as Bonnard's *Table Laid for Dessert* and Utrillo's *The House of Berlioz*, both purchased in 1935), but more typically by sudden bursts of enthusiasm for a particular school or movement. Among the few acquisitions made during the thirties, two of the most important were portraits by Augustus John: in 1933, his *Lady Cynthia Asquith: Portrait of a Lady in Black*, and, a year later, the arresting *Marchesa Casati*. Another important British picture came to the Gallery in 1936, Stanley Spencer's *Jubilee Tree, Cookham*, painted the same year. Frank P. Wood was responsible for all three purchases. Works by Roger Fry and Duncan Grant were acquired in 1935. In 1946 Vincent Massey, Canada's high commissioner to London from 1935 to 1946, gave works by Sickert, Hillier, Nash and Smith. Massey also represented the Gallery in dealing with the Contemporary Art Society, an organization under the auspices of the Tate Gallery, of which the AGT became a subscriber. The first gift from the society, Sickert's *St. Jacques, Dieppe*, was presented in 1946. Subsequent gifts included Moore's *Group of Shelterers during an Air Raid*, in 1951 – the first work by the great sculptor to enter the permanent collection.

The Gallery's history of collecting contemporary international art – that is, recent work by living artists – may date back to 1906, but a more convenient point of departure for the contemporary non-Canadian section was the purchasing in 1950 by the Women's Committee of Ben Nicholson's 1948 *Still Life*. This area of collecting, however, did not acquire a full-time curator until 1964, when Brydon Smith joined the Gallery. In the interim, the committee took on the project of donating works of art to the permanent collection, but most specifically directed its energies to the building up of the international contemporary holdings.

The acquisition of the Nicholson was completed under the guid-

Over, Figure 8: Installation view of *The European Iceberg: Creativity in Germany and Italy Today*, an exhibition organized by the AGO in 1985. Work displayed in the foreground: Michelangelo Pistoletto, *Figures Looking Down a Well*, 1983.

ance of Anthony Blunt, who, acting as the Gallery's London representative for over a decade, recommended several contemporary British works. This led to the devising of a specific Women's Committee policy to buy contemporary British paintings, a decision that necessitated the striking of an English Committee, composed of the painter Edward Bawden, Philip Hendy, director of the National Gallery, London, and Mrs. K.L. Somerville, secretary of the Fine Arts Department of the British Council. This "experiment," as it was called, yielded sixteen purchases between 1951 and 1953, including paintings by Piper, Hitchens, Sutherland and Richards, and Moore's *Working Model for Upright Internal and External Forms*. Blunt himself was responsible for recommending three of the most significant sculptures to find their way into the Art Gallery of Ontario's collection: Picasso's 1909 Cubist *Head of a Woman (Fernande)*; Matisse's 1916 *Jeanette V*, and Moore's 1953-54 *Warrior with Shield*.

Perhaps in reflection of the evolving ethnic nature of its home city and of the north-south reorientation of Canada's economy and culture, the Gallery redirected its focus away from British art first to contemporary European and then to American art during the latter half of the 1950s and the early 1960s. In 1953 the Women's Committee oversaw the acquisition of Dufy's *The Harbour at Le Havre*, and in 1955 the Junior Women's Committee funded the purchase of Gleize's *The Port*. Jean Sutherland Boggs was instrumental in securing Léger's *Kneeling Woman* and Picasso's Blue Period *Crouching Woman*, both in 1963. Other noteworthy acquisitions of the 1960s included Metzinger's *Still Life*, in 1964, and Dix's *Portrait of Dr. Heinrich Stadelmann*, in 1969. A standout purchase of 1971 was the Belgian Surrealist René Magritte's 1959 canvas, *The Birthday*.

In the spring of 1970, shortly before his death, Sam Zacks and his wife Ayala donated their private collection of late-19th and 20th-century art, consisting of 385 paintings, sculptures, prints and drawings by, among others, Degas, Picasso, Bonnard, Chagall, Matisse, Marquet, Rouault, Léger, Dufy, Modigliani, Soutine, Hepworth and Moore. Of this gift, unprecedented in Canadian museum history, Professor Robert Welsh has written:

> A number of paintings from the collection stand recognized as having been of pivotal importance in the career of the artist represented, and...many others are classic examples of a particularly significant phase in the artist's development.... [T]he Zacks collection comprises a veritable compendium of historical developments within the periods and movements involved – which is virtually to say, of the major developments in the history of twentieth-century painting and sculpture.

An index of the importance of this gift is the fact that, until then, the AGO did not own a single example of classic Cubism; as a result of the donation, the Gallery can display illustrative pieces by Gris, Braque and Lipchitz, in addition to the previously unrepresented Arp, Giacometti, Laurens and Maillol. These, in turn, provide a context for the Gallery's single most concentrated modern collection, that of the works of Henry Moore.

Both Sam and Ayala Zacks were closely involved in the plans to establish the Henry Moore Sculpture Centre to house the 101 sculptures, 57 drawings and 150 prints presented by the artist in 1974. This collection, augmented by recent bronzes purchased directly from Moore, and by early Moore drawings and prints acquired from dealers and private collectors, has been curated since that date by Alan Wilkinson, the present curator of twentieth-century art.

In 1980 the Modern Sculpture Committee replaced the Henry Moore Sculpture Committee, its mandate being to seek out, as Moore had suggested, important works of modern sculpture. A number of late 19th- and early 20th-century carvings and bronzes were acquired,

Figure 9: Main gallery of the Henry Moore Sculpture
Centre, which opened in 1974 to house Moore's generous gift to the AGO of over 100 sculptures, 57 drawings
and an almost complete set of prints. The sculptor, who
worked closely with the architect John C. Parkin on the
design of this gallery, suggested the natural, overhead
lighting that so powerfully displays his sculptural works.

several examples of which reflect, as does much of Moore's work, the influence of African and Oceanic art: Gauguin's *Hina and Fatu*, in 1980; Picasso's *Poupée*, in 1980; Brancusi's *The First Cry*, in 1981; and Giacometti's *Three Figures Outdoors*, in 1984. The modern British sculpture collection was strengthened with the addition of works by Gaudier-Brzeska, Epstein, Fry and Hepworth. In 1986, to celebrate their 40th anniversary, the Volunteer Committee acquired Gabo's *Linear Construction in Space No. 1*, and assisted with the purchase of his *Construction in Space, with Net*. At this time, the Gabo family generously donated an important early constructivist sculpture, *Model for a Fountain*.

Chief Curator Roald Nasgaard was responsible for the acquisition of Gorky's *They Will Take My Island* in 1980, and in 1981 for an early, untitled surrealist oil by Miró. In 1983 Mrs. Margaret Dunlap Crang donated Picasso's Blue Period oil *The Soup*. Giacometti's *Still Life with Bottles* was donated by Amy and Clair Stewart in 1984. David McTavish acquired Gontcharova's Cubist *The Bridge* in 1988. And Alan Wilkinson was responsible for securing Tanguy's *The Satin Pillow*, in 1986, and Arp's painted relief, *Nose and Cheeks*, in 1988 — two significant contributions to another project of the 1980s, that of providing a strong Surrealist context for the Moore Collection.

The International Contemporary Collection

In the early 1960s the Gallery's director, William Withrow, working closely with the Women's Committee, was instrumental in acquiring a number of works by such modern American Abstract Expressionists as Motherwell, Kline, Hofmann, Diebenkorn, and Rothko. Thereafter, from the mid-1960s to the early 1980s, under the curatorships successively of Brydon Smith (1964-67), Dennis Young (1967-71), Alvin Balkind (1974-75), and Roald Nasgaard (1976-present), concentration in the area of contemporary non-Canadian art would almost exclusively be on American painters and sculptors, though the occasional British acquisition came through. The Gallery moved with the times to embrace the second generation of American abstractionists – Kelly, Stella, Louis, Noland – and such mid-sixties Pop icons as Warhol's *Elvis I and II*, Segal's *The Butcher Shop*, and Oldenburg's *Giant Hamburger*. It then expanded into Minimal Art – Flavin, Lewitt, Judd – and subsequently into the various Post-Minimal and Conceptual modes – Serra, Smithson, Oppenheim, Barry and Weiner – that followed.

The steady growth of the international collection warranted the appointment in 1979 of a separate curator of contemporary art, in the person of Roald Nasgaard, and the establishment of a corresponding International Contemporary Collection Committee. The following year, with the purchase of Gerhard Richter's *Abstract Painting*, of 1980, the Gallery initiated a fresh reorientation toward European art, not only to reflect current production but also to register something of the depth of the history of contemporary art in Europe that was only then becoming apparent to North American eyes. The landmark exhibition, *The European Iceberg*, guest-curated by Germano Celant in 1985, served to crystalize this new awareness of the re-emerging continental scene (fig. 8). Alongside the work of Richter and Sigmar Polke, and a group of German and Italian Neo-Expressionists, perhaps the most important focus of attention has been a concentration of major works by Italian Arte Povera artists, including Michelangelo Pistoletto, Jannis Kounellis, Mario Merz, Luciano Fabro and Giulio Paolini. In general, the perspective of the 1980s has become more truly international, with an ongoing interest in acquiring works by the most significant emerging artists from both sides of the Atlantic.

If one can discern a pattern in the AGO's collecting in the contemporary international area, it has been the building of clusters of work around a few specific styles or movements, rather than the seeking of geographical or demographic comprehensiveness. The rapid escalation of market prices for modern works, which far outstrips the growth of available revenues and which forces increased reliance on donors and corporate fund-raising, has frustrated the Gallery's efforts to build in real depth. Nevertheless, the surprising strengths of the international contemporary holdings will be revealed when, for the first time, the collection moves into its own permanent installation galleries on completion of Stage III of the AGO's expansion program.

The problems faced by the European and international contemporary departments have also long challenged the curators of the Canadian historical, the contemporary Canadian, and the print and drawing sections, though in somewhat different forms.

The Canadian Historical Collection

A distinct committee to oversee the building of the Canadian Historical Collection may not have been established until 1974, but there was an evident readiness to reflect the history of art in this country soon after the foundation of the Gallery. Among the pictures that came from The Grange in 1910 are a number of Canadian works of historical interest, such as G.T. Berthon's pair of portraits of William Henry (p. 240) and Harriette Boulton (fig. 10). A loan exhibition in January 1911 of *Paintings by Deceased Canadian Artists* manifested a continuing commitment to this area, and among the gifts received following the opening of the first proper galleries in 1918 were three Canadian pieces from Sir Edmund Walker: a Paul Peel, a Lucius O'Brien and an Edmund Morris. That same year, Sir Edmund Osler donated a Daniel Fowler watercolour of 1875.

The first purchase of a Canadian historical work — another

Fowler – came in 1920, and was paid for from a fund raised through public subscription. This demonstration of interest in the finest Canadian watercolourist of the 19th century elicited a gift from the artist's daughter the following year of twenty-two of his European and British topographical views dating from 1837 to 1839. With no funds, and with only a rudimentary sense at the time of the history of Canadian art, there could hardly be a coherent collecting program, but the Council of the Gallery continued to respond to gifts when they were offered, and sometimes actively sought desirable pieces, such as when the Canadian Club of Toronto was asked to purchase Tom Thomson's *The West Wind* for the AGT at the time of the opening of the first expansion in 1926. On the same occasion, both the curator, E.R. Grieg, and the chairman of the Exhibition Committee, Dr. H.M. Tovell, put up the money to acquire two early sculptures by the famous Quebec carver, Louis Jobin.

That same year also saw the establishment of a permanent purchase fund, incorporating the designated Reuben and Kate Leonard Canadian Fund, and the authorization of the Council to approve less expensive purchases, primarily contemporary paintings from exhibitions at the Gallery. We should be grateful that the committee saw fit to turn a portion of the Leonard Fund and a new Friends of Canadian Art Fund, raised among members of the Gallery in 1929 exclusively for contemporary purchases, to the acquisition of major works by the Group of Seven.

Members of the Group had been close to the Gallery for some years, staging regular exhibitions there since their first joint one in 1920, and it was A.Y. Jackson and Arthur Lismer who found the two Jobins and encouraged their acquisition. Lismer ran the education program at the Gallery from 1926 to 1938 (fig. 1). This relationship was reinforced when the Group's early supporter and sometime employer, Albert H. Robson, became vice-president of the Council in 1929, and

Portraits of Harriette and Goldwin Smith, owners of The Grange to whom Edmund Walker appealed for the dedication of their home to the cause of a public art museum for Toronto.

Left, Figure 10: George Theodore Berthon (Canadian, 1806-92) *Portrait of Harriette Boulton*, 1847; oil on canvas, 59.1 x 44.5 cm. AGO, Goldwin Smith Collection. *Right*, Figure 11: J.W.L. Forster (Canadian, 1850–1938) *Portrait of Goldwin Smith*, 1906; oil on canvas, 152.4 x 111.8 cm. AGO, Goldwin Smith Collection.

most of the contemporary purchases of the next decade or so reflect their influence.

There is no pattern evident in the few historical acquisitions of the same period; that there were any at all during those Depression years is remarkable. Paul Kane's *Indian Encampment on Lake Huron* was offered at an attractive price by its owners in order to encourage the development of a Canadian collection on a solid historical basis, and J.W. Morrice's *Landscape, Trinidad* was bought from the Galerie Pierre Matisse in Paris for the same reason. The Albert H. Robson Memorial Subscription Fund, established following his death in 1939, encouraged interest in the Group and their circle through the next decade, and supported a number of important purchases of a historical nature, among them F.H. Varley's *Dhârâna* of 1932, A.Y. Jackson's *Maple and Birches* of 1915, and Emily Carr's *Guyasdoms D'Sonoqua* of 1928-30, all acquired in 1942. The spectacular Antoine Plamondon canvas of 1853, *Passenger Pigeon Hunt*, was purchased using the fund the following year.

Established as a sub-committee of the Exhibition Committee in 1938, the Canadian Collection Committee began to report directly to the Council in 1947. Its activities were further encouraged by the Fund of the T. Eaton Co. Ltd. for Canadian Works of Art, set up the following year. The curator at the time, Martin Baldwin, in 1945 organized the first serious historical survey exhibition of Canadian art, *The Development of Painting in Canada 1665-1945*, following it up in 1950 with *Fifty Years of Painting in Canada, 1900-1950*.

During his five years at the Gallery, Sidney Key organized retrospective exhibitions of the Group of Seven veterans Harris, Lismer and Jackson, which constituted the first serious cataloguing of the work of living Canadian artists. He also supported the purchase of both historical and contemporary Canadian work. The former category was represented by Homer Watson's *The Old Mill*, of 1886, acquired in 1948, and the latter by Goodridge Roberts's *Pleasant Island, Georgian Bay*, and Elizabeth Wyn Wood's cast tin sculpture, *Reef and Rainbow*, in 1950.

Most of the Canadian Collection Committee purchases of the 1950s were contemporary, although earlier works by Carl Schaefer, Maurice Cullen and David Milne, among others, were acquired through the new J.S. McLean Canadian Fund, established in 1953. An assistant curator, Nancy Robertson (1959-62), was interested in Canadian historical art, as reflected in her organizing of the J.E.H. MacDonald retrospective in 1965. However, her replacement in 1964, Brydon Smith, concentrated the Gallery's collecting activities on the contemporary American area, where they remained throughout the 1960s.

At the same time, a growing academic interest in the history of Canadian art encouraged the Gallery in the spring of 1965 to engage Helen Pepall Bradfield to prepare a catalogue of the complete Canadian holdings, the research for which was funded by a grant from the J.P. Bickell Foundation. The Gallery's importance as a major repository of Canadian historical art was further strengthened in 1965 with the transfer of title of 340 works purchased since 1912 from the annual exhibitions of the Canadian National Exhibition, which hitherto had been only on extended loan.

Two splendid donations brought more attention to Canadian historical art in 1970. The gift from the J.S. McLean Collection included a large amount of Group of Seven-related material, and several of David Milne's best oils and brush drawings, notably his *The Blue Rocker*, of 1914, and *The Camp*, of c.1930. The bequest of Charles S. Band, while including many important Group pictures, also boasted well-known paintings by leading figures of the forties and fifties, such as Paul-Émile Borduas and J.W.G. Macdonald. These two major collections were, remarkably, augmented by yet two more significant gifts that year, one of works from the Douglas M. Duncan Collection, the other from that of Sam and Ayala Zacks.

Joan Murray had joined the staff as research curator the year
before these benefactions, in 1969. She was appointed the first curator
of Canadian art in 1970, and in 1971 a Canadian Collection Committee was re-established as a sub-committee of the Contemporary Committee. With few resources, Murray nonetheless was able to contribute
substantially to the building of the historical collection, particularly
when in 1972 the transfer to the AGO of the Government of Ontario
Art Collection added a number of important 19th-century paintings,
including Paul Peel's famous *After the Bath*.

When Murray left in the fall of 1973, the Gallery, determined to
capitalize on the impetus, hired the dean of Canadian art historians,
J. Russell Harper, and established an independent Canadian Historical
Collection Committee with responsibilities for Canadian art dating
prior to 1945. Harper left within the year because of bad health, and
was replaced by Jeremy Adamson, who was able to add a number of
significant pictures to the first permanent collection installation in the
new Canadian wing of the Gallery, which opened in 1977. Among
these were Joseph Légaré's *The Fire in the Saint-Jean Quarter, Seen
Looking Westward*, of c.1845, and Varley's *Liberation*, of 1936.

Armed with a clear mandate, dedicated galleries, and an enthu-
siastic committee, Dennis Reid, the collection's curator since 1979,
has been able to develop a broad program of acquisitions through
purchase and donation. Whole periods of Canadian art history previously ignored are now receiving attention. George Heriot's *Village of
Chippawa* is but one of a number of pre-Confederation-era watercolours that are beginning to flesh out evidence of the earliest British-
trained artists to work in this country. Lucius O'Brien's *Northern
Head of Grand Manan* is the finest of a group of landscapes by the post-
Confederation painters that have recently been acquired, and George
Reid's *The Other Side of the Question* is perhaps the most impressive of
a range of paintings in the French academic tradition that lately have

illuminated that part of the history of Canadian art. The period of the 1930s has been amplified with major canvases, such as Paraskeva Clark's *Portrait of Philip*, and Bertram Brooker's *Phyllis*. The presentation by Katharine Helm of her collection of paintings, drawings and sketches by her father, C.W. Jefferys, was followed by the Jefferys estate's gift of the artist's papers to the Edward P. Taylor Reference Library. The donation of some 185 pieces of sculpture from the estate of Frances Loring and Florence Wyle in 1983 has given the AGO a solid base for the study of sculpture in Toronto during the first half of this century, and the acquisition through purchase (assisted in part by the Volunteer Committee) and gift of Jack Bush's family of his paintings and watercolours, represented by over 100 works, has reinforced the importance of the Canadian Collection both as a pre-eminent showplace and an essential centre for the study of Canadian art.

The Contemporary Canadian Committee

The present designation of the Contemporary Canadian Committee, with responsibilities from 1960 on, does not at all imply that present-day Canadian art has always been a distinct area of collecting at the Gallery. In the early 1960s the committee, in addition to acquiring works from current exhibitions, was still collecting landscapes by painters belonging to or associated with the Group of Seven and their successors, the Canadian Group of Painters. And until 1980, when a separate curator in the person of David Burnett (1980-84) was hired to take charge of the section, contemporary Canadian art was considered part of a Canadian-American — later the Contemporary — Committee.

The struggle to establish a presence for Canadian art as a distinct cultural entity was hampered by its inclusion with American, and its submission to the more advanced and powerful American art was a serious concern during the later 1960s and early 1970s. Not only

Over, Figure 12: Bernie Miller (Canadian, b.1948) *Future Use* (installation detail), 1985; steel, Styrofoam, light fixtures, film projector, various found objects, 260.0 (variable) x 488.0 x 366.0 cm. Purchase, 1988. This installation was included in an exhibition of Miller's work at the AGO in 1986.

was modern American art more aggressively collected during this period than Canadian, but its champions were more vocal on the committee. The Gallery's emphasis on contemporary Canadian art, therefore, has always been a reflection of the vigour with which it has been collected outside the institution. Thus it was that the core of the now historical part of the collection should have been established in the early 1960s, and that the principal source of acquisitions was current exhibitions, especially ones held in Toronto. Although there was a marked interest in sculpture (then newly resurgent in Toronto), the purchase of paintings in the early to mid-1960s set the collection's dominant tone.

These purchases were made in the context of the American Abstract Expressionist paintings then being bought and donated by the Volunteer Committee. The affinities of the younger Toronto artists of the day, however, were with the American Pop painters and sculptors. Painters Eleven had disbanded by late 1960 (although Harold Town and William Ronald were only being acquired by this time), and a predominantly figurative style, influenced by Pop and Neo-Dada, was apparent in the paintings and constructions of Michael Snow, Dennis Burton, Graham Coughtry, Joyce Wieland, Gordon Rayner and John Meredith. Snow's *Walking Woman* series is perhaps most emblematic of the inventiveness of that era, and is strongly represented in the collection (and also, along with Les Levine's work of the same period, pointed to the more conceptualized object-art of the 1970s).

Simultaneously with this expression of Toronto's new attitude toward itself and its new-found status as Canada's commercial centre for art, the bases in the collection for other regions of Canada were also established. In one foray in 1965, a whole block of work from the Prairies and West Coast, including Arthur McKay, Claude Breeze, Ted Godwin, Dorothy Knowles, and Ernest Lindner, was added to the canvases of Kenneth Lochhead and Ronald Bloore then recently

purchased. These acquisitions were made by Director William
Withrow with the aid of funds made available by the Canada Council
to enable galleries to buy art from other provinces. The energetic art
scene of London, Ontario, which would take on significance in the
collection during the 1970s, began to be represented by complementary paintings by Greg Curnoe and Jack Chambers. The consoli-
dation of Montreal's artistic tradition following upon Paul-Émile
Borduas's departure for Paris was documented with the first gifts and
purchases of paintings by Yves Gaucher and Guido Molinari in the
mid-1960s, which would be substantially augmented in the mid- and
late 1970s. This work was resolutely abstract, in contrast to the
predominately figurative mode of the Toronto and the mixed modes
of the Western Canadian painting then being collected. Only with
Jack Bush, who had broken with the Abstract Expressionist aesthetics
of his Painters Eleven past, does a strong presence of post-painterly
abstraction enter the Toronto core of the collection. Pursuing his own
version of colourfield painting, Bush influenced a whole generation
of younger artists whose works would find favour with the committee
in the 1970s and 1980s.

In response to the dominant shift of art in the mid-1960s away
from painting toward sculpture or object-art midway between the two
media, a decision was made in 1967-68 to improve the Gallery's
holdings in this area. The collecting of modern sculpture was pursued
in concert with the purchase of the important American minimal and
post-minimal pieces in the collection. Perhaps 1974 marks the recognition of substantial shifts in Canadian art, with the acquisition of
major installations by Colette Whiten and Murray Favro. This was
followed in 1975 with a serious commitment to contemporary Canadian art, commensurate with the number of outstanding mature and
younger artists then working in Montreal, Toronto and London.

Funds from the provincial lottery substantially aided the carrying out of this program in the latter part of the 1970s and into the next decade. These years saw the acquisition of major works by David Rabinowitch, Royden Rabinowitch, Betty Goodwin, Ron Martin, Paterson Ewen, Alex Colville and Christopher Pratt. The funds also allowed the collection to become representative of a larger number of artists and directions than normally would have been possible, and permitted retrospective buying of works by such important figures as Gaucher, Molinari, Bush, Snow and Charles Gagnon. (The extensive collecting of the Rabinowitches' sculpture and works on paper would take place in the 1980s.) Usually acquisitions have been concurrent with production, except in periods when concentrated efforts have been made to fill in gaps in the history of contemporary Canadian art, as first occurred in 1970 (also the year of the Zacks gift), and then in the late 1970s and mid-1980s.

The latter period was marked by curatorial concentration on the art of Toronto during the 1970s and 1980s. Here, as documented by Philip Monk, appointed curator of the Contemporary Canadian section in 1985, the devolution of sculpture under the influences of language and photography to the diverse forms we know today is recorded; and there has been special emphasis, for instance, on the sculpture and installations of Robin Collyer, Ian Carr-Harris and Liz Magor. Photo-based work has come to the fore in the collection, in recognition of the ways in which photography, along with film and video, has inflected all art practice, including that of such divergent figures and strategies as Jeff Wall and General Idea.

A contemporary collection can never be defined. By definition, its limits always extend to the present to include current artistic forms and practices. But at the same time, what is already secure within the collection becomes redefined, and thus the profile of the collection varies over time as reputations wax and wane, as the historical importance of a work or school is confirmed or discounted, and as historical patterns assert their contours. The Contemporary Canadian Collection has now had long enough to begin to find its history, both within and without the Gallery.

The Inuit Art Collection

The collecting of Inuit art at the AGO was initially dictated more by chance than by design. Fitful and limited activity resulted in the acquisition of only ten Inuit works before 1978. In 1954 the Canadian Collection Committee approved the purchase of the Gallery's first piece of Inuit art, *Woman Holding A Fish and a Ulu*, by Pinnie Nuktialuk, of Inukjuak. A second piece, *Hunter*, by Peter Qiluqi, from Povungnituk, was acquired in 1957. Both were obtained through the Fund of the T. Eaton Co. for Canadian Works of Art. In 1960 the first annual catalogued collection of Eskimo graphics, produced in Cape Dorset in 1959, was released. An exhibition of these works, hosted by the newly formed Canadian-American Committee, used the J.S. McLean Canadian Fund to purchase six prints.

This promising, though modest, collecting activity then ceased for the next sixteen years – a period characterized, coincidentally, by an efflorescence of artistic activity in the Far North. In the rest of Canada, it was a time of evaluation and of ongoing discussion as to the proper place for the display and documentation of Inuit art in public institutions.

The first exhibition of Inuit art to be organized by the Gallery, *The People Within*, held in 1976, occasioned the next acquisition. The curator, Reissa Schrager, of the AGO's Extension Services department, enthusiastically recommended that one of the show's major pieces, a tapestry by the renowned Jessie Oonark, be considered for purchase. This piece catalyzed ongoing discussion regarding the status of Inuit art, and the Contemporary Collection Committee sought a clear policy regarding its acquisition. Although the tapestry was added to the collection in 1977, the issue itself remained unresolved.

The Gallery's first gift of Inuit art, a sculpture by Peter Itukalla, was accepted in 1976. The second was a portfolio of six works, *Art of the Eskimos*, donated by Mrs. Richard Ivey and accepted by the Print and Drawing Committee in the watershed year of 1978. Belated involvement in the area of Inuit art meant that the AGO, like many institutions, had to depend on donations by private individuals to build a significant public collection. Near the end of 1978 the Contemporary Collection Committee accepted a major donation of Inuit art from the Klamer family. With a single stroke, 602 sculptures, drawings and prints transformed the collection. *Migration*, by Joe Talirunili, *Figure with Ulu*, by Aqjangajuk Shaa, and *Caribou Head*, by Osuitok Ipeelee, reflect the scope and quality of this legacy. Also included are a number of small ivory and wooden pieces from the Prehistoric and Historic periods.

The Klamer Collection resulted in the ongoing display of Inuit art at the Gallery, an international travelling exhibition titled *Grasp Tight the Old Ways*, and the hiring of Jean Blodgett as adjunct curator in 1979. Blodgett was instrumental in developing the collection and in laying the groundwork for the eventual establishment of an Inuit Art Department.

The Gallery's total commitment to Inuit art came in 1988 with Samuel and Esther Sarick's decision to donate over 1,600 sculptures and 1,200 prints and drawings. One of the largest concentrations of contemporary Inuit art to be assembled by private hands, the Sarick Collection, formed over twenty years, represents over 400 artists from thirty-three communities across the Arctic. The AGO responded to the Saricks' initiative by establishing a permanent exhibition space for Inuit art, and by creating an Inuit Art Department supported by an active collection committee and staffed by a full-time curator. Norman Zepp was appointed to this position in 1989. One of his first acts was to secure the impressive Inuit sculpture collection of Dr. Robert Williamson, which includes works by such Keewatin district artists as Tiktak, Tikeayak, Andy Miki and John Pangnark.

Although the history of Inuit art extends back over 4,000 years and is not subject to national boundaries, the major focus of collecting will continue to be works produced in Canada during the Contemporary Period (1948-present). In this area, thanks chiefly to the Klamer and Sarick donations, the AGO's Inuit Collection is close to becoming truly comprehensive. The representational nature of the holdings does not preclude areas of particular concentration and their strengthening through focused collecting, thereby establishing the potential for concentrated study and thematic exhibitions.

The Print and Drawing Collection

There remain to be discussed three separate departments whose holdings and functions have traditionally been somewhat interrelated at the Art Gallery of Ontario: prints and drawings, photography, and the reference library.

The vexed economics of print collecting were thoroughly studied by the father of the Print and Drawing Collection, Sir Edmund Walker, president of the Canadian Bank of Commerce, who began to pick up engravings and etchings by the likes of Dürer, Rembrandt and Whistler from prominent dealers in New York, London and Amsterdam at the height of the so-called "Etching Revival" in the 1870s and 1880s. Walker, as chairman of the Advisory Arts Council, had been deeply involved in the establishment of the National Gallery of Canada's Department of Prints and Drawings, but after his death in 1924 his executors decided that his extensive European collection should come to the Art Gallery of Toronto, where it formed the nucleus

Figure 13: Installation view of the exhibition *The Etchings of James McNeill Whistler*, organized by the AGO in 1984.

of the present holdings. These had been augmented by the regular purchase of works on paper from the Canadian National Exhibition, and by a series of large donations from such private collectors as Frank M. Kimbart, who gave the Gallery several hundred engravings and etchings; John Ross Robertson, who in 1947 presented a fine group of Victorian engravings; and Mrs. David Johnson, who in 1950 donated over 800 17th- and 18th-century *intaglio* prints, including a fine group of Canaletto etchings, from the collection of the late Frederick W.R. Johnson.

Walker was also an active patron of contemporary Canadian artists, and ensured that examples of prints, drawings and watercolours by his compatriots were prominently featured in the Gallery's collection of historical works on paper. Since 1979, the curators of the Canadian Historical Art and Contemporary Canadian Art departments have been responsible for building the works-on-paper collections of their respective areas.

The heritage of the institution's founders notwithstanding, it was to an expatriate English potter and collector, William B. Dalton, of Stamford, Connecticut, rather than to local benefactors, that the Gallery owed its first important acquisition of watercolours by key early members of the British school. Dalton's advisory role was taken up in the late 1970s by Andrew Wilton, keeper of the Turner Collection at the Tate Gallery, London. Other collecting areas also have been associated with the dedication and generosity of private individuals, such as Dr. Walter Vitzthum, professor of Fine Art at the University of Toronto, who was voted a small purchase fund by the Old Masters Committee. The first president of this committee, Arthur Gelber, together with his late wife Esther, presented many notable gifts, ranging from Annibale Carracci's *Studies for the Hand of an Angel Holding a Violin Bow* to Whistler's *Nocturne, Palaces*. In 1970 Sam and Ayala Zacks added to the collection an important group of early 20th-century European drawings, including a number of works by Russian Constructivists and Italian Futurists.

In acknowledgement of the importance of these media to the Gallery, Katharine Lochnan, formerly assistant to Chief Curator Mario Amaya, was appointed curator of prints and drawings in 1976. The Prints and Drawing Collection Committee, chaired by David McTavish, an Italian drawings specialist, was formed the following year. Dr. McTavish continues to advise the Gallery on addition of Italian drawings to the collection as begun by his teacher, Dr. Vitzthum.

Since 1976 the phenomenal growth of the collection – represented by such stand-out acquisitions as Dürer's *Adam and Eve*, Gainsborough's *Wooded Landscape with Herdsman and Cattle*, and van Gogh's *The Vicarage at Neunen* – has largely been attributable to gifts from collectors or from earmarked funds established by individuals, foundations and corporations. Witness such signal contributions as that of Mr. and Mrs. Ralph Presgrave, over 200 of whose prints came to the Gallery in three sections in 1976 and 1979; Elizabeth Dale's collection of 19th-century etchings; John T. Johnson's collection of Thomas Rowlandson drawings; and Gilbert and Stewart Bagnani's collection of master prints and drawings, presented in 1988-89. With the help of Vincent, Walter and Harold Tovell, the Gallery has been able to reunite many of the sheets that formed part of the first truly avant-garde collection to be put together by Torontonians, that of Dr. Harold and Ruth Tovell. The future of the department as a vigorous pursuer of prints and drawings was ensured by the founding, in 1975, of the Master Print and Drawing Society of Toronto, led by Sidney Bregman, which is supported by the Fraser Elliott Foundation, and by the dedication of purchase funds by the firms of Touche Ross, Norcen, and Brascan; the Dorothy Isabella Webb (*née* Walker) Trust, the Esther Gelber Fund, the Marvin Gelber Fund, and the Makepeace Investment Fund.

The department's single largest fund was established by the Trier-Fodor Foundation in 1975 for the purchase and display of "humorous, satirical and representative graphic art" by the popular European artist and toymaker Walter Trier. This fund has made possible the building of a collection of caricatures ranging from the 15th to the 20th centuries, including over 300 late-18th- and early-19th-century British and French caricatures.

The collection of works on paper will be housed in the Marvin Gelber Print and Drawing Study Centre on completion of the Stage III expansion. Adjacent to this complex are four galleries dedicated to displaying the permanent collection of prints and drawings and to travelling exhibitions: Esther and Arthur Gelber Treasury, Trier-Fodor Gallery, Margaret Eaton Gallery, and Marvin Gelber Gallery.

This space will also be available to the Gallery's small but growing photography collection. A hiatus of nearly sixty years intervened between the mounting of the first exhibition of photographs at the Art Museum of Toronto, in 1917, and the 1974 decision that curators within their specific disciplines could begin to purchase photographic images of historic and artistic importance. Since then Maia-Mari Sutnik, head of the Gallery's Photographic Services department, has mounted numerous exhibitions, published catalogues, and made strategic purchases to augment gifts from such collectors as Skip Gillham, Valerie Burton, David Milman, S.P. Ball and M.E. Reid, which began to flow to the AGO from collectors of 19th- and 20th-century photographs during the 1980s.

The Edward P. Taylor Reference Library and Archives

For almost forty years, the Gallery's library occupied that of Goldwin Smith's in The Grange, although his personal collection went to Cornell University. The earliest collection of books to come to the

Gallery was made up of titles from two donations: a gift from the first curator, Edward Grieg, and another from the estate of the artist Edmund Morris. These largely consisted of 19th-century "view books," such as *The Holy Land... after lithographs by Louis Haghe from drawings made on the spot by David Roberts, R.A....* (London, 1855), in six volumes.

The library remained relatively dormant until 1933, when the Gallery received from the Carnegie Foundation a gift of books, prints and reproductions, and a cash grant for educational purposes. The books resulted in a properly systematized catalogue of all books in the library, and the design of a bookplate for the collection by A. Scott Carter. The Carnegie gift constituted not only the first but also the most important donation of scholarly titles in the library's history; almost without exception they are still of basic significance in their fields. Another 127 titles came to the library in 1935 from the library of the photographer and journalist M.O. Hammond.

The Gallery's first full-time librarian, Grace Pincoe, was appointed in 1941; she was succeeded briefly by Elinor Baker, and then, in 1948, by Sybille Pantazzi. Under the able leadership of Miss Pantazzi, who retired in 1980 after thirty-two years as head librarian, the library underwent constant metamorphosis. In 1971 the facility moved to temporary premises on College Street, which it occupied for six years, while awaiting the completion of Stage II, when it moved back to the Gallery and assumed the name of its principal benefactor, the late Edward P. Taylor. Karen McKenzie, who has served as head librarian since 1980, has initiated the automation of the catalogue, the expansion of the library's collecting mandate, and the establishment of an international catalogue exchange program. She also supervised the planning of the new Chalmers Wing of Stage III, which increases the stacks, office and reading-room space of the Edward P. Taylor Reference Library and Archives to a total of 11,693 square feet.

Today, the library boasts over 100,000 books and exhibition catalogues. In its acquisition, the reference library reflects the collections of the Gallery itself. An international selection of catalogues of exhibitions and of permanent collections, in all languages, comprises a large part of its holdings. Together with periodicals, auction catalogues, and works of reference, such museum and gallery publications form the backbone of the library.

What sets an individual library apart from others, however, are its special collections and holdings of rare books and manuscripts. Through the generosity of individual donors, several fine illustrated folios have been acquired over the years. In 1936 the recently established library was given over 68 titles by S. George Curry, an architect with the firm of Darling, Curry and Pearson, among them Letarouilly's *Édifices de Rome moderne* (Paris, 1840-57), in three volumes. Other and subsequent additions to the collection include Chamberlaine's *Imitations of Original Drawings by Holbein* (engraved by Bartolozzi and published in London at the end of the 18th century), the finest example of early English colour printing; two volumes of reproductions of artworks from the collection of William Young Ottley, published in 1823 and 1829; and a notable early archaeological work, Robert Adams's *Ruins of the Palace of the Emperor Diocletian at Spalatro*, published in 1764. In 1954 a collection of 19th-century British books and engravings clipped from magazines, representing the golden age of English illustration, was presented to the library by Alan Garrow.

Yet another active collecting area is that of the library's archives, which contain manuscripts, printed ephemera, sketches and sketchbooks, and are not to be confused with the archives of the Gallery itself; the latter, originally under the aegis of The Grange and then of Administration, are now also the responsibility of the library. (The Gallery's archives were organized and maintained by Margaret Machell, the former keeper of The Grange, from 1974 to 1984.)

Included in the library's archives are such unusual items as two large scrapbooks compiled by G.A. Reid; two letterbooks of Edmund Morris, secretary of the Canadian Art Club; the F.S. Challener notes on Canadian artists; four volumes of proof engravings of illustrations by Henry Sandham; the Newton MacTavish papers; the C.S. Band papers; and the papers of such leading 20th-century Canadian artists as C.W. Jefferys, F.H. Varley, Arthur Lismer and Jack Bush. These unique materials augment the library's collection of over 35,000 artists' files, which it began to compile in 1912.

As AGO Director William Withrow wrote at the end of the preface for the previous handbook of the collection, published in 1974 to coincide with the opening of Stage I,

> Ideas about the nature of art museums have [changed] and will change the way in which this art gallery serves its community. But certain absolutes remain constant. One of these is the necessity for a collection which, within the limits of the community's financial powers, must strive for excellence rather than quantity, for integrity rather than representativeness. The Art Gallery of Ontario enters the last quarter of this century with enthusiasm and optimism that these ideals can be maintained.

As we approach 2000, the devotion and sense of purpose that have guided this institution since 1900 remain steadfast in the face of challenges posed by the new as well as the old constraints – economic, cultural, demographic – which confront all museums in the last decade of this century. This book is intended to affirm a commitment to past, present and future that is manifested with equal conviction in the collecting, scholarship and publishing activities of the Art Gallery of Ontario as a whole.

European Art

Giovanni del Biondo (Florentine, active c.1356-99)

Vision of St. Benedict
Tempera on panel. 35.8 x 39.3

St. Benedict Restores Life to a Young Monk
Tempera on panel. 33.7 x 37.5

Probably painted in Florence in the late 1350s or in the 1360s, these panels are among
the earliest works in the permanent collection. Like much 14th-century Florentine
painting, the pictures reflect the influence of Giotto, whose naturalism and monumentality had set European painting on a new course 50 years earlier. Giovanni del Biondo
gave bulk to his small figures by naturalistically shading the folds in their habits and
has given animation by using specific gestures and facial expressions. He lavished particular care on the face of the bald, white-bearded St. Benedict, depicted in front
of an attractively coloured but rather clumsily drawn porch.

   These panels and three others in private collections in Italy once formed part of
an altarpiece dedicated to St. Benedict, the 6th-century father of Western monasti-
cism. In one panel St. Benedict is shown shielding his eyes as he marvels at the small-
ness of the world, represented as a little globe, in contrast to the immensity of heaven,
which is conveyed entirely by radiant gold leaf. The other panel shows the story of a
monk, who was killed when the devil made a wall collapse on top of him but was
then miraculously restored to life by St. Benedict. In this panel the two episodes are
placed in a continuous and somewhat more naturalistic landscape.

   Purchased with funds donated by gift of A. L. Koppel, 1953
   Upper: 52/37   Lower: 52/36

Unknown (Italian, 15th century)

Adoration of the Magi (within the initial letter *E*)
Ink, gouache, gold leaf on parchment. 13.0 x 12.2

From classical times to the Renaissance, important manuscripts were decorated with ornamental borders and were often "illuminated" with gold leaf. After the invention of printing in the 15th century, these manuscripts gradually went out of fashion.

The decoration of initial letters was a popular application of the art of manuscript illumination. This historiated initial, showing the letter *E*, has been cut from a much larger sheet and was probably taken from a gradual, the musical portion of the missal, which was used in the celebration of the Mass. The nativity subject would tend to indicate that this initial was the beginning of the introit for the Feast of the Epiphany: "Ecce advenit dominator dominus." Graduals, which all medieval and Renaissance churches and monasteries owned, were usually large in size, because the words and music had to be visible to all members of the choir.

The manuscript can be dated to the second half of the 15th century, but it has not yet been determined where it was made; both Ferrara and Florence have been suggested. Although the drawing style, especially of the figures, is somewhat primitive, a convincing illusion of space has been created in the landscape.

Formerly in the collection of Dr. and Mrs. Harold Murchison Tovell and purchased from their son, Dr. H. M. M. Tovell of New York, with the assistance of the Government of Canada through the Cultural Property Export and Import Act, 1987   88/90

Simon Marmion (French, 1420/25–1489)

The Mass of St. Gregory c.1460/70
Oil on panel. 45.1 x 29.4

Precise detail and extreme naturalism, achieved through the use of oil paint, characterize 15th-century painting in Flanders and neighbouring territories. Much influenced by Flemish art, Simon Marmion worked primarily in Valenciennes, in northeastern France near the Flemish border. In this panel the dialect of the region (Picardy) is used in the long inscription at the bottom. It relates that once, when Pope Gregory the Great was celebrating mass, he miraculously saw a vision of the suffering Christ — the subject of this painting. The inscription adds that Gregory and other popes granted indulgences to those who made devotions connected with this subject.

Known both as a panel painter and a manuscript illuminator, Marmion used oil paint with considerable refinement. The body of Christ is delicately modelled, and the liturgical garments of St. Gregory and his attendant are harmoniously arranged. Both the fall of light and the linear drawing of solid objects have been studied with a new care. In contrast, the Instruments of the Passion, symbolizing Christ's suffering, are spread out on a gold ground, by now an old-fashioned treatment of the panel's surface.

Purchase, 1979   79/121

71

Bartolommeo di Giovanni (Florentine, active 1442-97?)

Lamentation with Saints and a Donor c.1490
Oil on canvas. 163.8 x 191.7

Probably done in Florence about 1490, this picture was originally painted on a wood panel, but later the paint layer was transferred to canvas. The lamentation over the dead body of Christ, which has just been taken down from the Cross, was a popular religious subject, although not one recounted in the Bible. To the group of Christ's immediate followers, seen mourning their Saviour's death, the artist has added later saints such as St. Jerome, the 4th-century translator of the Bible. St. Jerome kneels at the left while at the right the enormous figure of St. Andrew presents the man who probably commissioned the altarpiece. But neither the donor's identity nor the original location of the altarpiece is known.

Bartolommeo di Giovanni's ambitious painting presents the large group of varied figures with clarity and dignity, in a setting of fitting amplitude. During the 1480s Bartolommeo seems to have been associated with the thriving Florentine workshop of Domenico Ghirlandaio, whose influence is evident in this painting, but in the 1490s he worked in Rome and in Perugia. His paintings represent a conservative aspect of Florentine art on the eve of the High Renaissance.

Purchase, 1970   70/10

Tommaso di Stefano called **Lunetti** (Florentine, active c.1490/6–1564)

The Adoration of the Shepherds
Oil on panel. 75.6 x 49.5

Known by the nickname of Lunetti, Tommaso di Stefano was apprenticed in Florence with Lorenzo di Credi, who in turn had trained alongside Leonardo da Vinci. Both Lorenzo di Credi and Lunetti produced carefully executed but restrained paintings. At the same time, Leonardo, Michelangelo and Raphael were creating the masterpieces that distinguish the High Renaissance.

The biblical story of the angel's appearance to the humble shepherds in the fields and their reverent adoration of the newborn Christ child in the stable at Bethlehem was a popular subject of Renaissance painting. Lunetti's composition is a simplified version of a large altarpiece that Lorenzo di Credi painted before 1510 for the Floren- tine church of Santa Chiara. Both teacher and pupil were deeply influenced by the Adoration of the Shepherds in Hugo van der Goes's *Portinari Altarpiece*, the great Flemish triptych that was in Florence since the 1480s. Because of its modest size, it is likely that Lunetti's panel was commissioned by a private patron for personal devotions in an intimate setting. The painting once belonged to the Bourbon kings of Spain, one of whom presented it to the first Duke of Wellington.

Gift of Joey and Toby Tanenbaum, 1985   85/313

Bernard van Orley (Flemish, c.1491–1542)

Rest on the Flight into Egypt c.1518
Oil on panel. 88.9 x 70.5

Mary and her suckling child are the principal figures in a narrative that is spelt out
in the extensive landscape. To escape the wrath of Herod, Mary, Joseph and the newborn
Jesus fled Bethlehem for Egypt. Joseph is seen as a tiny, elderly figure in the middle
distance, while at the left Herod's soldiers enter in pursuit of the "King of the Jews."
According to an old legend, the troops abandoned their chase when farmers said
that they were planting their crops when the Holy Family passed. Since the fields had
miraculously ripened overnight, the soldiers concluded that it was impossible to
overtake their prey. The slender column in the left background refers to the legend
that relates how pagan idols collapsed when Jesus entered Egypt, and the solitary tree
beside Joseph refers to the palm that miraculously bent down to provide dates for
Mary. On the illuminated page in the foreground, blind "Synagogue" is shown as
a personification of the Old Order before the coming of Christ.

The brilliant colour and acute detail – as in the jewelled hem of Mary's mantle –
epitomize the oil technique perfected by Flemish artists. The leading member of the
Brussels school, van Orley produced work that reveals the influence of Italian Renaissance art, even though he may not have journeyed south of the Alps.

Gift by subscription, 1938   2456

Albrecht Dürer (German, 1471–1528)

Adam and Eve 1504
Engraving on laid paper. 24.7 x 19.1 (sheet)

Dürer was the greatest master of the Northern Renaissance and one of the outstanding
artistic geniuses of all time. Like his Italian contemporary Leonardo da Vinci, he was
a painter and writer of treatises on measurement, proportion, and artistic theory. Unlike
that of Leonardo, his fame rests more on his prints than on his work in other media.

    This superb impression of Dürer's masterpiece *Adam and Eve* demonstrates the
synthesis of the Northern and Italian Renaissance styles, which he effected following
his first trip to Italy in 1494. Dürer's extraordinary ability to capture texture and detail,
so characteristic of the Northern tradition, demonstrates his powers of observation
and his technical virtuosity as a goldsmith, while his attempt to create ideal human
proportions reflects his study of Italian art. The significance of this plate to Dürer is
indicated in part by the large number of preparatory drawings, many of which have survived, and the fact that it is the only plate on which the artist has signed his full name.

Purchase, 1984   84/2

Francesco Salviati (Italian, 1510-63)

Lamentation over the Dead Christ c.1540
Brown ink and wash, over traces of black chalk, heightened with
white gouache on laid paper. 24.1 x 16.1

This elaborately worked drawing is characteristic of Florentine Mannerism. Francesco
Salviati was trained in Florence but produced his first important paintings in Rome in
the 1530s. He fully assimilated the High Renaissance style of Michelangelo and Raphael
and added his own sophisticated elegance and inventive wit. Like other Mannerists,
he showed more interest in artistic refinement than in naturalistic depiction. Although
Salviati spent short periods in Bologna, Venice and France, he executed most of his
major works in Florence and Rome.

   This drawing appears to be one of Salviati's earliest surviving pen-and-ink drawings. It is related to a large altarpiece painted by Salviati about 1540 for the Venetian
church of the Corpus Domini. The dedication of the church to the body of Christ must
have dictated the subject of the painting. Although the composition is reversed and
the figures differ in detail in the drawing, the proportions of the composition and the
unusual addition of an angel holding the Instruments of the Passion at the top are
analogous to those of the painting.

   Purchase, 1981   81/4

Hendrik Goltzius (Dutch, 1558–1617)

Hercules and Cacus 1588
Chiaroscuro woodcut (three blocks) on laid paper. 41.2 x 33.2 (composition)

A brilliant and prolific engraver, Goltzius developed a distinctive style that was
widely copied in the northern Netherlands. He also made approximately 20 woodcuts;
Hercules and Cacus is his earliest and only dated print that employed the unusual
chiaroscuro woodcut technique.

The chiaroscuro or "light-dark" woodcut was invented in Italy and northern
Europe during the first half of the 16th century. To make a chiaroscuro woodcut,
several blocks are necessary, one for each colour or tone. In Italy the line block often
provided only a few accents, while the design was worked out in broad areas of tone.
In the North the image was fully worked out in the line block, and the tone or colour
blocks were used to add depth to the composition. The white of the paper was
used to create dramatic highlights.

The present woodcut depicts the mythological Greek hero Hercules, cloaked
in his lionskin and wielding a heavy club, as he prepares to administer the fatal blow
to the fire-breathing god Cacus. The ambiguous spatial recession of the composition
and the exaggerated gestures of the figures are characteristic of Goltzius's Northern
Mannerist style.

Purchase, 1983   83/254

Jacopo Robusti called **Tintoretto** (Italian, 1518-94)

Christ Washing His Disciples' Feet c.1545-55
Oil on canvas. 154.9 x 407.7

Tintoretto's *Christ Washing His Disciples' Feet* testifies to how 16th-century Venetian artists used oil paint on canvas to produce works of opulence and grandeur. Large canvases decorated both public and private rooms in Venice, just as frescoes decorated rooms of central Italy. But invariably the oil paint of the Venetians created a heightened richness of colour and texture. Showing the biblical event that preceded the Last Supper, this picture is a variation of an even larger canvas Tintoretto painted in 1548 for the church of San Marcuola in Venice. This painting was probably done shortly after for a private setting, where it hung with another canvas of similar dimensions by Tintoretto, *The Miracle of the Loaves and Fishes*, now in the Metropolitan Museum, New York. Both paintings include a large number of figures, depicted in a wide variety of poses and dressed in rich attire. Gold has even been used in the AGO's painting to adorn some of the costumes. Tintoretto also relied on Michelangelo for the inspiration of some of the figures and the architect Sebastiano Serlio for the inspiration of the architectural setting.

For more than 50 years Tintoretto produced a steady stream of such canvases, all impetuously executed, dramatically composed and teeming with figures. His vigorous brushwork and resonant colour exerted a profound effect on Italian Baroque painting of the 17th century.

Gift by general subscription, 1959   58/51

Pieter Brueghel, the Younger (Flemish, 1564–1637)

The Peasants' Wedding
Oil on panel. 36.2 x 44.2

This painting is one of the finest versions of an immensely popular subject. The composition originated with Pieter Bruegel the Elder, who made a practice of depicting peasants honestly and sympathetically. His son Pieter Brueghel the Younger painted many copies with variations after his father's compositions. But since the young Brueghel was only five when his father died, he usually relied on prints after his father's paintings rather than on the paintings themselves. In the case of *The Peasants' Wedding*, the original painting by the older Bruegel is lost, but the composition is known through an engraving.

In contrast to the idealizing tendencies of most Italian art, this painting celebrates everyday life. Depicted with sympathetic candour, the colourful peasants dance and carouse, while the sullen bride avidly eyes the gold accumulating in the platter before her. This well-preserved panel is distinguished by the lively touch with which it is painted.

Gift of Mr. and Mrs. W. Redelmeier, 1940   2557

Jan (Velvet) Brueghel, the Elder (Flemish, 1568–1625) and
Hans Rottenhammer (German, 1564–1625)

The Dream of Raphael 1595
Oil on copper. 35.6 x 51.4

This jewel-like picture combines an Italian allegorical subject and a detailed Northern technique of painting. The composition is based on Giorgio Ghisi's enigmatic
engraving of 1561, which includes an inscription saying that the design is by Raphael.
Although Raphael's authorship is now refuted, his name has given rise to the title of
the engraving and thus of this painting. The exact meaning of *The Dream of Raphael*
remains obscure, but it is likely that it is an allegory of life.

Jan Brueghel was the son of the famous Flemish artist Pieter Bruegel (the Elder).
In the late 1580s Jan travelled to Italy, where in 1595 he entered the services of
Cardinal Federico Borromeo, Bishop of Milan. The cardinal also patronized Hans
Rottenhammer, a German artist who probably painted the female figure and the baby
angels. Jan Brueghel specialized in painting nature in an extremely detailed manner.
In 1596 he returned north and established himself as the most original creator of
landscape and still life in Antwerp.

Gift of Joey and Toby Tanenbaum, in loving memory of Max Tanenbaum,
1986   86/238

Giuseppe Cesari called **Cavaliere d'Arpino** (Italian, 1568–1640)

Study of a Standing Male Nude c.1595
Red chalk on laid paper. 26.1 x 14.6

Giuseppe Cesari, known by his papal title, Cavaliere d'Arpino, rose rapidly to prominence in Rome and Naples during the last decade of the 16th century. But ultimately his painting failed to fulfill its early promise. Unlike his contemporaries Annibale Carracci and Caravaggio, d'Arpino did not conduct a rigorous examination of nature in order to fortify his art; instead, he allowed recollection and repetition to produce a predictable and eventually vacuous style.

A characteristic example of d'Arpino's draughtsmanship in red chalk, this beautiful sheet was once considered the work of Pietro Testa. The drawing may be a study for a martyrdom of St. Sebastian, since the figure's pose is similar to that in a drawing of the saint by d'Arpino in the Uffizi. The languorous attitude and exaggerated *contrapposto* appear to be paraphrases of Michelangelo's *Dying Slave*, sculpted in Rome c.1513-16.

Gift of Marvin B. Gelber, Toronto, 1989   89/1

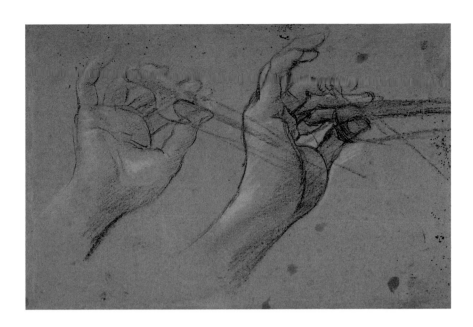

Annibale Carracci (Italian, 1560–1609)

Studies for the Hand of an Angel Holding a Violin Bow (recto) c.1585;
Study for the Figure of St. Jerome Reading (verso)
Charcoal and white chalk on blue laid paper. 28.3 x 40.8

Between them, Caravaggio and Annibale Carracci created the Baroque style in Rome
about 1600. But whereas no securely attributed drawings by Caravaggio are known,
a rich legacy of Annibale Carracci's drawings survives. Widely varied in technique and
subject matter, Annibale's drawings exercised a profound influence on the Baroque
artists of succeeding generations.

This remarkable drawing is a study for one of the angels in the upper part of *The
Baptism of Christ* (San Gregorio, Bologna), a signed and dated altarpiece of 1585. The
painting was Annibale's second major public commission, and the earliest altarpiece for
which preparatory drawings survive. Only two other drawings are firmly accepted as
studies for it. In the present drawing the artist finalizes the position of the hand and
fingers of the angel, creating an image of great beauty and refinement.

The drawing on the verso of the sheet relates directly to a painting of St. Jerome
reading (now in the Banca Popolare, Modena) that has been attributed to both Annibale
and his cousin Ludovico Carracci. With the firm attribution of the drawing to Annibale,
this painting can also be reliably attributed to him and dated to about 1585.

Gift of Arthur Gelber, 1988   338

Artus Wolfort (Flemish, 1581–1641)

Christ Healing the Lame
Oil on canvas. 170.0 x 226.8

This painting depicts Christ's visit to the pool of Bethesda in Jerusalem, where at certain times an angel "troubled the water"; whoever then stepped into the water first was healed of any illness. At Bethesda there was a man who had been lame for 38 years and had not succeeded in entering the pool. Here, Jesus says to him, "Rise, take up thy bed, and walk." The miracle of Bethesda was traditionally related to the cleansing power of the sacrament of baptism.

A contemporary of Rubens, Wolfort was less innovative, but he still could paint with an impressive realism, as is evident in the torso and bedding of the lame man.

Anonymous gift, 1983   83/304

Frans Snyders (Flemish, 1579–1657)

Still Life with Figures c.1625
Oil on panel. 124.5 x 177.8

Frans Snyders, a contemporary and collaborator of Rubens, specialized in painting large and robust still lifes. He was a pupil of Pieter Brueghel the Younger and a friend of his brother Jan Brueghel. He travelled to Italy but by 1609 was back in his native Antwerp, where he brought "kitchen piece" still lifes to a Baroque fullness.

It was common for Snyders to feature wild game and fowl; in this excellent example, he also included a lobster, grapes, apples, a lemon and an artichoke. In typical fashion he has painted the various textures with remarkable assurance and the colour with notable richness, especially the red of the lobster. Another typical feature is the view to the sky through an opening at the left. The figures were probably painted by Snyders's brother-in-law Cornelis de Vos, such collaboration being common in the paintings produced in Rubens's circle in Antwerp.

Gift from the John Paris Bickell Bequest Fund, 1952   51/71

Peter Paul Rubens (Flemish, 1577–1640)

The Elevation of the Cross c.1638
Oil on paper mounted on canvas. 72.1 x 132.7

Rubens, the leading Flemish Baroque artist, painted this turbulent oil sketch toward
the end of his highly successful career. In the centre, the cross on which Christ was
crucified is laboriously hoisted into place. The extreme physical activity of the men is
juxtaposed with the extreme emotional intensity of the women at the left. Only John
the Evangelist and the Virgin Mary witness the harrowing event with restraint. Throughout, the dynamism of the composition is heightened by the vibrant brushwork, at its
most dazzling in the Roman soldiers at the right.

This large oil sketch combines the groups that appear in the three central panels
of Rubens's enormous altarpiece painted in 1610-11 for the church of St. Walburga,
Antwerp. The sketch is also directly related to a large engraving of 1638, dedicated to
Cornelis van der Geest, a lifelong friend of Rubens and the man largely responsible
for the commission of the St. Walburga altarpiece almost 30 years before. Since van der
Geest died in 1638, it is likely that this event prompted the execution of this masterful oil sketch and the related engraving.

Purchase, 1928   906

Sir Anthony van Dyck (Flemish, 1599–1641)

Michel le Blon c.1630-35
Oil on canvas. 78.1 x 61.0

Among 17th-century Flemish painters, Anthony van Dyck was second only to Rubens.
Maturing quickly, van Dyck became Rubens's chief assistant before he was twenty.
For six years van Dyck travelled in Italy, then re-established himself in Antwerp about
1627, and from 1632 until his death lived in England as court painter to Charles I.
Throughout his career van Dyck readily took on portrait commissions; the portraits
from his second Antwerp period – such as this example – combine a remarkable
sensitivity to character with an exceptional refinement of paint handling.

The sitter has been identified by the inscription on a 17th-century engraving of
the portrait. A well-known engraver, diplomat and picture dealer, Michel le Blon acted
as agent for the Swedish Crown in London and may have been instrumental in van
Dyck's being invited to England. In contrast to his portraits of aristocrats, van Dyck has
here severely reduced colour and eliminated extraneous detail, but thereby the lively
intelligence of le Blon's face shows through. While the composition is a stable triangle,
the surface of the canvas is brilliantly animated by van Dyck's deftly varied brushwork.

Bequest of J. J. Vaughan, 1965   64/45

Frans Hals (Dutch, 1581/5-1666)

Isaak Abrahamsz. Massa 1626
Oil on canvas. 79.7 x 65.1

This engaging portrait is one of Hals's most innovative works. Although born in Catholic
Antwerp, Hals spent most of his life in Haarlem, where for over 50 years he specialized in doing portraits distinguished by technical virtuosity and psychological insight.

The sitter has been identified by the inscription on a 17th-century engraving.
A personal friend of Hals, and also of Michel le Blon (whose portrait by van Dyck is also
in the AGO's collection), Isaak Abrahamsz. Massa (1585-1655) was a commercial agent
in Russia. This may account for the unusual inclusion of the window with a view of fir
trees, perhaps painted by the Dutch landscape artist Pieter de Molijn (1595-1661).
The pose of Massa, the most original aspect of the portrait, departs radically from the
stiff formality of earlier Dutch portraits. As if to greet an unexpected visitor, Massa
turns in his chair, his eyes focused on the extreme left while his body is still turned to
the right. His mouth appears to speak and his elbow to invade the spectator's space. In
his hand Massa holds a sprig of holly, the evergreen plant symbolizing constancy.
Although painted when both Hals and Massa were in their 40s, this portrait radiates
youthful vitality.

Bequest of Frank P. Wood, 1955   54/31

Frans Hals (Dutch, 1581/5–1666)

Vincent Laurensz. van der Vinne c.1655
Oil on canvas. 64.7 x 48.9

As Hals got older, his portraits became more restrained in colour and his interpretation of character more penetrating. The influence of Rembrandt became deeper, but Hals still retained his own use of light and his own manner of painting in fragmented brush strokes.

The identification of the sitter relies on a print by van der Vinne himself. A minor artist, van der Vinne (1629–1702) worked in Hals's studio for about six months in 1655. Also a diarist, he kept an illustrated journal of a three-year trip he made throughout Europe. In this mature portrait, the composition is simple and the sitter's expression detached, the result being unpretentious but profoundly human. In the figure the paint has been applied thinly, with bold strokes fracturing the surface – a daring technique not fully appreciated until the time of Courbet and the French Impressionists.

Bequest of Frank P. Wood, 1955   54/32

Salomon van Ruysdael (Dutch, 1600-70)

The Ferry Boat 1656
Oil on wood. 77.5 x 114.3

This composition was a favourite of Salomon van Ruysdael. Only somewhat younger
than van Goyen, Ruysdael also painted tonal landscapes in the earlier part of his career.
But this landscape, dated 15 years after van Goyen's *View of Rhenen* (see opposite page),
epitomizes Ruysdael's mature style. Now individual colours are more distinct and tonal
differences more dramatic. The composition is also more deliberately organized, with
the horizontals of the low horizon and flat-bottomed ferry boat balanced by the commanding vertical of the feathery trees. The trees testify to Ruysdael's acute observation
of nature and to his consummate dexterity in translating those observations into paint.
Especially beautiful is the silver-green willow at the foot of the clump of trees. It was
usual for Ruysdael to show such scenes against the pale blue and yellow colour of an
early evening sky.

Bequest of W. Redelmeier, 1956   56/20

Jan van Goyen (Dutch, 1596–1656)

View of Rhenen 1641
Oil on canvas. 143.5 x 222.9

Until the 17th century, landscape mostly appeared in art as a backdrop for religious and mythological subjects. Then, the depiction of landscape evolved as a magnificent end in itself, both north and south of the Alps. But whereas most artists in Italy imaginatively recreated nature, artists in the Netherlands usually painted their immediate surroundings in a more naturalistic way.

Although exceptionally large, this canvas exemplifies the subject matter and subdued tonality of van Goyen's painting from the 1640s. The overcast sky, occupying a major part of the composition, governs the mood of the entire painting. The sombre tonality of the water, riverbank and tree is matched by the calm restraint of the various figures – fisherman, boatman, and travellers arriving at an inn. Throughout, the paint has been applied freely, but thinly. Van Goyen painted at least 18 views of Rhenen, which is located on the Rhine in Central Holland.

Purchase, Frank P. Wood Endowment, 1960   60/5

Rembrandt Harmensz. van Rijn (Dutch, 1606-69)

Portrait of a Lady with a Lap Dog c.1665
Oil on canvas. 81.3 x 64.1

Both as a teacher and a painter, Rembrandt dominated Dutch 17th-century art, even though his work increasingly departed from fashionable taste during the second half of his career. Although he painted many biblical subjects, which helped to create a new Protestant iconography, the majority of his pictures are portraits. For ten years after he settled in Amsterdam in 1631/32, the prosperous burgher class flocked to him for portraits painted in carefully detailed style. In contrast, many of his later, more penetrating portraits were not commissioned, being studies of his family or of his Jewish neighbours.

The sitter of this late portrait has not been conclusively identified, although it has been suggested that she is Magdalena van Loo, Rembrandt's young daughter-in-law. Posed against a dark, indefinite background, a device Rembrandt used to great effect, the young, rather plain woman stares pensively into space. The introspection of her demeanour contrasts sharply with the outward splendour of her dress, which creates a deeply compelling yet enigmatic image.

Bequest of Frank P. Wood, 1955   54/30

Rembrandt Harmensz. van Rijn (Dutch, 1606-69)

Christ at Emmaus: The Larger Plate 1654
Etching and drypoint on laid paper. 21.3 x 16.2 (impression)

Rembrandt's work as an etcher is legendary; his experimental technique has been widely admired and emulated throughout the centuries. He was also a supreme story-teller, often selecting dramatic episodes from the Bible. *Christ at Emmaus* dates to a time when Rembrandt was preoccupied with recording events from the life of Christ. The incident represented in this print occurred soon after the Resurrection, when two disciples met Christ on the road to Emmaus and did not recognize him. They invited him to a meal, and when they finally did discern his identity he vanished.

With his characteristic blending of the everyday and the divine, Rembrandt has depicted the two incredulous disciples, along with a portly innkeeper dressed in home-spun clothes; at the same time, he has portrayed Christ's divinity by drawing rays of light around his head. The pose with outstretched hands is reminiscent of the Christ figure in Leonardo's *Last Supper*.

Etched with boldly hatched lines, the plate was then completed with drypoint. In contrast to other prints in which Rembrandt left films of ink on the plate to create deep tonalities, the dramatic effect in this print depends primarily on his masterful manipulation of the white of the paper.

Gift of the Sir Edmund Walker Estate, 1926   1495

94

Jacques Callot (French, 1592–1635)

Two Zanni c.1616
Etching on laid paper. 9.6 x 14.4 (impression)

Callot was born in France but spent much of his career in Italy, where he became court artist to the Medici in Florence. There he had many opportunities to witness *commedia dell'arte*, a popular form of impromptu theatre. Following basic plots, actors would improvise much of their performances and dialogues, which were characterized by wild, mannered gestures and comic actions.

Although Callot's etching traditionally has been called *Two Pantaloons*, neither of the dancers resemble the popular *commedia dell'arte* character Pantalone; rather, they appear to be *zanni*, comic manservants or buffoons who combined the skills of clowns and acrobats and entertained crowds during carnival time.

Although Callot began his career as an engraver, he became a prolific and innovative etcher. He worked his plates with a special tool called an *échoppe*, twisting its oval point to make swelling and diminishing lines that animated his forms; he also employed multiple biting. The foreground figures, which were exposed to acid for a longer period, were more deeply bitten and printed more darkly, while the fainter lines in the background help create a sense of aerial perspective.

Gift of the Trier-Fodor Foundation, 1983   83/251

Jan Weenix (Dutch, 1640–1719)

Still Life with Dead Hare 1703
Oil on canvas. 121.9 x 101.6

Still lifes of dead game and fowl were not as popular in the Netherlands as in Flanders.
Hunting wild game was restricted to the Dutch upper class, and only at the end of the
17th century did they begin to decorate their houses with pictures of dead animals.
Jan Weenix catered to this taste.

    This fine example comprises the usual components of Weenix's art, a dead hare
most often being the central feature. Here, the fur is juxtaposed with the feathers of a
dead turkey, and both are contrasted with lush fruit at the right and live flowers behind.
The marble urn and the view into a park at sunset are also typical features. In sum,
the painting is a study of the contrasts between live and dead, animate and inanimate
objects – all imbued with an 18th-century refinement and gentle melancholy.

    Gift of Miss L. Aileen Larkin, 1945   2805

Lambert Doomer (Dutch, 1622/3-1700)

Noah's Ark on Mt. Ararat, a Camel Train outside a City in
the Foreground c.1678-79
Brown ink, watercolour on laid paper. 26.7 x 41.1

Doomer may have been apprenticed to Rembrandt in the late 1630s or early 1640s,
although he was not called a Rembrandt pupil until the mid-19th century. He was
influenced by Rembrandt's drawing manner, but the majority of his works are topographical in nature and executed in his own distinctive poetic style. Sketches made
during his extensive travels through Germany, France and the Netherlands were often
used for larger, more elaborate drawings such as this one.

    Doomer was a master of anecdotal detail. With lively pen work and luminous
washes he has created a vivid image of travellers on a journey. The roofs of a town
can be seen in the distance, with the massive presence of Mt. Ararat beyond. A classic
example of Doomer's work, this drawing illustrates the artist's skill at combining
landscape with biblically inspired narrative.

Purchase, 1978   78/98

Eustache Le Sueur (French, 1616/17-55)

The Raising of Tabitha c.1640/45
Oil on canvas. 185.4 x 137.2

Tabitha (Dorcas), who was known for her charity to the Christian community at Joppa, was deeply mourned at her death. Her friends summoned St. Peter, who "[was] brought ... into the upper chamber: and all the widows stood by him weeping, and showing the coats and garments which Dorcas made, while she was with them" (*The Acts of the Apostles* 9:39). In this painting, St. Peter, clad in his usual copper-coloured mantle over a blue tunic, is seen at the left, just as he enters Tabitha's death chamber. After dismissing the mourners, St. Peter miraculously raised Tabitha from the dead. Although the subject is reasonably rare in art, in this case it is fitting: the painting was undertaken as an altarpiece for the chapel dedicated to St. Peter in the church of St-Étienne-du-Mont, Paris. The artist himself was buried in this chapel.

Le Sueur espoused classical ideals, and though he did not go to Rome he admired the work of Raphael and Poussin above all else. This fine example of Le Sueur's work reveals his preoccupation with clearly organized compositions and decorous, sculptural figures, expressing themselves through rhetorical gestures and unambiguous glances. The bright, clear colour is also typical.

Gift from the Contributing Members' Fund, 1960   59/31

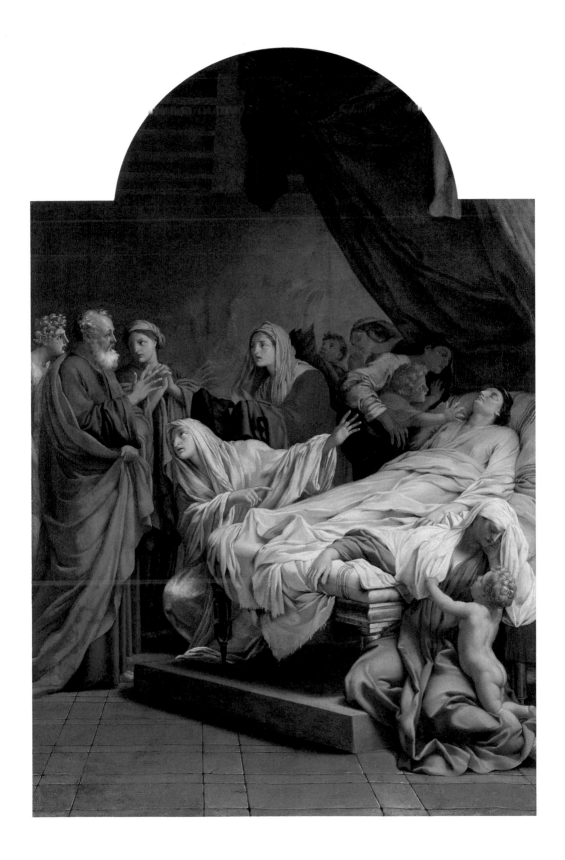

Nicolas Poussin (French, 1594–1665)

Venus, Mother of Aeneas, Presenting Him with Arms Forged by Vulcan c.1636/37
Oil on canvas. 108.0 x 134.6

Aeneas, the hero of Virgil's Latin epic *The Aeneid*, is here being shown the arms that
Venus persuaded Vulcan to forge for him. A refugee from the ruins of Troy, Aeneas was
then able to establish himself on Italian soil and fulfill his destiny of founding Rome.
        Such stories appealed to Poussin, who though French by birth did most of his
painting in Rome. He worked mostly for the educated upper middle class and favoured
subjects with moralizing or stoical themes. The greatest of French classicists, Poussin
sought clarity and balance in his painting and looked to such High Renaissance artists as
Raphael for inspiration. In this painting the figure of Aeneas is based directly on one
by Raphael in a fresco in the Vatican. In contrast, the golden light and craggy landscape
reveal Poussin's fascination with 16th-century Venetian painting, an interest he later
abandoned. A second version of the subject was painted by Poussin in 1639.

        Gift of Reuben Wells Leonard Estate, 1948   48/5

Salvator Rosa (Italian, 1615-73)

A Poet Seated by a Tree 1640s
Brown ink on laid paper. 16.8 x 10.8

A major painter of the Neapolitan school, Salvator Rosa is perhaps best remembered
for his turbulent and moody landscapes. He was also a prolific draughtsman and a
poet-satirist.

In 1639/40 Rosa settled in Florence, where he continued his interests in the pictorial arts and became absorbed in writing poetry and satire and in composing music.
This drawing belongs to a group of related sheets from the 1640s executed while
Rosa was associated with the Medici court. Far from reflecting this environment, the
drawing relates to the simpler life that Rosa enjoyed at a country retreat, a Tuscan villa
at Monterufoli. This image of an introspective, brooding poet shows the side of Rosa
that appealed strongly to the 19th-century Romantics and illustrates one facet of his
preoccupation with artistic genius, which, he maintained, should be completely
unfettered.

The majority of Rosa's drawings consist of a tangle of hastily executed lines
and rapid washes. This sheet, with its precise network of clean hatching, comes closer
to his etchings; it may thus have been undertaken as a design for a print that was
never executed.

Gift from the Volunteer Committee Fund, 1977   76/216

Claude Lorrain (Claude Gellée) (French, 1600-82)

Coast View with the Embarkation of Carlo and Ubaldo 1667
Oil on canvas. 92.7 x 138.4

Claude, like Poussin, was a Frenchman who spent most of his life in Rome. But whereas Poussin usually focused on the human figure, Claude always featured the landscape setting. In this splendid landscape, the subject is taken from the great 16th-century Italian epic *Jerusalem Delivered* by Torquato Tasso. Although Claude accurately depicted the two Christian knights Carlo and Ubaldo as they embark for the Fortunate Islands, he did not let the narrative distract from his principal concern: the evocation of an idyllic landscape bathed in radiant light. The coastline is largely imaginary but seems entirely plausible, because Claude so carefully studied the various aspects of nature. Combining refinement of observation, subtlety of composition and delicacy of execution, this serene masterpiece was painted in Claude's 67th year. It is one of four landscapes that the artist painted for the Florentine-Roman nobleman Prince Paolo Francesco Falconieri.

Gift of Group Captain H. L. Cooper, AFC, Salisbury, England, in appreciation of the contribution of Canadians in the Armed Services in two World Wars, 1962   62/12

Pier Francesco Mola (Italian, 1612-66)

Boy with a Dove c.1652-56
Oil on canvas. 99.1 x 74.9

This canvas typifies Roman Baroque painting at the middle of the century. Although born in the canton of Ticino in Italian Switzerland, Mola trained in Rome with the late Mannerist Cavaliere d'Arpino. Of greater consequence, he closely studied the canvases of the great 16th-century Venetians and also those of Guercino.

The compositional motif is a favourite one with Mola. What is basically a genre subject is rendered dramatic by the fancy dress and liveliness of the boy's pose and expression. The effect is further enhanced by the strong contrasts of bright light and dark shadow, and the rich colour applied with a vigorous brush. The result produces an arresting immediacy both of subject and painterly technique. From at least the mid-18th century until 1951, this painting belonged to the Dukes of Bedford.

Gift from the Corporations' Subscription Fund, 1959   58/25

Pietro da Cortona (Italian, 1596–1669)

Tobias and the Archangel Raphael late 1640s
Black chalk on laid paper. 23.6 x 16.7

Pietro da Cortona was the leading Italian painter from the 1620s until the 1660s. His frescoes in Rome and Florence constitute one of the chief glories of the High Baroque style; he also designed buildings of great importance.

A prolific and gifted draughtsman, Cortona made drawings in various media and a succession of styles. His drawings, like his paintings, frequently show sensuous figures in an abundant landscape. This drawing was engraved by G. B. Bonacina, who settled in Rome about 1650, and also by Francesco Cassart. Cortona repeated the composition in a painting of the Guardian Angel done for Pope Alexander VII in 1656.

The story of Tobias's journey to collect money due his blind father is found in the Old Testament Apocrypha. In this well-preserved drawing, Tobias looks expectantly up at his guide, the Archangel Raphael. In his hand, Tobias carries the fish from the river Tigris, which protected him from evil and then helped restore his father's sight.

Purchase, in memory of Dr. Walter Vitzthum, 1971   71/1

Mattia Preti (Italian, 1613-99)

St. Paul the Hermit c.1656-60
Oil on canvas. 233.7 x 181.0

Born in southern Italy, Preti made a significant contribution to the High Baroque painting of Rome, Naples and Malta. His bold and frequently penetrating style successfully
combines elements from Caravaggio and his followers and 16th-century Venetian painters such as Paolo Veronese. This painting, probably undertaken in Naples between 1656
and 1660, admirably demonstrates Preti's fondness for powerful, diagonal compositions
and for dramatic contrasts of light and dark. Preti liked to depict his principal figures
from a low point of view and at a moment of emotional intensity.

St. Paul the Hermit was a 4th-century ascetic, who lived in isolation in the
Egyptian desert. Here, the saint's meditations are interrupted by the arrival of a raven
with his daily ration of bread. Eventually St. Paul the Hermit was sought out by St.
Anthony Abbot, an equally dedicated hermit, who is seen approaching from the right.

Purchase, Frank P. Wood Endowment, 1968   67/36

Luca Giordano (Italian, 1634–1705)

Battle of the Gods and the Giants
Oil on canvas. 221.5 x 258.5

Famed for the speed with which he worked, Luca Giordano produced an enormous
number of paintings during a 50-year career. He made his birthplace, Naples, his home,
but he travelled widely, absorbing a variety of artistic influences – the 16th-century
Venetians, Ribera, Pietro da Cortona and Mattia Preti. He undertook important commissions in Venice and Florence and spent the years 1692–1702 in Spain at the court
of Charles II.

    This mature painting represents Giordano at the height of his powers. Freely
painted, with flashes of bright colour emerging dramatically from the dark ground, the
picture represents the type of dynamic subject Giordano relished. According to Greek
mythology, a band of giants piled one mountain on top of another, in order to assault
Olympus and overthrow the gods. Jupiter, seen here at the upper right, hurled his
thunderbolts and flung the mountains down on the giants. In this painting the beautiful
figure of Minerva, in armour and a blue mantle, also plays a major role in combating
the brutish giants.

    Gift of Dr. and Mrs. Gilbert Bagnani, 1988   88/300

Giovanni Battista Foggini (Italian, 1652–1725)

The Rape of Orithyia by Boreas
Bronze. H. 54.5

The Rape of Proserpine by Pluto
Bronze. H. 54.5

After training in Rome, Foggini returned to his native Florence in 1676, where he established himself as one of the most significant Late Baroque sculptors. Appointed grand-ducal sculptor in 1687 and official architect in 1694, he devoted most of the rest of his life to commissions for the ruling Medici family.

Foggini's virtuosity is epitomized in this carefully balanced pair of bronzes, which must have been modelled before 1702 when they were depicted in a fresco in a Florentine palace. Both male figures daringly support themselves and their abducted victims on one leg. Appropriately Boreas, God of the North Wind, treads on a cloud, while Pluto, King of the Underworld, steps on flames. Representations of similar rapes are common in Baroque sculpture and painting, but no other artist so audaciously balanced the figures or contrived such marvellously agitated silhouettes. The contrast of rippling drapery and smooth, glistening flesh is also typical of Foggini's sculpture.

Purchased from the collection of Margaret and Ian Ross with assistance from the Volunteer Committee Fund, 1982
Left: 82/71   Right: 82/70

François Lespingola (French, 1644–1705)

Hercules Delivering Prometheus
Bronze. 45.5 x 59.5 x 36.0

Lespingola was French by birth and is best known for his large-scale sculpture, done for Louis XIV at Versailles. His training, however, largely took place in Rome, where he lived from 1666 to 1675.

This imaginative sculpture is the only small bronze reliably attributed to Lespingola. Several other casts of the bronze are known, but they all show variations of detail. The bronze celebrates Prometheus, the mortal who stole fire from the gods. As punishment, Prometheus was chained to a rock and his ever-replenished liver daily devoured by an eagle. In the sculpture, Hercules prepares to kill the aggressive eagle and free Prometheus from his torture. The striking pictorial treatment of the narrative is analogous to that of many small-scale Florentine bronzes of the second half of the 17th century. Although Lespingola may have studied such bronzes when he was in Italy, it is also possible that this sculpture predates most comparable Florentine examples. In any case *Hercules Delivering Prometheus* attests to a remarkable artistic imagination and technical facility.

Purchased from the collection of Margaret and Ian Ross with assistance from the Volunteer Committee Fund, 1982   82/73

Massimiliano Soldani-Benzi (Italian, 1656–1740)

The Guardian Angel
Bronze. 41.2 x 28.0

Like Foggini, who was four years older, Massimiliano Soldani-Benzi studied in Florence and then in Rome at the Grand-Ducal Academy. Soldani-Benzi specialized in medals but by the turn of the century was also active as a sculptor of three-dimensional bronzes.

This relief is a translation into bronze of Pietro da Cortona's painting *The Guardian Angel*, done in 1656 for Pope Alexander VII. A closely related subject, *Tobias and the Archangel Raphael*, appears in a drawing by Pietro da Cortona in the AGO's collection (see p. 105). Although Soldani-Benzi altered small details of Cortona's painting, he brilliantly succeeded in reproducing such features as the rippling drapery. To heighten the pictorial effect of the relief, Soldani-Benzi thoroughly worked the surface of the bronze with several different tools.

Purchased from the collection of Margaret and Ian Ross with assistance from the Volunteer Committee Fund, 1982   82/73

Massimiliano Soldani-Benzi (Italian, 1656–1740)

Castor and Pollux
Bronze. H. 52.7

Many of Soldani-Benzi's free-standing bronzes are reductions of famous marbles from antiquity or the Renaissance. The AGO possesses an unsurpassed series of single-figure reductions, in addition to other Soldani-Benzi bronzes related to Roman and Greek sculpture. This superb bronze is based on a marble statue that enjoyed wide fame during the 17th century. A celebration of idealized male beauty, the marble was an antique Roman copy of a 4th-century BC Greek statue in the style of Praxiteles. The marble was in Rome when Soldani-Benzi was a student there, but it later passed to Spain and is now in the Prado, Madrid. Posed frontally, the two nude athletes wear laurel wreaths and hold objects related to the games — torches and a *patera*, the flat dish from which wine was poured to the gods in thanksgiving for victory. The two athletes are traditionally called Castor and Pollux, but the identification has often been challenged. Once in the possession of the Dukes of Marlborough at Blenheim Castle, this fine bronze testifies to the enduring interest of European culture in classical art.

Purchased from the collection of Margaret and Ian Ross with assistance from the Volunteer Committee Fund, 1982   82/66

Giovanni Paolo Panini (Italian, 1692–1765/8)

A Capriccio of Roman Ruins with the Arch of Constantine c.1755
Oil on canvas. 99.1 x 135.3

A Capriccio of Roman Ruins with the Pantheon c.1755
Oil on canvas. 99.1 x 135.3

Views of Rome and its classical ruins were immensely popular in the 18th century, both with Italian connoisseurs and foreign travellers on the Grand Tour. Of the many artists who painted Rome, Panini was the most celebrated. Born in northern Italy, he settled in Rome when he was 20. His influence was strong among French artists, especially Hubert Robert.

These paintings, which unite the widespread 18th-century fascination with ruins and the concurrent love of fantasy, are *vedute ideate e rovine* – fanciful views of Rome. They show well-known Roman buildings arranged according to the imagination, not reality. Ruins of monumental architecture, together with intact buildings and sculpture, form a stage on which Romans listen to unidentified orators. The actions of these anonymous figures are typically casual and their attitude languorous.

Purchase, Frank P. Wood Endowment, 1963
Upper: 62/32   Lower: 62/33

Antonio Canaletto (Italian, 1697–1768)

Al Dolo
Etching on laid paper. 29.7 x 42.5 (sheet)

The best known of all the view painters, Canaletto brought the long tradition of recording the buildings and canals of Venice to its highest achievement. He attempted to record topographical detail accurately and to convey a sense of the light and mood of the city. Canaletto made only 34 etchings, which were completed between 1741 and 1744; they are unsurpassed in the history of *veduta* prints for their light and colour, brilliance of line and expressive power. Eleven of his etchings, including this one, depict actual views of sites in the outlying areas of Venice.

This plate shows the town of Dolo, which is situated about 15 miles west of Venice on the Brenta canal. The view was taken looking west along the canal, with the Church of S. Rocco on the right and the Villa Zanon-Bon on the left. Using long, trembling parallel lines, Canaletto has captured both the vibrant Venetian sunlight and the cool, dark shadows of the buildings.

Gift of Mrs. David Johnston in memory of W. R. Johnston, 1951   50/27

Giovanni Battista Tiepolo (Italian, 1696–1770)

Caricature of a Man with a Sword 1754-62
Brown ink and wash on laid paper. 19.6 x 14.2

Although Giovanni Battista Tiepolo's fame rests firmly on his revival of the glorious tradition of 16th-century Venetian history painting, he was also a brilliant and influential draughtsman who worked in a variety of media.

Few Italian artists devoted themselves to caricature professionally, and Tiepolo appears to have considered the execution of his caricature drawings a private activity for the entertainment of friends and colleagues. Exaggerating the unique characteristics of the individual, he often drew single figures in profile or from the back. His subjects — who remain anonymous — were taken from a wide cross-section of society.

The present drawing was included in *The Third Volume of Caricatures*, an album of 106 caricatures that date to the period from 1754 to 1762. The artist's enormous signature is in itself a caricature and states that he "invented and drew it." In this sketch, the figure has been reduced to elementary geometric shapes; the circular head is topped by a ridiculously tiny hat; the legs and feet become sticks, and the hands resemble animal paws. The result is a deliberately naïve but remarkably clever caricature of the human body.

Gift of the Trier-Fodor Foundation, 1986   86/38

Giovanni Battista Piranesi (Italian, 1720–1778)

Carceri d'Invenzione (Prisons) 2nd edition 1761
16 etchings on laid paper bound in original paper cover. 57.2 x 45.4 (closed)

Although Piranesi trained as an architect, he could not establish himself in the field; instead, he turned to printmaking after becoming absorbed in the study of Roman antiquities and mastering the etching technique. He was influenced by Canaletto's etchings, and from them he learned how to use the white of the paper most effectively. Around 1745 he began the *Carceri d'Invenzione*, known in English as *Prisons*.

This series, originally conceived as light-filled architectural caprices, had changed character by 1761, when Piranesi re-issued it. The second edition included two new prints, while the original fourteen were reworked. Using heavy etched lines, the artist solidified the forms, intensified the shadows and added sinister elements that included instruments of torture, watchtowers, chains and walkways. Although the *Carceri* etchings have generally been interpreted as nightmare visions or inner psychic landscapes, recent scholarship suggests that the images may in fact represent Piranesi's fantasies about ancient prisons and expressions of his admiration for the grand architectural achievements of the Romans.

Gift of Dr. and Mrs. Gilbert Bagnani, 1988   88/221

Hubert Robert (French, 1733–1808)

View of the Vaulting of St. Peter's Taken from an Upper Cornice c.1760-63
Red chalk on laid paper. 33.5 x 45.4

Under the tutelage of the director of the French Academy in Rome, Charles Natoire, Robert was encouraged to sketch the Roman landscape and its ancient buildings during his studies from 1754 to 1765. The drawings, which he made while he was still a student, earned him considerable fame.

The French Academy was located on the Corso, across the street from Piranesi's print workshop, and it is not surprising that this drawing shows the influence of the latter's *Carceri* (see opposite page), published while Robert was still in Rome. The vast spaces, peopled with tiny figures, are reminiscent of the Italian printmaker's compositions.

The drawing shows two figures crouching on the edge of the cornice under the coffered vault of the nave of St. Peter's Basilica. The crossing beneath the dome, the right transept, and the apse are visible in the background, flooded with light from above. The composition is unusually dramatic and memorable, and the sheet is a classic example of Robert's masterful use of red chalk to create a wide range of tones and textures.

Purchase, 1984   83/312

François Boucher (French, 1703-70)

The Wooden Shoes (Les Sabots) 1768
Oil on canvas. 62.2 x 52.1 (oval)

As the chief exponent of the Rococo style championed by the court of Louis xv,
Boucher enjoyed enormous success. After study in Italy, he quickly re-established
himself in Paris as a painter of religious and mythological subjects, in addition to
portraits, landscapes, pastorales and genre scenes. As the director of the Gobelins
Factory he also designed tapestries. Only in the 1760s did his work come under attack
by Diderot, who remarked that Boucher had everything "excepté la verité."

Bucolic love scenes were favourite subjects in 18th-century France, both as a
reaction against the high-minded art of the previous century and as an adjunct to the
frivolous life of the royal court. Such subjects preoccupied Boucher almost exclusively
during his last years. This painting illustrates a scene from a short-lived comic opera,
also called *Les Sabots*, performed by the Italian Comedians in Paris in October 1768.
One critic noted that the opera offered "a dramatic tableau in the taste of those that
M. Boucher gives us in his ingenious compositions."

Purchase, Frank P. Wood Endowment, 1978   78/6

Jean-Baptiste Siméon Chardin (French, 1699–1779)

Jar of Apricots 1758
Oil on canvas. 57.2 x 50.8 (oval)

An exception among 18th-century French artists, Chardin did not study in Italy and never attempted the heroic subjects of the ancients. Nor was he interested in the fashionable fêtes and pastorales typifying French Rococo painting. Instead, Chardin firmly devoted himself to genre and still-life subjects, usually painted on a small scale. Composed with unusual rigour and executed with a special appreciation for oil paint's granular properties, Chardin's humble subjects invariably possess an immutable and timeless quality. Despite their middle-class subject matter, his pictures were collected by the king of France, the king of Sweden and Catherine the Great of Russia.

Oval paintings are rare by Chardin; this one has a pendant featuring a melon and peaches, in a private French collection. Although the objects are unpretentious, their shapes have been arranged with careful deliberation – a series of ellipses played off against the oval of the canvas itself. Colour is similarly deployed, with touches of red and blue stabilized in the middle by the orange-yellow of the round lemon.

Purchase, 1962   61/36

Jean Honoré Fragonard (French, 1732–1806)

Melissa leads Astolfo and Ruggiero to Logistilla 1780s
Black chalk, brown wash, traces of graphite on laid paper. 40.0 x 25.8

Fragonard was a brilliant draughtsman and one of the great masters of the 18th century.
He had an instinctive gift for narrative and during his career made illustrations for a
number of texts that were never published in book form. His 160 drawings for Ludovico
Ariosto's *Orlando Furioso* were executed when he was at the height of his artistic powers and are among his finest works. The complex narrative of this 15th-century epic
poem describes the struggles between Christianity and paganism and between love and
folly. The present drawing appears to illustrate an event in the tenth canto and shows
the good sorceress Melissa guiding the two knights Astolfo and Ruggiero to the safety
of Logistilla's island.

   Fragonard's drawing is grandly conceived and alive with movement. Beginning
with a sketchy underdrawing in charcoal, he added rapid brushwork composed of
rococo arcs and curves and applied wash, boldly creating alternate areas of dark and
light. The perpetual motion balances a classical sense of order that is embodied in the
position of the central female figure, who glances back over her left shoulder while
gracefully moving forward to the right.

Purchase, Walter C. Laidlaw Endowment, 1978   77/207

Charles Joseph Natoire (French, 1700-77)

The Park at Arcueil 1748
Brown ink, watercolour, black and red chalks, heightened with white gouache, on green laid paper. 24.4 x 33.2

Natoire's drawings were so greatly admired in 18th-century France that he became the rival of the famous painter and draughtsman François Boucher. Natoire was appointed director of the French Academy in Rome in 1751 and had a significant impact on the many French artists who studied there. Natoire encouraged his students to venture into the countryside around Rome to draw after nature. Since he spent over 25 years in Rome, it is not surprising that he completed many drawings of Italian gardens. His drawings of French gardens, however, are rare and date to his early career in Paris from 1730 to 1751.

The park and gardens of the Château d'Arcueil were perhaps the most beautiful in France and provided a favourite subject for landscape draughtsmen in the 1740s. Although only three have survived, Natoire is known to have made 14 drawings of the gardens at Arcueil.

This sheet shows the artist's unique variation on the technique of *trois crayons*, a mixture of red and black chalk heightened with white, together with ink and wash. The composition recalls the festive mood and rococo elegance of Watteau's *fêtes galantes*. Characteristically Natoire introduces rustic elements derived from 17th-century Dutch art, giving the scene a distinctly genre flavour.

Purchase, 1987   87/35

William Hogarth (British, 1697–1764)

Portrait of a Boy in a Green Coat c.1756
Oil on canvas. 63.5 x 48.3

Hogarth is best known for his satirical "moral histories" such as *The Rake's Progress* and for his promotion of nationalism in British art. He was the first significant native-born portraitist, an occupation previously dominated in England by foreigners, most notably Hans Holbein and Anthony van Dyck. Hogarth preferred to depict his sitters informally and to execute all the details of a picture himself, contrary to the usual practice of the day.

This appealing portrait is a good example of Hogarth's sympathetic but unsentimental portrayal of children. The artist has skilfully captured the unaffected personality of the rosy-cheeked boy and has suggested by the untied neck ribbon and rumpled sleeve his spirited nature. This effect is further heightened by the fluid, painterly brushwork, seen to perfection in the woolly dog. The sitter has never been identified conclusively.

Gift of Reuben Wells Leonard Estate, 1936   2371

Thomas Gainsborough (British, 1727-88)

The Harvest Waggon c.1784
Oil on canvas. 121.9 x 149.9

Esteemed as one of Britain's ablest portraitists, Gainsborough himself always professed a greater interest in landscape. While his early landscapes are full of specific detail, reflecting the influence of Dutch 17th-century works, his mature landscapes are more generalized, in a manner similar to much 18th-century French art. These imaginary landscapes were composed at home and inspired by pieces of cork and coal, sand and clay, mosses, lichens and broccoli.

The Harvest Waggon, a late masterpiece bought by the Prince of Wales, is an ambitious variation of a composition Gainsborough painted about 1767 (now in the Barber Institute, Birmingham). Figures, landscape and sky now combine to produce a rhythmical Rococo composition. Typical of Gainsborough's late work, the paint has been applied with dazzling freedom, contributing significantly to the unity of the whole.

Gift of Mr. and Mrs. Frank P. Wood, 1941   2578

Thomas Gainsborough (British, 1727-88)

Wooded Landscape with Herdsman and Cattle c.1775-80
Black chalk and grey-black washes heightened with white chalk on laid paper.
28.0 x 36.7

During his lifetime Gainsborough was best known for his society portraits, but they
were not his preferred subject matter. They were a reliable way to make a living.
Throughout his life he expressed a wish for "the People with their damn'd Faces" to
leave him alone so that he could draw and paint landscapes to his heart's content. His
first love was the countryside around Suffolk, where he grew up, and the first paintings
he admired were the realistic Dutch landscapes imported through the nearby East
Anglian ports.

Gainsborough drew thousands of landscapes, and in later years, when this work
appears to have been made, he drew for pleasure, as a release from the pressure of
business, and also to stimulate ideas for finished landscapes in oil. Although this drawing is similar to one or two of his paintings, it was not used as a study to be slavishly
copied when worked up. The sheep, cattle and herdsman are typical of the sort he used
to "fill a place . . . or create a little business for the Eye to be drawn from the Trees in
order to return to them with more glee."

Purchase, 1985   85/272

John Robert Cozens (British, 1752-97)

The Lake of Albano and Castel Gandolfo
Watercolour over graphite on wove paper. 36.1 x 52.8

Constable described Cozens's work as "all poetry" and the artist as "the greatest genius that ever touched landscape." His influence on Constable and Turner made Cozens one of the most important landscape watercolourists of the 18th century. This view of volcanic Lake Albano, with the Pope's summer residence on its rim, is a characteristic example of the artist's work.

Cozens first visited the Continent in 1776, when he accompanied Richard Payne Knight on his trip through the Alps to Rome. Cozens spent the next two years studying Rome, Naples, and the surrounding countryside. The singular landscapes he produced quickly created a demand for his work, and he executed several versions of his favourite compositions. The present work is probably the earliest of ten watercolours based on this particular view; the other nine are more contrived, and the brush strokes more mannered. The delicate greens and blues found here are typical of Cozens's earliest watercolours, while the faint touches of mauve and orange enliven this fresh work.

Gift of Midland Bank Canada, 1986   86/197

Richard Earlom (British, 1743–1822)
after Joseph Wright of Derby (British, 1734–1797)

An Iron Forge 1773
Mezzotint on laid paper. 48.7 x 60.1 (sheet)

The work of Joseph Wright — who lived and worked for most of his life in Derby, an early centre of the Industrial Revolution — combines an 18th-century intellectual fascination with science and a proto-romantic sensibility. He often painted interior night scenes, and one of his absorbing interests was the observation of unusual artificial light sources. The dramatic chiaroscuro effects of his oils were ideally suited for translation into mezzotint.

Although Earlom made mezzotints after a wide variety of subjects, *An Iron Forge* was one of his largest and most brilliant plates. In mezzotint, the engraver works from dark to light, scraping out the design on a copper plate that has been uniformly roughened with a tool called a rocker. Mezzotints in pristine condition have rich, velvety surfaces that are extremely fragile. This impression of *An Iron Forge* has been particularly well preserved.

Purchase, 1983   83/249

Henry Fuseli (Swiss, 1741–1825)

Lear Banishing Cordelia c.1786-89
Oil on canvas. 267.3 x 364.5

Swiss by birth, Fuseli studied in Rome in the 1770s and worked for the rest of his life in England. Apart from painting, he was active as a translator and as professor and keeper of the Royal Academy.

This massive painting was commissioned by Josiah Boydell, who in 1789 exhibited 34 paintings by various artists in his Shakespeare Gallery in Pall Mall. The venture was intended to establish a British school of history painting and to profit from the sale of prints engraved after the pictures. Fuseli was always attracted to scenes of emotional conflict and dramatic intensity. When in Rome he frescoed a room with episodes from Shakespeare's plays, and he contributed no fewer than nine paintings to Boydell's gallery. *Lear Banishing Cordelia* illustrates the opening scene of *King Lear*. Lunging at Cordelia, Lear disinherits his faithful daughter for not matching her sisters' overt assertions of love. The exaggerated gestures and artificial figure-types, together with the theatrical spotlighting, recall 16th-century Mannerist painting, which had strongly attracted Fuseli in Rome.

Gift from the Contributing Members' Fund, 1965   64/21

Saverio della Gatta (Italian, active 1777–1828)

View of Naples from Portici, with Peasants Dancing to the Music of
an Itinerant Band
Gouache on laid paper. 45.8 x 36.3

Della Gatta specialized in gouache views of Naples, southern Italy and Sicily, no doubt influenced by the technique of Marco Ricci. Combining the contemporary taste for views of the Bay of Naples – so popular with British tourists – with that for the picturesque, he animated the foreground with genre elements: wayfaring children, a woman nursing a baby while seated on a donkey, a group of musicians and dancers, and a ragged youth teasing a dog. Beyond them, the vista stretches across the bay, past the lighthouse and the port of Naples to the Carthusian monastery of San Martino and Castel Sant'Elmo on the hill behind the city.

Purchase, Estate of Mrs. Dorothy Whealy, 1971   70/140

George Stubbs (British, 1724–1806)

A Horse Frightened by a Lion 1788
Etching, engraving, mezzotint, stipple on wove paper. 24.9 x 33.7 (impression)

Stubbs's first prints were made after his anatomical drawings for scientific texts. In the late 1770s he began making engravings that reproduced his paintings of wild animal subjects. Stubbs was particularly preoccupied with themes of animal combat. He first engraved the subject of a horse frightened by a lion in 1777, placing the animals in a spacious, rugged landscape, as in the related paintings. His engraving of 1788 omits the landscape and focuses exclusively on the drama that takes place between the two animals. In this later work, the artist combines romantic realism with a classical aesthetic by placing the terrified white horse parallel to the picture plane in a pose that evokes Greco-Roman reliefs.

Stubbs's printmaking technique was based on careful craftsmanship and the masterful manipulation of the engraving tools. In the present work the artist combined etching, line-engraving, mezzotint and stipple-engraving to create subtle transitions in tone that approximate the tonal values of painting. Stubbs's images were important inspirations for French Romantic artists, notably Théodore Géricault and Eugène Delacroix, when they visited England in the 1820s.

Purchase, 1981   81/99

VAUX-HALL.

Robert Pollard (British, 1755–1838) and **Francis Jukes** (British, 1747–1812)
after Thomas Rowlandson (British, 1756–1827)

Vaux-hall 1785
Hand-coloured etching and aquatint on laid paper. 53.9 x 75.5 (sheet trimmed)

As the best-known social caricaturist of the Georgian period, Rowlandson was adept in finding humour in everyday situations. He had his drawing *Vaux-hall* exhibited at the Royal Academy in 1784. Within a few months, a copper plate reproducing the drawing was expertly etched and aquatinted by Pollard and Jukes, and impressions were delicately coloured by hand in the publisher's studio. Through the print the image gained wide recognition in England and abroad.

By the 1780s London had over 60 pleasure gardens where one could go for an evening's entertainment. Vauxhall, located by the Thames on the Surrey side, became the most fashionable of all. Rowlandson's friend Henry Angelo later recalled that "Rowlandson the artist and myself have often been there, and he has found plenty of employment for his pencil. The *chef-d'oeuvre* of his caricatures, which is still in print, is his drawing of Vauxhall, in which he has introduced a variety of characters known at the time...." Included among the personalities that Angelo refers to are the Prince of Wales, accompanied by his mistress, Perdita Robinson, and her suspicious husband (in the right foreground), and the beautiful Duchess of Devonshire, with her sister, Lady Duncannon (in the centre).

Gift of J. T. Johnson and Marion Darte Johnson, 1982   82/227

James Gillray (British, 1757–1815)

The Zenith of French Glory 1793
Hand-coloured etching on wove paper. 35.5 x 25.0 (impression)

The period between 1780 and 1820 has been called the golden age of English caricature
because of a remarkable boom in the production of humorous prints and drawings.
The momentous events of the French Revolution and the Napoleonic Wars were
favourite subjects for caricature.

Gillray became the supreme master of political satire. His genius is demonstrated
in his hand-coloured etchings, which are aggressively drawn and provide scathing cri-
tiques of the political life of the times. This print was intended as a condemnation of
the execution of Louis XVI, which occurred in Paris on January 21, 1793. Although the
English had been sympathetic to the French cause during the early years of the Revolution, they were alienated by the escalating violence. In Gillray's horrifying caricature,
a bishop and two monks hang from a lantern in the foreground, while above them a
ragged revolutionary, a *sans-culotte*, is obscenely perched and literally "without breeches."
In the distance a church burns and swarms of *bonnets-rouges* cheer on the execution.
This plate represents one of the earliest English attempts to realistically depict the
French guillotine.

Gift of the Trier-Fodor Foundation, 1982   82/245

Nicolas-André Monsiau (French, 1755–1837)

Zeuxis Choosing His Models 1797
Oil on canvas. 96.0 x 129.0

In his spacious studio Zeuxis, the 5th-century BC Greek painter, is seen awarding a
floral wreath to a beautiful nude woman. When Zeuxis was commissioned to paint an
image of Helen of Troy, the most beautiful of mortals, he selected the five most beautiful maidens in the town as models. He then combined the most flawless aspect of each
in his painting. The story is told both by Cicero and Pliny the Elder; later it came to
epitomize idealist art theory.

   Monsiau was born and died in Paris, but he trained in Rome from 1776 to 1780.
There, he absorbed the masterpieces of Antique and Renaissance art and also frequented
the studio of Jacques-Louis David, the greatest Neoclassical painter. These experiences
are fully evident in this painting. As a true Neoclassicist Monsiau has not only stressed
a clarity of line, but he has also lavished attention on beautifully deployed colour and
precisely observed detail.

   Gift from the Volunteer Committee Fund, 1988   88/100

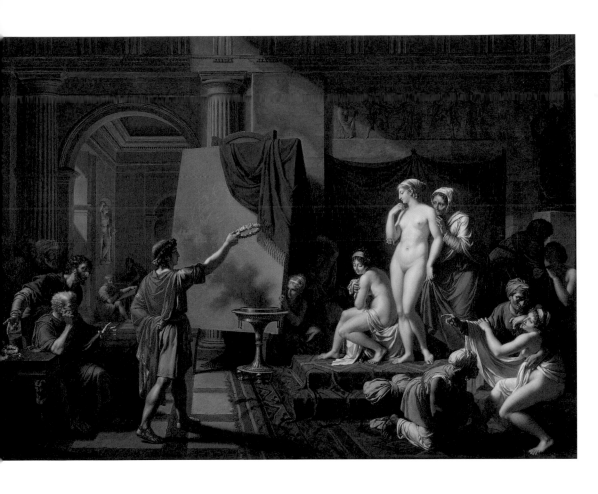

John Constable (British, 1776–1837)

Wooded Landscape 1801-02
Oil on canvas. 92.1 x 72.1

This landscape may be the first painting Constable exhibited at the Royal Academy,
London – in the summer of 1802. In the Academy's catalogue the painting is simply
described as "a landscape," but the size of the AGO's canvas is similar and the style
appropriate for an early date in Constable's career.

   Together with Turner, Constable was the leading English landscape painter of
the 19th century. Born in East Bergholt, Suffolk, Constable continued to be inspired by
the local landscape throughout his life. At the beginning of his career, Constable professed a special interest in the precise detail of Gainsborough's early landscapes, which
also depict Suffolk. This painting, too, contains a wealth of accurate detail, but it is
already painted with a rougher touch, heralding much landscape painting of the rest of
the century. The tree at the left was repeated by Constable in his well-known canvas
The Cornfield of 1826 in the National Gallery, London.

   Gift of Reuben Wells Leonard Estate, 1936   2373

Joseph Mallord William Turner (British, 1775–1851)

South-West View of a Gothic Abbey (Morning), [now Building at Fonthill, the Seat of W. Beckford, Esq.] 1800
Watercolour, gum arabic, traces of graphite on wove paper. 69.4 x 102.9

In May 1799 William Beckford, a wealthy English dilettante and author, requested that Turner visit Fonthill Abbey and make several views for him. Turner stayed there for two weeks in the autumn; by May of the following year he had finished five large watercolours of the abbey made from various vantage points at different times of day. Beckford earned himself a reputation as a difficult eccentric; he bought seven views from Turner (two are now lost) but quibbled over the price, paying only 35 guineas for each. By 1818 he had sold nearly all of them.

Turner held to a practice of working from pencil and wash sketches done on the spot; two sketchbooks survive from his trip to Fonthill showing an unfinished building (Beckford did not move in until 1807). Turner must have had access to James Wyatt's architectural plans, since all his finished views show the abbey as complete (they are important records, since the tower collapsed in 1825). Turner's large watercolours were virtuoso performances in the medium, well able to compete with oil paintings on the Royal Academy's walls. This sheet, which is sadly faded, reveals his characteristic compositional framing devices and his ability to capture the English countryside and atmosphere at any time of day.

Bequest of John Paris Bickell, Toronto, 1952   51/39

Richard Parkes Bonington (British, 1801-28)

Dutch Fishing Boats
Graphite, watercolour, and scraping out on wove paper. 23.9 x 17.8

Bonington has been described as the greatest exponent of pure watercolour painting. The son of an English drawing master who trained him in the British tradition of watercolour painting, Bonington was also taught in France from the age of fifteen. The large areas of independent wash in his work owe a debt to Thomas Girtin, one of the great masters of English watercolour, and the bright, fresh colours also evident in his work pay homage to Delacroix. He used the loosest of pencil sketches for composition and employed the brush only to achieve the necessary details. Delacroix remarked of him that "Nobody...possessed the lightness of execution, which...makes his work, as it were, diamond-like; charming and seducing the eye independently of the actual subject of imitation."

Gift of W. B. Dalton, Stamford, Conn., and the United Kingdom, 1961   60/12

Eugène Delacroix (French, 1798–1863)

The Fanatics of Tangier 1857
Oil on canvas. 47.0 x 55.9

The leading painter of the Romantic movement in France, Delacroix had to resist the opposition of the entrenched classicism of official art throughout much of his life. Yet, at the end of the 19th century, the leaders of the modern movement uniformly acknowledged the crucial influence of Delacroix – his acute observation of nature, mastery of colour and ability to convey emotion.

Delacroix's trip to North Africa in 1832 with the Count de Mornay, the French ambassador, left a deep impression. It exposed him to "living antiquity" and to a richness of colour and light that remained an inspiration for the rest of his life. While in Tangier Delacroix witnessed the frenzied Isawas, a fanatical Muslim sect, rampaging through the city. Delacroix painted the incident twice: first in a more conventional canvas of 1838 (now in the Minneapolis Institute of Art) and 19 years later in the present canvas. In the second version Delacroix moved the writhing mass of fanatics outside the city walls and enlivened the composition throughout. As he commented, "I did not begin to do anything passable from my North African journey until I had so far forgotten the small details as to recall only the striking and poetic aspects."

Purchase, 1962   62/5

De temps en temps j'aime à voir le vieux Père,
Et je me garde bien de lui rompre en visiere

Eugène Delacroix (French, 1798–1863)

Mephistopheles Flying (frontispiece from *Faust*) 1828
Lithograph on *chine collé*. 40.9 x 27.7 (sheet)

Rebelling against the idealism and heroic themes of Neoclassicism, the young French
Romantics of the 1820s and 1830s began to explore the inner world of the emotions
and the imagination. Delacroix, the greatest exponent of the French Romantic school,
was drawn to Goethe's *Faust*, the tragedy of a learned man who sells his soul to the
devil in exchange for superhuman knowledge and power.

Delacroix's 18 illustrations for *Faust* (the entire set is in the AGO's collection)
were inspired by a comic-opera interpretation of Goethe's play that the artist saw in
London in 1825. Using the *manière noire* lithographic technique, which he had perfected
by the early 1820s, Delacroix scratched through a coating of lithographic crayon to
create dramatic highlights and exploit the rich blacks of the medium.

In this frontispiece, Mephistopheles returns from a visit with the Lord to gloat
diabolically: "I like to see the Ancient One occasionally, and take care not to break
with him." Goethe praised the artist's work, saying that "Delacroix seems to have felt
at home here and to have roamed freely, as though on familiar ground, in a strange
fusion of heaven and earth...."

Gift of the Richard and Jean Ivey Fund, 1979   79/17.2

138

François Bonvin (French, 1817-87)

A Woman Knitting 1861
Charcoal and stump on laid paper. 42.2 x 31.4

Inspired by 17th-century Dutch art, Bonvin, friend of the painter Gustave Courbet and a fellow Realist, was instrumental in the revival of still-life painting and was also fond of genre subjects in which women go about their daily tasks.

Applying the charcoal with a firm hand, Bonvin has boldly structured *A Woman Knitting* in broad areas of black and white. The almost geometric division of space is reminiscent of the 17th-century Dutch painter Pieter de Hooch. The subject reflects Bonvin's intimate knowledge of the work of his countrymen J. B. S. Chardin (see p. 119) and Jean-François Millet.

Purchase, 1985   85/83

Narcisse-Virgile Diaz de la Peña (French, 1807/8-76)

Autumn in the Forest 1866
Oil on canvas. 41.9 x 59.7

Diaz belonged to the Barbizon School, which promoted landscape as a legitimate subject rather than as a background for narrative pictures. Greatly admired by the Impressionists, these artists worked outdoors in the forest of Fontainebleau, beyond the village of Barbizon, but completed their paintings later in the studio. Although a great part of Diaz's work was romantically or classically inspired, it was the execution of landscapes such as this that impressed his successors.

This view of an untamed stretch of land, featuring gnarled and moss-covered oak trees, a rock-strewn slope and a peasant gathering twigs, is typical of Barbizon subject matter. Here Diaz chose a view with large trees at the sides, framing an open, sunlit centre – a classical composition he frequently favoured. His sensitive depiction of unkempt nature and close observation of natural colour and light made him unusually successful during his lifetime.

Gift of Mrs. John W. Simpson, New York and Vermont, 1943   2608

Alfred Sisley (French, 1839-99)

View of St-Cloud: Sunlight 1876
Oil on canvas. 54.2 x 73.2

Born in Paris of British parentage, Sisley met Monet and Renoir in Gleyre's class at
the École des beaux-arts in 1862. More than any of the other Impressionists, Sisley
restricted his subject matter to landscape. His canvases testify to an unflagging interest
in observing nature and in reproducing atmospheric effects with the Impressionists'
technique of broken brush strokes. "The method of painting must communicate...the
emotion the painter has experienced," wrote Sisley. "I am in favour of different techniques in the same painting, for if the sun tones down certain parts, it brightens others
and these effects of light must be rendered on the canvas."

View of St-Cloud's date corresponds to a crucial period in the history of Impressionism when the young painters organized a series of exhibitions of their own works,
thereby challenging the prevailing structure of state-run exhibitions in France. Like the
best of his early paintings, this oil combines a loaded brush stroke with a tightly structured composition. The viewer's eye is led gently from the shadowed pasture in the
left foreground, down a little path, behind the stand of trees, and finally to the brightly
lit cluster of houses dominated by a soaring steeple and a lone cyprus positioned squarely
at the centre of the canvas. This broad sweep is crowned by a vast expanse of sky and
a row of fluffy clouds whose importance to the shaping of landscape composition was
clearly defined by Sisley: "the planes [of the sky] give depth...and the shapes of clouds
give movement to a picture."

Gift of Mr. and Mrs. R. Fraser Elliott, 1989   89/402

Claude Monet (French, 1840–1926)

Vétheuil in Summertime 1879
Oil on canvas. 67.9 x 90.5

Monet was a leading member of the Impressionists, the informal group of painters who between 1874 and 1886 exhibited together as a protest against the French academic system. Working outdoors, the Impressionists used bright colours, applied in short, visible brush strokes. They were fascinated with the relationship between colour and light, and frequently painted subjects involving light affected by various atmospheric conditions or reflected from different surfaces. Their vivid, freely executed paintings stood in sharp contrast to the high-minded narrative and smooth surfaces of conventional academic art.

In 1878, the year after the third Impressionist exhibition, poverty drove Monet from suburban Argenteuil to rural Vétheuil. In the three years Monet spent at Vétheuil, he painted many views of the village and the Seine featuring the light effects of different times of day and year. This painting was purchased in 1880 by Dr. Georges de Bellio, an important friend and doctor of the Impressionists. Monet himself chose it to be shown in the *Exposition centennale de l'art français* held in Paris in 1900.

Purchase, 1929   1354

Camille Pissarro (French, 1830–1903)

Pont Boieldieu in Rouen, Rainy Weather 1896
Oil on canvas. 73.7 x 91.4

The eldest of the Impressionists, Pissarro was both instrumental in organizing the first Impressionist exhibition in 1874 and the only participant in all seven succeeding shows. He remained a staunch friend of the Impressionist painters and acted as mentor to the Post-Impressionists, Cézanne, van Gogh and Gauguin. Although his work in many media reveals a deep feeling for nature, he did not ignore the effects of the Industrial Revolution on the landscape of late 19th-century France.

    This painting is perhaps the finest of a series Pissarro made of the Seine at Rouen, beginning in 1883. Between January and March 1896, Pissarro stayed at the Hôtel de Paris, from the windows of which he would look down on the recently completed Pont Boieldieu and across the busy Seine to the Gare d'Orléans and the Place Carnot. "What particularly interests me," Pissarro wrote, "is the motif of the iron bridge in wet weather with all the vehicles, pedestrians, workers on the embarkments, boats, smoke, haze in the distance; it's so spirited, so alive."

Gift of Reuben Wells Leonard Estate, 1937   2415

Edgar Degas (French, 1834–1917)

Danseuse vue de dos. 'Grand battement à la seconde' c.1885-90
Black chalk heightened with white chalk on green laid paper. 30.6 x 24.0

Degas's art was largely devoted to themes of modern urban life. Unlike his fellow Impressionists, he had little interest in landscape and found his favourite subjects at the racecourse, the ballet, the circus and the theatre and in the cafés of Paris. By 1872 he had become fascinated with the ballet, a theme that allowed him to observe and analyze the human body in motion. The unusual viewpoints and asymmetrical compositions of these works owe much to Degas's interest in photography and Japanese woodblock prints.

Degas often inscribed his drawings of dancers with specific information regarding the position of the body. In *Danseuse vue de dos*, he notes the lively play of light as it falls on the right arm and leg, shown in second position. In the 1880s Degas preferred to work with charcoal or black chalk and pastel rather than with ink, pencil or gouache, and his drawings took on a new freedom and forcefulness. Here the strongly defined contour lines, along with the vigorous zigzag strokes in the shadows, emphasize the two-dimensional surface and give the drawing a daring, modern appearance.

Formerly in the collection of Dr. and Mrs. Harold Murchison Tovell
and purchased from their son, Dr. H. M. M. Tovell of New York, with
the assistance of the Government of Canada through the Cultural
Property Export and Import Act, 1987   88/85

Pierre Auguste Renoir (French, 1841–1919)

Studies for Mother and Child (Maternité) c.1885
Red crayon, white chalk on wove paper. 58.7 x 80.1

Renoir painted a picture of a world in which life was bright, carefree and easy. His early work was impressionistic in style and employed loose brushwork and vibrating colour to capture the flickering effects of light. By the mid-1880s he had lost interest in capturing the transient effects of nature and his compositions had become more structured and the forms more solid.

Renoir's first son, Pierre, was born in March 1885, and by the following year he had produced three oil paintings and a number of related drawings of his wife, Aline, feeding the baby. Renoir's fascination with the subject of the nursing mother was in part inspired by the Madonnas of Raphael, which he studied during a trip to Italy in 1881-82.

The central study on the *Maternité* sheet, with its pyramidal format, presents an informal yet timeless view of motherhood. The two remaining studies contrast the calm presence of the woman with the active movements of the baby. Drawing rapidly with red crayon, the artist has emphasized the contours of the figures and then used broad modelling with white chalk to create solid sculptural forms. The drawing appears to be a study for a lithograph that reproduces the composition almost exactly.

Gift of Sam and Ayala Zacks, 1970   71/309

Edgar Degas (French, 1834–1917)

Woman in Bath c.1892
Oil on canvas. 71.1 x 88.9

Although numbered among the Impressionists, Degas deplored the sobriquet and was only superficially sympathetic to rapid *plein air* painting, preferring to work indoors from both memory and sketches. He was a gifted draughtsman but later developed a passion for colour that culminated in his paintings of the 1890s. His subjects are usually mundane figures in natural attitudes: entertainers, laundresses, and anonymous nudes presented as if viewed "through a keyhole."

Degas painted *Woman in Bath* after he had explored the subject in monoprints, lithographs and pastels in addition to oils. Here the artist depicts the sensuous, vulnerable form of the bather with a minimum of strokes, modelling the form in rich colours, so that it blends and harmonizes with the pink and violet garments hanging against the wallpaper behind the bath. The shallow and simply outlined composition and the cropped figure of the maid reflect Degas's long-held interest in photography and Japanese prints. The intense colour and expressive line of this painting are typical of his work of the 1890s.

Purchase, Frank P. Wood Endowment, 1956   55/49

Pierre Auguste Renoir (French, 1841–1919)

The Concert 1918-19
Oil on canvas. 75.6 x 92.7

In 1906 Renoir settled in Cagnes in the south of France, where despite crippling arth-
ritis, he continued to paint a prodigious number of pictures. One of Renoir's last
paintings, this sensuous masterpiece was completed within a year before the artist's
death. *The Concert* attests not only to Renoir's longtime interest in Rubens, Boucher,
Fragonard and Delacroix, but also to an indomitable will to create art, undeterred
by old age and disabling illness.

For over 50 years Renoir devoted himself to the female figure, painted lovingly
in many guises. But in few paintings did he so thoroughly blend voluptuous figures,
opulent accoutrements and a lush setting. The colour, warm with the sun of the south,
and the brush strokes – orchestrated from thin glazes to accents of impasto – rhythmically bind the various elements together. Renoir even introduced distortion – as
in the head of the woman at the right – when aesthetically necessitated by the overall
design. Roses appear throughout like a visual counterpoint, while music, suggested
by the mandolin languorously strummed by the woman and proclaimed by the title
itself, heightens the sensuous effect.

Gift of Reuben Wells Leonard Estate, 1954   53/27

Edgar Degas (French, 1834–1917)

Horse with Jockey
Bronze. 17.8 x 29.5

Sculpture was the most intensely private of Degas's activities as an artist. Whereas his paintings, drawings and prints were widely exhibited and collected during his lifetime, he exhibited only one work of sculpture – his famous clothed *Petite danseuse de quatorze ans*, shown in Paris in the Sixth Impressionist exhibition in 1881. Degas likely began modelling in clay or wax in the mid-1870s. After 1900, as his eyesight worsened, it would appear that sculpture occupied more and more of his time. At the time of his death, some 150 sculptures were found in his studio, many of them badly damaged. Of these, 73 works were cast in bronze by the Hébrard Foundry.

Degas was obsessed in his sculpture with many of the same subjects that preoccupied him as a painter and draughtsman: the movement of classical ballet dancers on- and offstage, women washing and drying themselves after a bath, and studies of horses. Throughout the 1880s Degas's brilliant sculptures of horses reflect his awareness of Eadweard Muybridge's series of photographs of horses in movement. *Horse with Jockey* is one of three surviving sculptures of horses that includes the rider. Despite the lack of details such as the reins and stirrups, one senses the active rapport between horse and jockey.

Gift of R. W. Finlayson, 1969; donated by the Ontario
Heritage Foundation, 1988   L74/15

Auguste Rodin (French, 1840–1917)

Adam c.1880
Bronze. H. 182.9

Rodin, and he alone, was responsible for the rebirth of interest in the art of sculpture.
He was the dominant personality, as no single artist had dominated the art of painting.

After failing to gain admission to the École des beaux-arts, Rodin worked for the
fashionable sculptor Carrier-Belleuse and later worked in Belgium, where he produced
ornamental sculpture for public buildings. In the Paris Salon of 1877 Rodin exhibited
The Age of Bronze. In contrast to the sterile Salon sculpture, the lifelike character of
this work led to Rodin being accused of making a *surmoulage*, casting directly from
the male model.

In 1880 Rodin was commissioned by the Minister of Fine Arts to design an
entrance portal for the new Museum of Decorative Arts. His ambition was to do something akin to Ghiberti's bronze doors for the Baptistery of the Cathedral in Florence.
Rodin himself chose the subject based on Dante's *Inferno*. *Adam*, *Eve*, *The Three Shades*
and *The Thinker* were the four largest works associated with *The Gates of Hell*. *Adam* and
Eve were intended to flank the portal of the gates, to represent the origins of sin and
the suffering portrayed on the main panels.

For Adam Rodin borrowed directly from the work of Michelangelo – the point-
ing finger of the right hand is that of Adam in the Sistine Chapel, while the bent right
leg and the inclination of the head against the left shoulder derive from the figure of
the dead Christ in Michelangelo's marble *Pietà*.

Purchase, 1929   1336

James Abbott McNeill Whistler (American, 1834–1903)

Nocturne: Palaces from The Second Venice Set 1879-80
Etching and drypoint printed with plate tone on old laid paper. 29.6 x 20.1
(trimmed to the plate line and signed on the tab with a butterfly)

Whistler devoted himself to etching throughout his life, and his novel concept of line
and space not only revolutionized the medium but also exerted enormous influence
on his followers in Europe and North America. His *Venice* etchings represent the climax
of his printmaking career. In them, his experiments with artistic printing reached
their highest level of sophistication, and he achieved the synthesis of Occidental and
Oriental styles that he had been seeking throughout the 1870s.

In *Nocturne: Palaces*, arguably Whistler's most beautiful print, the artist combined
the picturesque form and spatial geometry learned from Rembrandt and the Dutch
with the two-dimensional decorative patterns derived from Japanese woodblock prints.
His etched line provides only the most elementary grid for the effects to be achieved
by creative printing. By varying the colour and amount of ink on the surface of the
plate, he could change the temperature, mood, and time of day from a cool, early
morning to a late, hot night.

Gift of Esther and Arthur Gelber, 1982   82/45

James (Jacques Joseph) Tissot (French, 1836–1902)

The Milliner's Shop c.1883-85
Oil on canvas. 146.1 x 101.6

Tissot worked independently in Paris and London, having refused Degas's invitation to
participate in the first Impressionist exhibition. He was essentially a conservative
artist but was not unreceptive to modern ideas. His paintings of middle-class people,
viewed as if by the "objective" eye of the photographer, have been described as
"human still lifes." Tissot was immensely successful during his lifetime, but after his
death his work was ignored for many decades.

    The Milliner's Shop is from a series of 15 paintings called *La Femme à Paris*, which
show women of different social backgrounds in contemporary Paris. Tissot hoped to
re-establish himself in Paris with these paintings and to have them published as prints,
with accompanying short stories. The detailed depiction of the interior of the milliner's shop testifies to Tissot's academic sympathies, but the composition and subject
matter suggest an awareness of the paintings of contemporary urban life by Manet and
Degas. In part the treatment of the background also reveals an interest in Impressionist technique.

Gift from the Corporations' Subscription Fund, 1968   67/55

Vincent van Gogh (Dutch, 1853–1890)

*The Vicarage at Neunen: Seen from the Back, with the Artist's Studio
on the Right* c.1884
Graphite and stump, brown ink, brown wash heightened with white. 25.6 x 37.8

The Vicarage at Neunen is a pivotal work, summing up van Gogh's development during
his early Dutch period and anticipating his later work in France. A striking visual
record of the artist's immediate surroundings, this drawing also symbolizes his lifelong
preoccupation with documenting the places where he resided and worked.

Van Gogh's father, Theodorus, a Protestant pastor, lived with his family in the
vicarage at Neunen from 1882 until his death in 1885. In the spring of 1884 van Gogh
executed a group of highly finished drawings of scenes in or near the garden. This view
shows the back of the house; the laundry and storeroom on the right became the artist's first studio. One of his sisters is shown sewing or spooling yarn on a porch while
a Brabant peasant woman stoops to tend the spring garden.

The moody character of this drawing, with its grey-brown tonality and expressionistic tendencies, is typical of van Gogh's Brabant period. The intricate and varied
calligraphy of his line and the spontaneous touches of body colour anticipate the artist's
later Paris and Arles drawings.

Purchased with proceeds from the Annual Giving Fund, 1982   81/556

153

Paul Gauguin (French, 1848–1903)

Hina and Fatu 1893
Tamanu wood. H. 32.3; D. 14.2

Painter, sculptor, printmaker and ceramist, Gauguin was the most versatile artist of
his generation. He left his occupation as a stockbroker in 1883 to devote himself to
painting, and two years later he abandoned his family to live in Brittany. He had a taste
of the Tropics in 1887 when he visited Martinique and Panama.

Gauguin's most concentrated activities as a sculptor date from his two trips to
French Polynesia, the first from 1891 to 1893, the second from 1895 until his death in
the remote Marquesas Islands. He sought in vain to find an ideal life far removed from
bourgeois European values. He was disappointed to find that little indigenous art
remained and religious traditions had all but disappeared.

A book on Oceanic religion and mythology published in 1837 was a source for
this sumptuous carving illustrating the dialogue between Hina, goddess of the moon,
and Fatu, god of the earth, concerning life and death and the eternity of matter. Gauguin,
the father of primitivism in modern art, has in this work adopted poses from Javanese
sculpture and decorative motifs from Marquesan art. In declaring "the great error is the
Greek, however beautiful it may be," Gauguin turned to non-European sources for
inspiration. His work, particularly his wood carvings that were included in the great
retrospective exhibition of his work held in Paris in 1906, undoubtedly inspired the
interest in tribal art of Picasso (see p. 165) and his generation.

Gift from the Volunteer Committee Fund, 1980   80/70

Paul Gauguin (French, 1848–1903)

Manao Tupapau 1894-95
Colour woodcut on wove paper. 24.6 x 39.4 (image)

Although Gauguin was not the first 19th-century artist to revive the woodcut technique, he was the most revolutionary. His earliest woodcuts illustrate *Noa Noa*, the autobiographical romance that he wrote after his first sojourn in Tahiti, from 1891 to 1893. In *Manao Tupapau*, one of ten images from *Noa Noa*, he re-interpreted a theme that he had explored in a previous painting. The mysterious title means "she thinks of the spirit" or "the spirit thinks of her." In the woodcut the girl is shown curled up in what is either a fetal or a burial position. Gauguin's search for meaning in Polynesian culture and religion often resulted in ambiguous and provocative images.

The *Noa Noa* blocks were originally printed in black ink, but in the spring of 1894, while working with the printer Louis Roy in Paris, Gauguin began to print them in colour. In the present work the red-brown was printed first, then the black, and lastly a stencil was used for the glowing yellow that surrounds the figure. Roy pulled perhaps only 25 to 30 impressions. His rather crude printings reinforced Gauguin's strong overall designs, and the expressive, emotive qualities of these woodcuts later had a profound impact on German Expressionist artists.

Formerly in the Collection of Dr. and Mrs. Harold Murchison Tovell and purchased from their son, Dr. H. M. M. Tovell of New York, with the assistance of the Government of Canada through the Cultural Property Export and Import Act, 1987   88/86

Adolf Menzel (German, 1815–1905)

Head of a Young Man 1893
Charcoal and stump on wove paper. 21.0 x 12.9

Menzel's early work was dominated by grand themes such as the one depicted in *Iron Rolling Mill* of 1875, a key painting that contributed to the development of industrial imagery in German Realism. Menzel was also an outstanding and prolific draughtsman, making over 5,000 drawings. In his later years he became increasingly devoted to drawing, restricting himself to a small format and continuing his search for new modes of expression. As is indicated by this drawing, Menzel's use of charcoal and stump was extremely sophisticated, and he was capable of creating images that are almost photographic in their subtle tonal range. The unusual vantage point of the viewer and the curious cropping of the figure may also owe something to his interest in photography.

Purchase, 1985   85/270

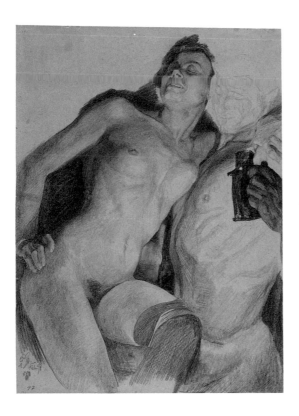

Otto Greiner (German, 1869–1916)

The Devil Showing Woman to the People 1897
Black and red chalks on wove paper. 40.3 x 28.2

Rejecting the need to paint objective, tangible reality, Symbolist artists of the late 19th
century sought to portray the realm of ideas, feelings and dreams. Symbolism manifested itself in several countries and in a wide range of pictorial styles. As is evidenced
by Greiner's work, German artists tended towards allegory, illustrative detail and dramatic action. Greiner met the Symbolist Max Klinger in Italy in the 1890s, and a work
such as the present one reflects the moralizing, literary qualities and dark mysteries
found in the work of his countryman.

    Greiner's drawing is a study for a large multifigured lithograph in which the
Devil is shown holding Woman high above a tumultuous crowd. She is the femme fatale,
the seductive, death-bringing female who appears in various forms in late 19th-century
art. The sense of evil that is implied in the drawing becomes more explicit in the
print in which the devil's face is transformed into that of an animal by the addition
of horns, pointed ears and a terrifying grin.

    Purchase, 1969   69/43

Frederick H. Evans 1893

Frederick H. Evans (British, 1853–1943)

A Souvenir of Aubrey Beardsley 1893
Platinum print mounted on decorative border mounted on paper folder.
Page: 20.2 x 14.0; Photograph: 5.7 x 4.4

Best known for his photographs of the interiors of cathedrals, Evans also made some memorable portrait studies. He strongly advocated the technique of unmanipulated photography, in opposition to many of his contemporaries. Although he practised and preached a doctrine of pure photography as the true art, Evans presented his work in elaborately decorated mounts and created a series of borders around the print, often of contrasting or harmonizing tints. Evans's concern with presentation was made explicit through the written instructions and demonstrations he gave to his colleagues.

The portrait of Aubrey Beardsley is an exceptional example, not only of Evans's presentation methods, but also as a striking image of his friend. It was at Evans's suggestion that John Dent, the publisher, hired Beardsley as the illustrator for the new edition of the classic *Le Morte d'Arthur* by Sir Thomas Malory. To commemorate their friendship, Evans made small prints of Beardsley's distinctive profile portrait and mounted them within a decorative border that the artist had drawn for *Le Morte d'Arthur*.

Gift of Mrs. Gordon Conn, 1979   79/129

Édouard Vuillard (French, 1868–1940)

Interior with Hanging Lamp, pl. 4 from *Landscapes and Interiors* 1899
Transfer lithograph in 5 colours on *chine volant*. 33.5 x 28.0 (composition)

In 1889 Vuillard joined the Nabis, a brotherhood of young artists who were united in their reaction against the naturalism of Impressionism and in their interest in the decorative and emotive use of colour and line. Vuillard and his friend Pierre Bonnard were given the nickname *Intimistes* by the group because of their predilection for domestic interiors. Vuillard repeatedly represented the rooms of his own apartment, and often included his mother engaged in various domestic tasks. His intention was never simply to record his surroundings but to imbue his subjects with symbolic meaning.

By 1891 Vuillard was sharing a studio with Bonnard, who encouraged him to try lithography. Like his friend, Vuillard owed much stylistically to Japanese woodblock prints, as may be seen in his use of curiously cropped compositions, distorted perspectives and sumptuous patterning.

The publisher Ambroise Vollard commissioned Vuillard in 1899 to produce *Landscapes and Interiors*, an album of 12 colour prints that was published in an edition of 100. The lithographs are a testimony to Vuillard's technical virtuosity and his fresh, brilliant colour and innovative designs have never been surpassed.

Gift of Touche Ross, 1987   87/20

Édouard Vuillard (French, 1868–1940)

The Widow's Visit 1899
Oil on paper mounted on wood. 50.2 x 62.9

Vuillard is best known for domestic scenes, which often featured family members and caused him to be known as an "Intimist." Under the influence of his fellow Nabis and Gauguin, he had rejected Impressionism in favour of simplified paintings in cloisonnist colour patches, ignoring perspective and depth, but, having, as he said, "a horror of general ideas which I haven't discovered for myself," he rejected these in favour of an independent, colourful, highly patterned style.

 This painting is a vignette showing two women, Vuillard's mother and sister, listening – the younger woman somewhat bored – to their visitor. Its gentle wit and hint of stage set recall the artist's early work in the theatre, while the depiction of figures in their home typifies the portraits inspired by Degas, which he painted throughout his life. The indication of space and detail in the room, and the sunlight casting shadows on the patterned wallpaper, contrast with Vuillard's earlier flat, tapestrylike, evenly lit pictures and mark his developing interest in naturalism.

Purchase, 1937   2422

Pablo Picasso (Spanish, 1881–1973)

The Soup 1902
Oil on canvas. 38.5 x 46.0

The Soup, originally in the collection of Gertrude Stein, is one of the best-known examples of Picasso's work from the Blue Period (1901-04). It was painted in Barcelona where Picasso lived from January 1902 to April 1904. The sadness, melancholy and spiritual alienation characteristic of late Symbolist art found a reflection in Picasso's compassionate rendering of the poverty and loneliness of the men and women with whom he identified.

    The Soup is one in the series of the mother-and-child theme found in Picasso's work of 1901-02. The resignation and weariness of life conveyed by the static, bowed body of the mother and her closed, unseeing eyes are contrasted with the light dance-like movement of the girl, eagerly reaching out for the bowl of steaming soup. The bare necessities of life are represented in an almost ritualistic act. The elongated figure of the mother and the simplified modelling of the drapery reflect influences as diverse as Gothic art and the work of El Greco. The economy of pictorial means is evident in the rigid geometry of the stark interior. Picasso's friend, the poet Apollinaire commented on the dominant blue tonality that reflects Picasso's admiration for Whistler and the late work of Cézanne: "For a year Picasso lived this type of painting, blue as the humid depth of an abyss, and full of pity."

    Gift of Margaret Dunlap Crang, 1983   83/316

Raoul Dufy (French, 1877-1953)

The Harbour at Le Havre 1905-06
Oil on canvas. 61.0 x 73.0

Dufy's early work of 1900-04 was influenced by the Impressionist and Post-Impressionist painters whom he admired: Monet, Pissarro, Degas, Cézanne and Gauguin. During these years he painted the streets of Paris and the resorts along the Normandy coast, employing a light blue-grey palette.

At the *Salon d'Automne* of 1905 Dufy saw Matisse's *Luxe, Calme et Volupté*. "On looking at that picture," he declared in 1925, "I grasped all the new reasons for painting; the realism of the Impressionists lost its charm for me as I contemplated the miracle of the imagination introduced into draughtsmanship and colour." He abandoned his Impressionistic style and began to adopt the bold, pure colours of the Fauves.

The Harbour at Le Havre is one of Dufy's early Fauve pictures. Despite his use of pure colours in an expressionist rather than in a descriptive manner, the palette is relatively subdued compared to the more audacious juxtaposition of colours in the work of his Fauve colleagues. The structure of the thick brush strokes and bold outlines reflects Dufy's interest in the overall rhythmical pattern of the masts, houses and boats. Dufy, like his friend Marquet, created a "gentle" Fauvism, pictures whose beautifully judged tonalities produce a mood of quiet gaiety and restraint.

Gift from the Women's Committee Fund to commemorate the
Golden Jubilee of the Art Gallery of Toronto, 1953   52/38

Pablo Picasso (Spanish, 1881–1973)

Nude with Clasped Hands 1905-06
Gouache on canvas. 96.5 x 75.6

Nude with Clasped Hands reflects the transition from the despair of the Blue Period to the work of the Rose Period. The model is Fernande Olivier, whom Picasso met in 1904 and with whom he shared his first deep emotional attachment. The melancholy and isolation of his earlier work gave way to the lighter, warmer, more delicate palette of the Rose Period, which was accompanied by a corresponding change in subject matter. Picasso concentrated on the full classical beauty of the female nude in contrast to the Mannerist elongations that characterized much of the work of the Blue Period.

This massive nude figure shows Picasso's concern with the defined outline of the figure. Though sculptural in feeling, the modelling is subtle, emphasizing the firmness of the small breasts and the curve of the stomach below the clasped hands. In contrast to the delicate modelling of the body, the face and hair, which have been worked in more detail, present a calm and serene portrait of Fernande. During the next few years, Fernande was the model for numerous paintings and drawings, and for the 1909 bronze in the AGO's collection (p. 166).

Gift of Sam and Ayala Zacks, 1970   71/297

Pablo Picasso (Spanish, 1881–1973)

Poupée 1907
Wood, paint, metal. H. 26.0
Purchase, 1980   79/315

Picasso was not only one of the most prolific painters, draughtsmen and printmakers of the 20th century, but also one of its most prolific sculptors, whose works in wood, stone, bronze, iron, sheet metal, and wire comprise more than 650 works. As with much of his three-dimensional work throughout his career, Picasso's carvings and bronzes made between 1901 and 1914 are closely allied to his preoccupations as a painter.

Poupée was carved in 1907, the most concentrated period of sculptural activity to date. That all but two of the ten known sculptures of 1907 were carved in wood is a reflection of the two dominant sources that informed Picasso's sculpture at the time: Gauguin's wood carvings that were included in the 1906 *Salon d'Automne* and the African and Oceanic art that Picasso saw when he visited the ethnographic collections at the Trocadéro in 1907. *Poupée* reveals the impact of Oceanic sculpture, in particular, the squat, blocklike forms of Marquesas Island tikis that Gauguin had incorporated into a number of his wood carvings.

The circular metal eyes could have been suggested by any number of examples of tribal art. Also, in common with some of Gauguin's carvings and with much tribal sculpture, Picasso painted this little sculpture. (Only traces of the paint remain.) A certificate signed by Picasso and dated 28–2–55 states: "Cette poupée a été faite pour Memène Ferrerod (Madame Masson)."

Purchase, 1980   79/315

Pablo Picasso (Spanish, 1881–1973)

Head of a Woman (Fernande) 1909
Bronze. 41.9 x 26.1 x 26.7

While spending the summer of 1909 with his mistress Fernande Olivier at Horta de
Ebro, Spain, Picasso executed a series of paintings and drawings of Fernande. In his
exploration of sculptural volume, the large, generally flat planes of his earlier studies
were replaced by more varied and tightly knit facets and lumps that mark the culmination of the first phase of Analytic Cubism. On his return to Paris in September,
Picasso modelled *Head of a Woman (Fernande)*. The sculpture is so closely related to
the paintings and drawings of the previous few months as to suggest that Picasso may
have based it on one of them, rather than working directly from the model.

Picasso's Analytic Cubist paintings were so sculptural that, as he told his friend
Julio Gonzalez, "it would have sufficed to cut them up – the colours, after all, being
no more than indications of differences in perspective, of planes inclined one way
or the other – and then assemble them according to the indications given by the colour, in order to be confronted with a 'sculpture.' "

The historical importance of this work as the first Cubist sculpture cannot be
overemphasized. Picasso was the first to realize the sculptural implications of two-
dimensional Cubism. This seminal work stands alone to mark the birth of Cubist
sculpture, a movement that slowly gathered momentum during the next five or six
years in the work of Boccioni, Archipenko, Gabo and Lipchitz.

Purchase, 1949   48/32

Raymond Duchamp-Villon (French, 1876–1918)

Baudelaire 1911
Terracotta. 38.7 x 22.3 x 24.8

Duchamp-Villon was the second of six children of an extraordinarily gifted family. His elder brother was Gaston (Jacques Villon), his youngest brother Marcel Duchamp (who did not modify his family name). Of the three brothers Duchamp-Villon was the only one to devote his efforts to sculpture. Raymond left Rouen for Paris to study medicine. About 1900 he became interested in modelling and decided to become a sculptor.

His early work reflects a variety of sources from Art Nouveau to the expressive surface modelling of Rodin. Gradually Duchamp-Villon began to simplify the surfaces of his sculpture, culminating in this portrait of the French poet and critic Baudelaire, his first mature work. The sculptor, like the poet before him, was concerned that art should interpret the unique character of the age in which it was made. Duchamp-Villon worked from photographs of Baudelaire by Paul Nadar and Étienne Carjat. The definitive version (which exists in terracotta, plaster and bronze) was based on a small wax study and at least one drawing (Centre Georges Pompidou, Paris). In contrast to the agitated surface of Rodin's 1898 bronze portrait of Baudelaire and to the deeply faceted surface of Picasso's 1909 Cubist bronze *Head of a Woman (Fernande)* (see opposite page), we are presented with an austere, simplified image that reflects Baudelaire's intellectual power.

Gift in memory of Harold Murchison Tovell and
Ruth Massey Tovell from their sons, 1962   62/1

Piet Mondrian (Dutch, 1872–1944)

Farm at Duivendrecht c.1905–07
Charcoal and stump on laid paper. 47.2 x 61.5

One of the founders of 20th-century abstraction, Mondrian is best known for the primary colours and simplified geometry of his mature paintings. His interest in analyzing form began during his early years in Holland, when his work was still essentially naturalistic.

Mondrian painted and drew this farmhouse at Duivendrecht, near Amsterdam, on numerous occasions. In a related painting that depicts the house from the same angle, the artist used the tonal, *plein air* approach of his Dutch predecessors, the Hague Impressionists. In this drawing, however, Mondrian seeks to extract a strong structural design from the picturesque scene. The house and its reflection in the pond are given almost equal scale and definition; the contour lines of the house, the verticals of the trees, and the division between water and land are emphasized. Although still naturalistic, the work foreshadows Mondrian's later attempts to reconcile the visible world with an abstractly conceived image of universal balance and harmony.

Purchase, Laidlaw Foundation, 1962   62/13

Maurice Utrillo (French, 1883–1955)

The House of Berlioz c.1909
Oil on canvas. 54.0 x 73.0

The illegitimate son of the model and artist Suzanne Valadon, Utrillo was born in the bohemian milieu of Montmartre. He became addicted to alcohol while a schoolboy. In 1900 he was treated in an asylum and from 1912 was in and out of hospitals and institutions. Utrillo, encouraged by his mother, began to paint in 1902 in a style influenced by the Impressionists. He had no formal training. The streets, houses and churches of Paris, particularly those of Montmartre where he lived, were the focus of his art. He sold his paintings cheaply to obtain money for drink. He first exhibited at the *Salon d'Automne* in 1909.

Although he often painted from postcards, this early canvas would appear to have been done from the elevated vantage point of Utrillo's private window. In this unusual composition, the walls and the solid facades and rooftops of the houses recede behind the tangle of leafless trees, with their web of delicate overlapping branches. The scene is at once intimate and yet lonely, as Utrillo has brilliantly captured the spirit of Paris, as he contemplates "the souls hidden away in these secretive houses."

Purchase, 1935   2319

Albert Gleizes (French, 1881–1953)

The Port 1912
Oil on canvas. 90.2 x 116.5

Parisian-born Gleizes began his career as an industrial designer before becoming an artist around 1900. His early work was influenced by Cézanne and the Fauves, but like many artists of his generation he became profoundly influenced by the work of Picasso and Braque, the cofounders of Cubism. Gleizes became a founding member of the *Section d'Or* in 1912 and with Metzinger wrote *Du cubisme*, a book dealing with the aesthetics and theory of the most important pictorial revolution since the Renaissance.

 While Gleizes adopted on a superficial level the obvious external features of Cubism, such as the overall geometric structure and the faceted forms, his work lacks the complex spatial ambiguities found in the work of Picasso and Braque. In *The Port* Gleizes has not abandoned traditional perspective or attempted to represent objects from various viewpoints; he simply has imposed a Cubist grid on the various forms of houses, ships and sails. *The Port* stands closer to the Futurists' interest in the dynamic energy of modern life than to the simple, everyday objects and figures depicted in the Cubist work of Picasso and Braque. The painting, both in its subject matter and lively palette, seems more like a Cubist version of Dufy's *The Harbour at Le Havre* (see p. 163) than a work contemporary with Analytic Cubism.

 Gift from the Junior Women's Committee Fund, 1955 55/13

Jean Metzinger (French, 1883–1956)

Still Life
Oil on canvas. 81.3 x 60.0

The early work of Metzinger reflects the influence of Neo-Impressionism and the work of the Fauves. He met Picasso in 1909 and soon, like all the lesser artists associated with Cubism, was deeply influenced by his work. Metzinger became an ardent dissemi-nator of Cubist ideas, when he co-wrote *Du cubisme* with Gleizes in 1912, which con-stituted the first major theoretical statement on the subject. As did other artists of the *Section d'Or* group, he sought eternal truths embodied in mathematics and geometry and explored their application in the compositional organization of his paintings.

Like Gleizes, Metzinger imitated the planes and faceted forms found in the Analytic Cubist paintings of Braque and Picasso without fully understanding their complex analysis of forms. Nor did he try to make tangible the space surrounding the objects. In *Still Life* the painter has tilted the tabletop toward the viewer, so that it is parallel to the picture plane rather than receding into depth. Metzinger has taken the still-life objects on the table – the bottle, pot and loaf of bread – and dissected them into planes and angles and faceted forms. His vision, despite the enormous debt to Cubism, was basically naturalistic.

Gift of Mr. and Mrs. Walter Carsen, Thornhill, 1964   63/26

Roger Fry (British, 1866–1934)

Group: Mother and Children 1913
Painted wood. 28.4 x 23.6 x 10.2

Painter, aesthetician, critic, curator and editor, Roger Fry introduced the work of the Post-Impressionists to the British public. In 1910 he organized the exhibition *Manet and the Post-Impressionists*, which brought paintings by Gauguin, van Gogh, Cézanne and Matisse to the centre of London's art scene.

In July 1913, along with the Bloomsbury Group painters Vanessa Bell and Duncan Grant, Fry founded the Omega Workshops Ltd., a design centre for artists, with a showroom in Fitzroy Square, London. Young artists were employed to design furniture, pottery, stained glass, floor and wall coverings, murals and sculptures.

Group: Mother and Children, Fry's only known sculpture, was based on a photograph of Vanessa Bell (Virginia Woolf's sister), seated and protectively hugging her two young sons, Julian and Quentin. The pyramidal form of sculpture, carved from a single block of wood and then painted, probably derives from traditional renditions of the Madonna and Child with St. John. The broadly chiselled, deeply faceted surfaces reflect the influence of Cubism and the sculpture of Gaudier-Brzeska. In October 1913 the sculpture was displayed on the mantelpiece of the sitting room designed and furnished by the Omega Workshops for the *Ideal Home Exhibition*. Two 1913 drawings by Duncan Grant, studies for Omega Workshops' Christmas card designs (which are also in the AGO's collection), were directly based on Fry's carving.

Purchase, 1987   87/1

Jacob Epstein (British, 1880–1959)

Birth 1913-14
Stone. 30.6 x 26.6 x 10.2

Born in New York City of Jewish Polish immigrants, Epstein studied at the Art Students' League from 1894 to 1902. In 1902 he went to Paris, where he enrolled in the École des beaux-arts. In Paris Epstein became interested in the "mass of primitive sculpture" at the Trocadéro (now the Musée de l'Homme). In 1905 Epstein settled permanently in London. Two years later he began work on 18 figurative carvings for the British Medical Association building, the first of many controversial public commissions.

Epstein's contact with the avant-garde dates from a visit to Paris in 1912 for the installations of his notorious *Tomb of Oscar Wilde* at the Père-Lachaise Cemetery. He met Modigliani, Brancusi and Picasso, and the dealer Paul Guillaume. At the time he may have acquired his first work of tribal sculpture. In 1913 Epstein did a series of stone sculptures that reflected his interest in both African and Oceanic art.

His drawings and sculpture of 1913-14 focus obsessively on themes of sexuality: copulation, pregnancy and birth. *Birth* depicts the splayed legs of the mother with the male infant at the moment of delivery. Iconographically, depictions of the actual moment of birth are rare in Western art, whereas the subject is not uncommon in Oceanic art and is also found but to a lesser extent in African sculpture.

Throughout his life Epstein assembled one of the finest and most comprehensive private collections of African and Oceanic art.

Purchase, 1983   83/235

173

Constantin Brancusi (Romanian, 1876–1957)

The First Cry c.1914
Polished bronze. H. 17.3

Born in Romania of peasant stock, Brancusi, like many painters and sculptors of his generation, was drawn to Paris, where he arrived in 1904. The following year he studied at the École des beaux-arts and by 1906 was exhibiting at the *Salon d'Automne*, where he met Rodin, who praised his work. Brancusi consciously avoided the dominant influence of the great French sculptor, declaring "nothing can grow in the shadow of the great trees." He became friends with many of the most avant-garde artists working in Paris: Picasso, Matisse, Modigliani, Léger and Lipchitz.

    The human head was one of the most important themes throughout Brancusi's working life. *The First Cry* was cast from the head of *The First Step*, his first wood carving, executed in 1913. Like many of his colleagues, Brancusi rejected the Greco-Roman tradition and turned to tribal art for inspiration. While the smooth, egglike shape of the head of *The First Cry* is typical of the purity of simplified forms that characterize his sculpture, the mouth and the deeply gouged out curved incision above it may have been directly inspired by an ancestor figure from the Upper Niger that Brancusi could have seen in the Musée de l'Homme in Paris. The sculptor has created a powerful, universal image of the first cry at birth.

Purchase, with assistance from the Volunteer Committee Fund, 1981   81/142

Constantin Brancusi (Romanian, 1876–1957)

Narcissus Fountain c.1922-23
Silver print. 39.8 x 29.9 (sheet)

Impressed by Edward Steichen's photographs *Rodin-Le Penseur* and *Balzac*, and with
rudimentary technical assistance from Man Ray, Brancusi in the early 1920s renewed
his interest in depicting his work in photographs. For the sculptor photography was an
expressive medium. Its affinity to light and space was the link that would bring his
sculptural forms to life, accentuate textures and articulate the order and volume of
his surroundings.

In *Narcissus Fountain* Brancusi has carefully stacked pedestals and blocks and clus-
tered various materials to emphasize the vertical, the horizontal, the spiral, the curve,
the angular and the oval to establish overlapping spatial relationships. A large, bend-
ing, never-realized funerary monument looms behind the studies of heads; the plaster
to the right relates to the detached head of *The First Step* (1913/14), which inspired
The First Cry (a polished bronze version of the latter is in the Gallery's collection,
see opposite page).

The art historian Carola Giedion-Welcker, an intimate friend of Brancusi, wrote
in her monograph on the sculptor: "These photographs taken with a camera wanting
in technical perfection are works of art of the first order.... Their psychic, as their
spatial, force communicates itself to the viewer with intensity. We perceive the work
as Brancusi experienced it and wanted to convey it, unadulterated in its creator's
attitude and interpretation...."

Gift from the Junior Committee Fund, 1984   84/52

Henri Gaudier-Brzeska (French, 1891–1915)

Torpedo Ornament 1914
Cut brass. 15.9 x 3.8 x 3.2

In 1906 Henri Gaudier won a travelling scholarship to London. The following year was also spent in England, where he made drawings of birds, animals and architecture. In early 1910 Gaudier returned to France to study art at the Ste-Geneviève Library in Paris, where he met Sophie Brzeska, a Polish woman 20 years his senior. When they moved to London soon after, Gaudier decided to add Sophie's surname to his own.

In June 1912, when Gaudier-Brzeska visited Epstein in his London studio, he was impressed by his stone carvings (see p. 173) and decided to concentrate on carving. During the next year and a half he met many of the leading artists and intellectuals in London. In late 1913 he worked at the Omega Workshops (see p. 172). He also contributed to the Vorticist magazine *Blast* proclaiming the importance of tribal sculpture.

Torpedo Ornament was made for the philosopher T. E. Hulme who had suggested that hard lines and geometric, cubic shapes were appropriate forms for modern art. In this remarkable small sculpture, the artist has pierced through the standing figure in three areas, as Archipenko had done in his 1912 *Walking Woman*. When the sculpture is positioned on its side, it resembles a torpedo fish. Little wonder that works such as this, as well as Gaudier's writings about sculpture, impressed Henry Moore during his student years in London in the early 1920s.

Purchase, 1985   84/930

Giacomo Balla (Italian, 1871–1958)

Linea di Velocità (Line of Speed) c.1914
Gouache and graphite on pressed board. 21.9 x 32.0

When Balla signed the official Futurist group manifesto in 1910, he joined a number
of revolutionary young Italian artists who sought to translate the dynamism of modern technological society into politics, poetry, music and the visual arts. Their concern
was with overthrowing all traditional values in favour of new expressions of art that
reflected modern life. The Futurists wished to represent machines or figures in motion;
as their manifesto proclaimed: "universal dynamism must be rendered as dynamic sensation . . . movement and light destroy the substance of objects." The city became a
symbol for the kinetic rhythms and continuous movement of the modern world.

     Balla's initial experiments with methods of representing motion and velocity
traced in abstract patterns the flights of birds. By 1913 he turned to a study of the speed-
ing automobile and presented its "line of speed" as schematic forms that approxi-
mated the structure of movement. These studies led to *Linea di Velocità* in which Balla
sought to transcend the mystery of speed on earth by an analysis of the dynamic forces
of nature. The whirling, vortexlike form in this drawing prefigures Balla's paintings
and drawings that delineate the movement of celestial bodies.

     Gift of Sam and Ayala Zacks, 1970   71/55

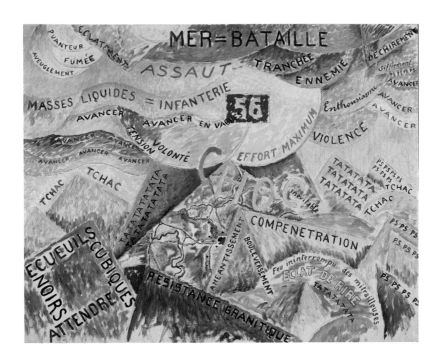

Gino Severini (Italian, 1883–1966)

Sea Equals Combat (Mer = Bataille) 1915
Oil on canvas. 48.5 x 59.6

Severini went to Rome in 1901, where he studied with Giacomo Balla and met Umberto
Boccioni. In 1906 he went to Paris, where he worked in close proximity to Braque,
Dufy and Utrillo. Initially interested in Neo-Impressionism and the work of Seurat,
Severini was introduced to Cubism after meeting Picasso and Apollinaire. In 1909 he
allied himself with the Italian Futurists. In revolt against social conventions and artistic
traditions, their manifesto, published in 1909, proclaimed that "the world's magnifi-
cence has been enriched by a new beauty: the beauty of speed. A racing car…is more
beautiful than the *Victory of Samothrace*."

Severini, in keeping with Futurist doctrine, wished to portray nature as dynamic
rather than static, to represent motion as a chronological sequence, and to show the
interaction between space and time. The Futurists also believed that war was an heroic,
noble cause. In *Mer = Bataille* Severini covers the canvas with words, commands and
indeed the noises – "tatatata…" – of war. Just below the centre is a topographical map
showing roads and railway lines. The bright yellows, reds, greens and blues give the
work a feeling of optimism, even cheerfulness. Never again was the subject of war
glorified with a naïveté that today seems ludicrous.

Gift of Sam and Ayala Zacks, 1970   71/325

Sonia Delaunay (Russian, 1885–1979)

Paris 1915
Coloured wax on laid paper. 32.6 x 44.3

Sonia Delaunay and her artist-husband Robert were painters concerned with the contrast and placement of colours to create movement and form independent of objects. Together they developed a new language for painting based on Eugène Chevreul's 19th-century theory of colour harmonies and contrasts. Sonia Delaunay applied these colour principles equally to painting, book covers, applied art and fabric design.

While in Portugal during WWI, Delaunay painted an extensive series of gouache and encaustic self-portraits in preparation for the catalogue cover of her exhibition in Stockholm in 1916. The right panel of one of these studies presents concentric and broken circles that not only provide a structure for colour contrasts but also create the abstracted features of the figure's head and hat. Delaunay incorporated printed letters in the left panel, which led to a whole new concept of adapting advertising and poster design in her work during the 1920s.

Gift of Sam and Ayala Zacks, 1970   71/117

Natalia Gontcharova (Russian, 1881–1962)

The Bridge c.1914
Oil on canvas. 65.0 x 50.0

Descended from an old noble family, Natalia Gontcharova was trained at the Moscow College where she met Mikhail Larionov, her lifelong companion. Soon both painters came into contact with Diaghilev and were participating in the most adventurous artistic activities in Russia. They visited Paris for the first time in 1906 and became fully familiar with avant-garde Western art. Gontcharova also took a keen interest in icon painting, which reinforced her own use of bright colour, flat decoration and emphatic linear rhythms.

Done in the middle of this century's second decade – a period of extreme social and political turbulence – *The Bridge* displays several features of Gontcharova's rapidly evolving style. By now she had assimilated the elements of the Cubist, Futurist and *Der Blaue Reiter* schools and had participated in Rayonism, promoted by Larionov. The intense colours are her own, as are the splintered and interpenetrating planes, barely held in dynamic equilibrium on the surface of the picture.

Purchase, 1988   87/200

Marc Chagall (Russian, 1887–1985)

Over Vitebsk 1914
Oil on paper mounted on canvas. 70.8 x 90.2

In 1914 Chagall returned to Russia after an absence of four years during which time he had emerged as an avant-garde artist in Paris. He was forced to remain in his homeland throughout the war. Compared to the excitement and artistic stimulation of the French capital, Chagall found life in his native city of Vitebsk provincial and boring.

Chagall soon began to paint scenes of his home town mixed with picturesque Judaeo-Slavic folkways. *Over Vitebsk* depicts the view from the artist's window with the Iltych church at the right, towering above the small houses. The deep perspective of the snow-covered road and the tilting buildings create a sense of disquietude. There is little evidence of the influence of the Fauve and Cubist painters, whose work had informed Chagall's formative years in Paris. The most striking and haunting aspect of the painting is the enormous figure of a man floating above the rooftops. It has been suggested that this incongruity of scale may relate to Russian Byzantine art in which the scale of the figure is based not on verisimilitude, but on its importance. The old bearded man, with his walking stick and sack thrown over one shoulder, is usually identified with the theme of the Wandering Jew and as such reflects both myth and for the artist present-day reality.

Gift of Sam and Ayala Zacks, 1970   71/260

Henri Matisse (French, 1869–1954)

Jeannette V 1916
Bronze. 58.4 x 19.7 x 29.3

Matisse, like Degas, Gauguin and Picasso, was a painter/sculptor whose reputation as a great artist would be secure even if all that survived were his three-dimensional works. His sculptural oeuvre was relatively small: some 70 bronzes and a little-known wood carving of 1907 entitled *La Danse*, which was inspired by Gauguin's Tahitian carvings such as the AGO's *Hina and Fatu* (see p. 154). Matisse focused his attention on sculpture during two distinct periods of his career – from 1900 to about 1916, and from 1924 to 1932.

Jeannette V, the last in the series of five heads based on the model Jeanne Vaderin, was executed between 1910 and 1916. They comprise one of the most remarkable portrait studies in 20th-century sculpture. *Jeannette I* and *II* were done directly from the model. As a point of departure for *Jeannette V*, Matisse began with a plaster cast of the third head in the series, which was the first he had worked on without the model. As in his four great relief sculptures of the female back, the heads of Jeannette became progressively bolder and less tied to the appearance of the model.

Like many artists of his generation – Picasso, Modigliani, Brancusi – Matisse turned to African art for inspiration. The rugged modelling of the head of *Jeannette V* is reminiscent of several tribal styles of African art, such as Cameroon and Bambara sculpture.

Purchase, 1949   49/45

Jacques Lipchitz (Lithuanian, 1891–1973)

Bather III 1917
Bronze. 71.7 x 23.4 x 26.0

Unlike many other foreign artists who were drawn to the artistic centre of Paris,
Lithuanian-born Lipchitz had no previous academic training when he arrived in Paris
in October 1909. He enrolled at the École des beaux-arts but soon transferred to the
Académie Julian. Lipchitz's early, academic sculpture reflects the influence of Art
Nouveau and is akin to the naturalism of Maillol.

In 1913 or 1914 Lipchitz visited Picasso in his studio, where he would have seen
not only the full range of the artist's Cubist paintings but also the few radical and
innovative Cubist sculptures (see p. 166). In 1914 Lipchitz began creating his own proto-
Cubist sculptures. A number of sculptures of 1915 were among his most abstract works,
some of which he destroyed "since I felt that I had lost the sense of the subject, of
its humanity...."

Bather III clearly illustrates the basic distinction between Analytic and Synthetic
Cubism. Instead of simplifying a realistic figure, in other words, working from nature,
Lipchitz was now building up the figure from abstract forms, working towards recognizable human shapes. In *Bather III* individual elements of the human anatomy – the
head, arms, finger, navel and crossed legs – are readily identifiable. Lipchitz's Cubist
sculpture was much influenced by Cubist painting, particularly by the work of his close
friend Juan Gris.

Gift of Sam and Ayala Zacks, 1970   71/226

Mikhail Larionov (Russian, 1881–1964)

Stage Mask 1916
Oil, ink, charcoal on wove paper. 77.4 x 55.1

Larionov belongs to the first generation of early 20th-century Russian artists who sought to develop alternatives to Cubism and Futurism. In 1912, in collaboration with Natalia Gontcharova, he formulated a movement of nonfigurative painting called Rayonism. Filled with intersecting rays of colour that interact dynamically, these paintings were principally concerned with colour combinations and heavy surface textures in linear arrangements.

In 1915 the theatrical impresario Sergei Diaghilev invited Larionov to join the Ballets Russes in Switzerland as a set and costume designer. This drawing is probably a study of a set design for *Histoires Naturelles*, which he choreographed with Michel Fokine. The ballet was rehearsed in Lausanne in 1916 by the Ballets Russes but never produced. This design may have been conceived for a three-dimensional moving relief planned as a backdrop for a series of dances.

Gift of Sam and Ayala Zacks, 1970   71/212

Aristide Maillol (French, 1861–1944)

Torso for Île-de-France 1921
Bronze. H. 120.0

Maillol, born at Banyuls-sur-Mer in the south of France, began his career as a painter
and a tapestry designer. By 1900 he abandoned his tapestries and devoted himself to
sculpture. The important Parisian dealer Ambroise Vollard gave Maillol his first one-
man exhibition in 1902.

    The subject of almost all Maillol's sculpture is the female nude. His works, like
the bronzes of Renoir, reflect a classical serenity that is far removed from demonic
power of much 20th-century sculpture that was inspired by tribal art and from Rodin's
penetrating, psychological studies of facial expression and the often tortured movement of the human figure. As Maillol stated: "I search for beauty and not for character."
Once he had found his ideal of feminine beauty – the nude, full, calm and serene –
his style changed little throughout his life. A number of bronzes, such as this one and
his monument to Paul Cézanne, may be said to personify their subjects only in the most
general way, more in name than in any specific iconographic references to the geographical region, or to the work of the French painter. Maillol's nudes embody in their
smooth, idealized forms the timelessness of the Mediterranean tradition.

    Courtesy of American Friends of Canada Committee, Inc.; gift of Peter D.
Meltzer in memory of the late David and Elise Meltzer, 1983 AL82.2

Amedeo Modigliani (Italian, 1884–1920)

Portrait of Mrs. Hastings 1915
Oil on cardboard. 55.5 x 45.4

Painter, sculptor and draughtsman, Modigliani was born in Livorno, Italy. He studied in Florence and Venice before moving to Paris in 1906. In his short career, during which he suffered from several attacks of tuberculosis, Modigliani produced some 22 stone carvings and numerous drawings, but he is best known for his portraits and evocative studies of the female nude.

During his formative years in Paris, Modigliani assimilated several influences – Fauvism, Cézanne, Brancusi and African tribal sculptures – which helped to shape but never dominated his personal style. This oil is one of many portraits of Beatrice Hastings, the English writer of South African origin. During the early years of WWI, the artist and writer lived together briefly in Montmartre. This portrait was executed soon after Modigliani had been concentrating on sculpture, and indeed the masklike appearance of Hastings's face recalls his stone heads. While the brownish tonality owes a debt to Cézanne and the Analytic Cubist paintings of Picasso and Braque, the elongated features such as the neck and nose reflect the influence of African art, which Modigliani, like Picasso, Matisse and Brancusi, greatly admired. With simplicity and economy of means, Modigliani has produced a tender, yet austere portrait in a style that has become instantly recognizable and uniquely his own.

Gift of Sam and Ayala Zacks, 1970   71/260

186

Chaim Soutine (Lithuanian, 1893/4–1943)

The Village Church c.1919-22
Oil on canvas. 57.8 x 81.3

Born in Lithuania, Soutine studied drawing in Russia before moving to Paris in 1913, where he enrolled at the École des beaux-arts. Soutine's unsettled life and the anguished emotionalism of his work earned him membership into a group of painters known as *peintres maudits*.

From 1919 to 1921 Soutine lived and worked at Céret, the small town in the French Pyrénées where Picasso and Braque had spent their summers ten years earlier. Although the scene represented in *The Village Church* is in the medieval town of Saint-Paul-de-Vence, the painting is closely related to Soutine's violent expressionistic landscapes painted at Céret. The emotionalism and neurotic intensity have an obvious precedent in the work of van Gogh, and yet Soutine goes even further in the way in which the paint seems to have been poured onto the canvas and then violently attacked with the brush. The work seems to be more about the action of painting as a reflection of the artist's state of mind than about representation. The church just right of centre and the roofs of the houses are about the only recognizable vestiges of reality. Indeed, without the title as a guide, one could easily read this work as non-representational, anticipating the paintings of the Abstract Expressionists of the New York School.

Gift of Sam and Ayala Zacks, 1970   71/333

Pierre Bonnard (French, 1867–1947)

Southern Landscape with Two Children c.1916-18
Oil on linen. 139.1 x 198.1

Bonnard, after studying law, began his academic training in Paris at the École des beaux-arts and the Académie Julian. He met Vuillard and Denis and through Sérusier became familiar with the theories of Gauguin. The decorative character of Bonnard's early work reflects the influence of Art Nouveau. As a member of the Nabis group, he was nicknamed "the Japanese Nabi" because of his love of Japanese prints.

In 1912 Bonnard rented a villa at Grasse, not far inland from Cannes on the Riviera. In his landscapes painted in the south of France, Bonnard abandoned the intimacy of his studio in which he painted nude studies of his wife Marthe and focused instead on the warmth of the Mediterranean light and the luxurious, semitropical foliage. In this oil, one of Bonnard's most ambitious landscapes, the two young children appear to be an extension of the colour and forms surrounding them, as they merge with the overall pattern and rhythm. The colours and delicate brush strokes owe something to the Impressionists, while the quality of decoration is a characteristic of the work of the Nabis. Like Matisse, Bonnard was one of the greatest colourists of the 20th century. In his southern landscapes, he created an idyllic Arcadia, a world, in the words of Baudelaire, of "luxe, calme et volupté."

Gift of Sam and Ayala Zacks, 1970   71/62

189

Augustus John (British, 1878–1961)

The Marchesa Casati 1919
Oil on canvas. 96.5 x 68.6

Later to become the pre-eminent British portraitist of his day, Augustus John studied at the Slade School of Fine Art in London and exhibited regularly with the New English Art Club. In 1919, while painting dignitaries at the Paris Peace Conference, he met the arresting Marchesa Casati, whose extravagance and narcissism were legendary. He was to draw or paint her four times in the course of their thirty-five year friendship.

Originally full length but cut down by the artist, this portrait depicts the Marchesa in silk pyjamas, which float elegantly around her slim, pale arms and torso. With her left hand provocatively on her hip, she turns to survey the viewer, her lips moist, her large, kohl-darkened eyes glowing beneath a mass of vivid, dyed curls. The amorphous mountain terrain in the background and the subject's smile allude to Leonardo's *Mona Lisa*, although La Casati is more seductive than mysterious. The Marchesa was notorious for her evocation of exotic and historical characters, typically at fancy dress parties. She appears in some guise or other in half of the over 125 known portrayals of her. The AGO's portrait is one of the most successful, John's bravura style matching the Marchesa's provocative gaze and pose.

Purchase, 1934   2164

Otto Dix (German, 1891–1969)

Portrait of Dr. Heinrich Stadelmann 1922
Oil on canvas. 90.8 x 61.0

The son of a foundry worker, Dix studied art in Dresden between 1909 and 1914. Early influences in his formative years include van Gogh, painters of the *Jugendstil* movement, *Die Brücke* and *Der Blaue Reiter* artists, and the works of the German Primitives. After WWI Dix was one of the principal exponents of the movement called *Neue Sachlichkeit* or New Objectivity, which arose as a reaction against German Expressionism.

In the early 1920s Dix developed a style characterized by merciless, often frightening realism as in this unforgettable portrait. Dr. Stadelmann was an unorthodox psychiatrist in Dresden, who practised hypnotherapy on wealthy hypochondriacs in a sanatorium that he called the "Bird House." (Each patient was classified as some species of bird.) In this extraordinary portrait, the viewer is confronted with the hypnotic stare of Dr. Stadelmann's bulging red/green eyes (the layers of paint on the surface of the canvas make the eyes bulge in reality). The starkness of his dark suit contrasts with the delicate patterns of the lace curtains in front of the window. Dix lays bare with an uncompromising honesty and truthfulness the ravages of old age and something of the subject's hypnotic if not magical powers.

Anonymous gift, 1969; donated by the Ontario Heritage Foundation, 1988   L69.2

Karl Schmidt-Rottluff (German, 1884–1976)

Seated Nude c.1913
Hand-coloured monoprint on laid paper. 50.3 x 40.6

Karl Schmidt was born in the German town of Rottluff and, like Emil Nolde, adopted the name of his birthplace. He moved to Dresden in 1905 and became a founding member of the German Expressionist group *Die Brücke* (The Bridge). Influenced early on by the African and Oceanic art housed in the Dresden Ethnological Museum, *Die Brücke* artists rejected Impressionism and turned toward a more introspective art. They desired to transcend the everyday world and to express emotions through distortions of colour and form.

From 1912 and 1920 Schmidt-Rottluff's works were among the most blatantly primitivistic of the early 20th century. Whether *Seated Nude* was inspired by a specific source is not known, but the work reveals the influence of primitive art in both form and spirit. The masklike face, the crudely drawn body, and the bright, jarring colours aggressively challenge traditional notions of female beauty.

The technique used in this work remains a mystery. While the black ink appears to have been applied by lithographic means, the colour was added by hand. No other impression is known, and the work appears to be unique.

Anonymous gift, 1982   82/230

Emil Nolde (German, 1867-1956)

Tändelei (The Flirtation) 1917
Woodcut on wove paper. 30.7 x 24.2 (composition)

Emil Nolde was born Emil Hansen but later adopted the name of his birthplace, a small town on the German-Danish border. He felt at ease with the peasants of the region and became fascinated with the primitive arts of all cultures. In 1906 he became a member of *Die Brücke* (The Bridge), a group of German Expressionist artists who rejected the naturalistic art of their predecessors and used colour, line and form in symbolic, emotive ways. The *Brücke* artists introduced Nolde to the woodcut technique; his prints in this medium became some of the most powerful graphic works of the 20th century. The present work is a superb early impression of the woodcut, printed in high relief.

  In 1913 Nolde visited the South Seas, where he found affirmation for the mystical content of his art and for his rhythmic, expressive use of colour and form. *Tändelei* illustrates Nolde's interest in the ritualistic dances of the people native to the islands. By distorting the human figure, compressing the picture space, and brutally simplifying the form, the artist has created a disturbing, emotionally charged image.

  Anonymous gift, 1985 85/111

Fernand Léger (French, 1881–1955)

Kneeling Woman 1921
Oil on canvas. 92.1 x 60.3

Born at Argentan, Normandy, Léger moved to Paris where he worked as an architectural draughtsman, and where he studied at the École des arts décoratifs and the Académie Julian.

Léger participated in the public debut of Cubism, when he exhibited in the spring of 1911 at the *Salon des Indépendants* with Le Fauconnier, Gleizes, Metzinger, Laurencin and Delaunay. From the outset, Léger rejected the static compositions of the Cubism of Braque and Picasso in favour of more dynamic effects. In 1913 he created his revolutionary series *Contrastes de formes*, which were among the first abstractions ever to be painted. When subject matter reasserted itself the following year, the still lifes, landscapes and figure studies were composed of geometric and tubular forms. One critic used the term "tubism" to describe Léger's brand of Cubism.

In 1920 Léger began to focus on the human figure as a subject in its own right. In *Kneeling Woman* the subject kneels in front of a busy abstract background, whose dominant vertical and horizontal forms reflect the influence of Mondrian. Her massive limbs seem closer to interlocking machine forms than to human anatomy. For Léger and the Purists, man was the most perfect of natural machines. In this work, there is a dialogue between abstraction and representation, a challenge that was to absorb Léger for the rest of his life.

Purchase, Walter C. Laidlaw Endowment, 1963   63/4

Picasso (Spanish, 1881–1973)

Seated Woman 1926-27
Oil on canvas. 130.8 x 97.8

"I am intent on resemblance," Picasso said, "a resemblance more real than real, attaining the surreal." Unlike the Surrealists, with whom he exhibited in 1925, Picasso did not depict fantastic, imaginary landscapes but based his work on the observation of nature and the events of his own life.

Seated Woman is one of Picasso's most complex and enigmatic figure studies done at the time when he was closely allied with the Surrealists. The figure is set against a background made up of large decorative areas of unmodulated colours that ultimately derive from Picasso's Synthetic Cubist work of 1914-18. Whereas one reads the decorative skirting at centre right as existing well behind the left shoulder, the diagonal skirting at left ends abruptly at the right shoulder, as if the woman is wedged into the corner of a very small room. The distortions of the figure itself and the confluences of facial features and multiple profiles in the area of the head are so complex that no single literal reading appears feasible. It has been suggested that Picasso has combined three heads in one: the head in profile on the left is that of the artist; the head in profile on the right is that of his son Paulo; and the one at centre that locks the other two heads together is that of Picasso's wife Olga.

Picasso has displaced the female genitals to the head, a much practised Surrealist device. Some of the disquieting and aggressive imagery found in Picasso's work of the period reflects the artist's borrowing from Oceanic sculpture, which he admired for its lyrical, grotesque and fantastic qualities and for its highly imaginative metamorphosis and displacement of anatomical forms, characteristics he found lacking in much of the African art that had been so influential in the development of his early Analytic Cubist work of 1908-09.

Purchase, 1964   63/44

Pablo Picasso (Spanish, 1881–1973)

Head of a Man 1967
Ink and watercolour on wove paper. 74.9 x 56.5

Picasso created thousands of drawings between 1966 and 1968 that recapitulated many of the themes and styles he had developed throughout his prolific career. In this drawing from Picasso's late period, a renewed interest in the art of the past, and particularly classical antiquity, is revealed.

    This drawing belongs to a series of large format sketches that recall Picasso's cubist concern with presenting simultaneous front and profile views of the head. That the subject may be a type derived from antiquity is evident from the dotted pattern used to render the hair and beard. Picasso's perpetuation of the simplicity characteristic of Neoclassicism in a spirit of modern invention reveals his genius as a draughtsman.

    Gift of Mr. and Mrs. Sidney Bregman, 1988   88/360

Henri Matisse (French, 1869-1954)

Seated Model with Guitar 1922
Charcoal and stump, black graphite on laid paper. 47.4 x 31.5

Beginning in 1916, Matisse spent a part of each year in Nice. The "Nice Period," which ended in 1929, was dominated by quiet interiors, exotic costumes, rich textures, and the presence of Henriette Darricarrere, a model who sat for numerous drawings between 1921 and 1927.

Matisse believed that drawing was the foundation of art and experimented with a wide variety of media. In the 1920s his favourite technique was charcoal and stump, in which a rolled wad of paper (stump) or a cloth was used to smudge the charcoal. The resulting tones range from pale greys to dense blacks. In the present drawing, dramatic highlights dissolve into deep shadows, and rounded curves and countercurves are carefully balanced by acute angles and flat decorative patterns.

Gift of Sam and Ayala Zacks, 1970   71/250

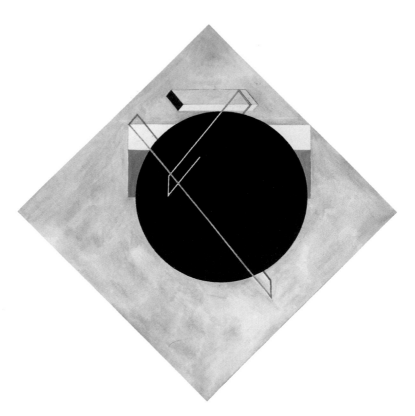

El Lissitzky (Russian, 1890–1941)

Study for 'Proun 8 Stellungen' (Proun 8 Positions) 1923
Ink, gouache, watercolour, graphite on laid paper. 24.5 x 24.8

Lissitzky contributed to a wide range of activities within the Russian avant-garde
movement as a painter, architect, illustrator, exhibition and interior designer, and
theoretician. Under the influence of Kasimir Malevich, Lissitzky abandoned figuration
in 1919 to create a new conception of nonobjective art for utilitarian purposes.

Lissitzky's *Proun* (Russian acronym for "Project for the Affirmation of the New")
is a composition of flat and three-dimensional geometrical forms that interact in a
neutral space. He considered the *Prouns* to be an intermediary step between painting
and architecture that would offer a radical way for viewers to re-evaluate both art forms.
This study – like the painting by the same title in the National Gallery of Canada's
collection – was intended by the artist to be viewed from any of eight possible positions (with no fixed top or bottom). Lissitzky thus affirmed his desire that the *Prouns*
act as metaphors for a revolution in society's understanding of space, material
and movement.

Gift of Sam and Ayala Zacks, 1970   71/228

Naum Gabo (Russian, 1890–1977)

Model for a Fountain 1923-24, reassembled 1985
Glass (replaced) and enamelled metal (repainted). H. 72.5

Although Gabo had no formal art school training, his varied intellectual background influenced his development as a sculptor and included studies in medicine, natural science and civil engineering. In 1912 and 1913 Gabo visited his brother Antoine Pevsner in Paris, where he saw the work of numerous avant-garde artists at the *Salon des Indépendants*.

Gabo's earliest constructions, made in such materials as plywood, galvanized iron, ivory, steel and cardboard, date from 1915-17. In these Cubist-inspired works, still figurative in nature, he was moving away from the monolithic conception of sculpture. In 1920, 5000 copies of Gabo's *Realistic Manifesto* were published in Paris in which he outlined his ideas for a revolutionary new art. Time and space were among the key elements of Constructivist art.

In 1918-19 Gabo began creating purely abstract constructions, innovative and experimental in nature, using modern industrial materials such as metal, plastic, Perspex, glass and aluminum. During the 1920s Gabo made a number of small models obviously intended to be enlarged and placed in public settings. Unfortunately none of these works were constructed on the monumental scale that the sculptor intended. Nevertheless, with *Model for a Fountain*, one of the masterpieces of Constructivist sculpture, the artist has created, in a modest scale, a work of great purity and elegance.

Gift of the Gabo family, in honour of the
Volunteer Committee's 40th anniversary, 1986   85/552

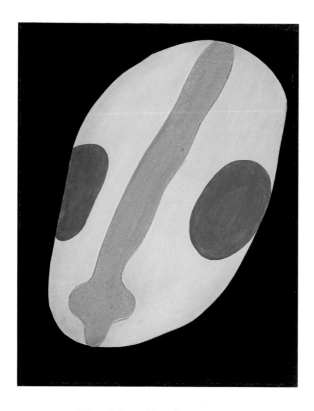

Jean (Hans) Arp (French, 1887–1966)

Nose and Cheeks 1925-26
Oil on laminated paperboard. 40.0 x 30.5

Painter, sculptor and poet Arp was born in Strasbourg, France. In 1916 he joined the
Dada group in Zurich, and later in 1925 he became a member of the Surrealist group
in Paris, participating in their first exhibition. In keeping with the Surrealists, Arp
experimented with free automatic drawing and the use of random, chance elements
in his work.

     This relief illustrates the continuity of the organic forms that characterized Arp's
Dada period work. He was a master at creating ambiguous, suggestive meaning and
whimsical visual puns. In this work the images may be read literally as a nose and cheeks
but equally obvious are images of the male genitals. In Arp's work sexuality, one of
the dominant themes of the Surrealists, has none of the morbid cruelty found, for
example, in Dali's paintings. Rather, in reliefs such as *Nose and Cheeks*, Arp focuses in
a playful way on the interchangeable forms of the human anatomy.

     His first fully three-dimensional sculptures were made in 1930-31; they were
multipiece compositions comprised of organic forms that greatly influenced the work
of Moore and Hepworth.

Purchase, 1988   88/111

Alberto Giacometti (Swiss, 1901-66)

Three Figures Outdoors 1929
Bronze. 51.5 x 38.5 x 9.0

Giacometti, sculptor, painter, draughtsman and printmaker was born in a village in the Italian-speaking Bregaglia Valley in Switzerland, the son of a Post-Impressionist painter.

Giacometti arrived in Paris in 1922 to study sculpture under Émile Antoine Bourdelle. He visited the studio of Cubist sculptors Lipchitz and Laurens and frequented the Trocadéro to view the collections of tribal art. André Masson introduced Giacometti to many of the most important members of the Surrealist movement.

Three Figures Outdoors marks the transition from the Cubist-inspired work of 1926-28 to the open, cagelike constructions of the late 1920s and early 1930s. It is probably the first of Giacometti's Surrealist sculptures to focus on an aggressive erotic theme, which culminated in *Woman with Her Throat Cut*, 1932. As with much Surrealist art, this bronze is open to various interpretations. The two phallic pointed prongs are indicative of some kind of sexual encounter, with the female figure being represented by the central zigzag form. The outer frame may be read as an abstract representation of an outdoor setting, possibly trees or architecture. The sculpture was almost certainly inspired by spikelike forms found in carvings from the Sepik River region of New Guinea. As with most of the Surrealists, including Picasso, Giacometti's interest in tribal sculpture had shifted, by the late 1920s, from African to Oceanic art.

Purchase, 1984   83/311

Joan Miró (Spanish, 1893–1983)

Untitled 1926
Oil on canvas. 100.2 x 81.5

In 1920 Spanish-born Miró settled permanently in Paris, where he soon befriended Picasso and other members of the avant-garde. He signed the Surrealist Manifesto in 1924 and joined the movement the following year.

Miró's untitled canvas belongs to an important early group of spontaneously executed canvases that not only possessed considerable appeal for painters after WWII, but also won the approval of André Breton at the time. It was, Breton wrote in 1928, "by such pure psychic automatism that [Miró] might pass for the most 'surrealist' of us all."

The first stage in the execution of this work must have involved the laying in of the grey-black ground, without any reference to the traditional horizon, but with distinct variations in density and texture. On this translucent ground, Miró has overlaid a space configuration – chalk-white angular lines, both curving and straight black lines, and patches of colour that differ in texture. In one area small touches of yellow and green paint have been squeezed straight from the tube onto the canvas. The first stage was free and unconscious, while the second stage was, as Miró has said, "carefully calculated." Many of the elements found in Miró's work can be identified as abstractions of real things, but in this work elements such as the black crescent moon/moustache hover on the brink of being recognizable, yet remain ambiguous, elusive and mysterious.

Purchase, with assistance from the Volunteer Committee Fund, 1981   81/158

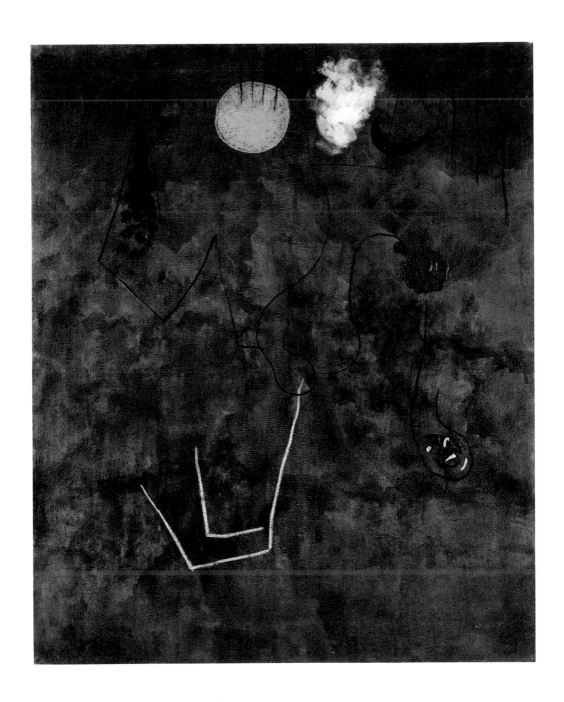

Jacques Lipchitz (Lithuanian, 1891–1973)

Figure 1926-30
Bronze. H. 216.6

In 1925-26 Lipchitz abandoned the traditional monolithic mass of stone and bronze that had characterized his Cubist sculpture of the previous decade and embarked on his series of innovative "transparents," which he described as "sculpture as space, as air or spirit rather than as solid mass."

Figure was based on a small maquette of 1926, which in turn evolved from a sculpture entitled *Ploumanach*. The latter bronze was inspired by offshore rock formations, where large stones were balanced on others that had been eroded by water. In the first of two studies for *Figure*, the top section included a reclining figure, but as Lipchitz wrote, "I must have begun to see this as a primitive totem, for in the next sketch I transformed the upper part into a head with an indication of staring eyes."

In 1930, at the request of a collector, Lipchitz enlarged the small 1926 *Study for Figure*. The sculptor saw *Figure* as the summation of his ideas dating back to 1915: "Specifically, it pulled together those different directions of massive, material frontality and of aerial openness in which I had been working during the 1920s. It is also very clearly a subject sculpture, an image with a specific and rather frightening personality." Of all Lipchitz's sculptures that reflect affinities with tribal art, *Figure*, with the hypnotic, staring eyes, comes closest to the demonic presence found in Picasso's work of 1907-08. Along with Moore's *Glenkiln Cross* (p. 224), Lipchitz's *Figure* is one of the greatest totemic images in 20th-century sculpture.

Gift of Walter Carsen, 1989   89/403

Yves Tanguy (French, 1900-55)

The Satin Pillow 1929
Oil on canvas. 130.5 x 97.2

Tanguy, born in Paris of a Breton family, decided to become an artist in 1923 after seeing two paintings by de Chirico in a gallery window. He soon became aware of Surrealism, and late in 1925 he met Breton and members of the Surrealist group.

Tanguy, like Dali and Magritte, belonged to the so-called Illusionist Surrealists. The setting in *Satin Pillow* is suggestive of an eerie desert landscape, a moonscape or the ocean floor, inhabited by strange forms, which seem suspended as they float across the canvas. In this painting a number of Surrealist predilections have come together, including the inexplicable juxtaposition of disquieting images and the hints of automatism in determining the appearance of that imagery. As with the paintings of Miró, the suggestive but ambiguous forms persist in teasing the imagination; but whereas the images of Miró's painting appear whimsical, Tanguy's are more disconcerting. One of Tanguy's finest paintings of the period, this canvas belonged to the poet Paul Éluard and then was acquired by the English Surrealist painter Sir Roland Penrose. That Dali's name appears on a label on the back of the stretcher suggests that he may also have owned the painting.

Purchase, 1986   86/39

Barbara Hepworth (British, 1903-75)

Mother and Child 1927
Hopton wood stone. 45.0 x 28.0 x 20.5

Hepworth, like her friend and colleague Henry Moore, was born in Yorkshire in the
north of England. They both studied at the Leeds School of Art and at the Royal College of Art in London. From the outset of her career, Hepworth followed the examples
of Brancusi, Modigliani and Gaudier-Brzeska in her commitment to carving directly in
stone or wood, in adherence to the doctrine known as "truth to materials."

    This rare early work is one of the few carvings that has survived from the 1920s,
when Hepworth's sculpture was firmly rooted in the figurative tradition. Since she
was working directly in stone, Hepworth was hesitant to free certain features of the
figures – the heads, necks and arms – from the monolithic block. In *Mother and Child*,
which is stylistically related to Moore's equally massive and powerful *Mother and Child*
of 1925-26, the two figures, while fully realized in the round, are shown in high relief.
Indeed the inseparable, tender mother-and-child relationship is enhanced by the
unity and sense of oneness created by the material itself.

    Purchase, with assistance from the Volunteer Committee Fund, 1983   82/278

Henry Moore (British, 1898–1986)

Seated Figure 1930
Alabaster. H. 47.0

When this beautiful alabaster figure was acquired by the Gallery in 1976, it represented not only the earliest Moore sculpture in the collection, but also the first and, to date, only carving. *Seated Figure* marks the culmination of varied influences that informed Moore's art during the 1920s – his interest in direct carving, which was partly inspired by his admiration for Pre-Columbian stone sculpture, and his interest in early Greek Cycladic sculpture and Sumerian art.

As is common in Moore's sculpture, the pose of *Seated Figure* is asymmetrical, including the base and block on which the figure sits. The head is turned to the right, the clasped hands rest on the right knee, the figure is twisted at the waist in a kind of *contrapposto* movement. The drapery, used for the first time in Moore's sculpture, is shown in a simplified, schematic way.

Moore eventually stopped using alabaster, he admitted, because of his concern that the soft, sensuous quality of the material would distract from the form of the sculpture itself.

Seated Figure, with its vestiges of the art of the past that had interested Moore during the first decade of his career, marks the end of the first major period in his art. His work of the next few years was influenced by the Surrealists – Picasso, Arp and Giacometti.

Purchase, 1976   76/164

Henry Moore (British, 1898–1986)

Montage of Mother and Child Studies c.1929-30
Graphite, ink, chalk, coloured washes on paper. 47.3 x 36.2 (sheet)

This is the only known montage of mother-and-child studies. As the inscription in her hand at the bottom sheet indicates, the montage was assembled by the artist's wife. (Irena is an alternative spelling of Irina.) She cut from Moore's notebooks all but the largest of the mother-and-child studies shown here and arranged them in their present order, before pasting them down on a board.

The reclining figure and the mother and child were the two dominant themes of Moore's sculpture, drawings and prints during the 65 years of his working life. Of the latter motif, he wrote: "from early on I have had an obsession with the Mother and Child theme. It has been a universal theme from the beginning of time and some of the earliest sculptures we've found from the Neolithic Age are of a Mother and Child. I discovered, when drawing, I could turn every little scribble, blot or smudge into a Mother and Child.... So that I was conditioned, as it were, to see it in everything."

These studies were done as a means of generating ideas for sculpture. Two carvings, one of 1929, the second of 1930, were based directly on preparatory sketches on this sheet.

Purchase, 1976   76/165

Henry Moore (British, 1898–1986)

Figures Sculptures 1931
Woodcut on paper. 12.7 x 19.7

The AGO collection includes all but 30 of the 719 prints that Moore made between 1931 and 1984. This is Moore's first print and one of two woodcuts executed in 1931. Like almost all of Moore's prints made between the early 1930s and the late 1960s, this woodcut is closely related to the drawings of the period in which he was generating ideas for sculpture. The massive reclining figure that dominates the central area of the sheet is surrounded by other figure studies, all of which reflect the influence of the organic, biomorphic forms found in the work of Arp and Picasso.

The technique of Moore's drawings of the early 1930s, which is also evident in this woodcut, reflects to some extent the automatic drawings of the Surrealists. As Moore wrote, he would begin a drawing "with no perceived problem to solve, with only the desire to use pencil on paper, and make lines, tones and shapes with no conscious aim; but as my mind takes in what is so produced, a point arrives when some idea becomes conscious and crystallizes, and then a control and ordering begin to take place."

Gift of Henry Moore, 1974   74/144

Henry Moore (British, 1898–1986)

Spanish Prisoner c.1939
Lithograph. 36.5 x 30.5 (image)

Spanish Prisoner, Moore's first lithograph, is not only the rarest of all the sculptor's prints, but also one of the most important. This is one of only three known trial proofs. Although the lithograph was never editioned, it was intended to raise money for the Republican Spanish prisoners of war who were interned in the south of France.

This work was based on the 1939 drawing *Spanish Prisoner*, one of four known preparatory studies for the lithograph. The figure is placed behind two rows of barbed wire. The head, imprisoned behind bars, is related to Moore's 1939 drawings of internal and external form motifs and anticipates *The Helmet* of 1939-40. This haunting image reflects Moore's deeply felt reaction to the political event and to the plight of the Spanish prisoners.

Gift of Henry Moore, 1976   76/63

Henry Moore (British, 1898–1986)

Two Women on a Bench in a Shelter 1940
Ink, wax crayon, chalk, wash, gouache on wove paper. 34.4 x 42.7

This work is one of the famous shelter drawings that Moore created during the early years of WWII. During the Blitz of 1940, Londoners began using the Underground platforms beside the tracks as air raid shelters. The positions of the shelterers and the setting had an overwhelming impact on Moore. They combined two of his favourite motifs: "I saw hundreds of Henry Moore Reclining Figures stretched along the platforms," and "even the train tunnels seemed to be like the holes in my sculpture."

Before the war, drawing had been, Moore said, "a second string in one's bow," although vitally important to his development as a sculptor. But the war temporarily diverted his attention away from sculpture, and for nearly two years he worked exclusively on drawing. Now that Moore had found a subject related to the war, his friend Kenneth Clark persuaded him to become a war artist. Dealing with a subject from life that profoundly moved him, the humanist side of his nature, which for so long had been in conflict with his interest in primitive art, found an outlet in the shelter drawings.

In these drawings Moore began to make a serious study of drapery, a motif that had a marked influence on his subsequent sculpture. In this drawing, as in much of his work, the drapery almost becomes the subject itself, existing as an independent form.

Purchase, 1974   74/337

Ben Nicholson (British, 1894–1982)

Composition c.1935-40
Oil on canvas. 122.2 x 92.7

Although born into an artistic family, Nicholson was, apart from a brief period at the
Slade School in London, without formal training. While visiting Paris in 1921, he saw
the work of Picasso and Braque. During the 1920s he focused on still-life and landscape
subjects that reflected an interest in Cubism.

After meeting Mondrian in 1934, Nicholson began creating his first carved and
painted white reliefs, composed of abstract circles and rectangles of great subtlety.
Throughout the 1930s Nicholson was closely involved with the abstract school of painting, and along with Moore and Hepworth – whom he married – he became a leading
member of the English avant-garde.

In *Composition* the way in which the flat planes of colour have been divided into
vertical and horizontal divisions reflects Mondrian's influence. The circle that hovers
just above centre is a personal stylistic trademark in Nicholson's work. Although later
in life he returned to landscape, still-life and architectural subjects, Nicholson
remained one of the most consistent exponents of the geometric abstract.

Gift of Sam and Ayala Zacks, 1970   71/276

215

Barbara Hepworth (British, 1903-75)

Two Figures 1943
Wood, redwood. One Figure: H. 50.8; Other Figure: H. 34.3;
Whole: 61.2 x 31.4 x 21.0

During the early 1930s Hepworth abandoned her figurative work of the previous decade and began creating abstract carvings. By 1931 she was no longer intimidated by the challenge of carving into and opening out the stone. In *Pierced Form* of that year, she carved a hole through the stone, a formal innovation initiated by Archipenko and Gaudier-Brzeska (see p. 176) in 1912 and 1914 respectively. Hepworth was also influenced by the purity of Brancusi's work and by the multipart compositions of Arp's sculpture.

In 1931 Hepworth met (and later married) the English abstract painter Ben Nicholson. The two artists with their children moved to Cornwall in 1939, where they were soon joined by Gabo. The landscape of Cornwall around St. Ives had a profound influence on Hepworth's work. She wrote: "I began to be hungry for landscape. Monoliths were creeping into my work." The use of strings in *Two Figures* is a feature found in her prewar sculpture. Whereas in Gabo's constructions of the period (see opposite page) the nylon filaments are totally integrated with the Perspex, Hepworth's strings serve a different function, as they cut across and make tangible the negative space surrounded by solid form. That she entitled this carving *Two Figures* is indicative of a return to figurative references and of her interest in the standing figure in relation to landscape, which echoes the prehistoric stone monoliths that dot the Cornish landscape.

Gift of Sam and Ayala Zacks, 1970   71/88

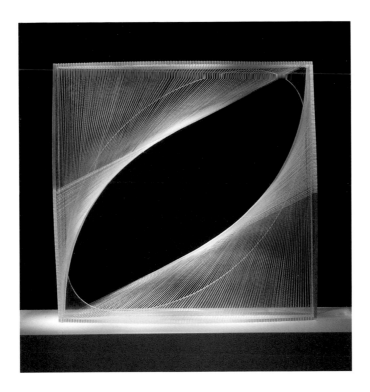

Naum Gabo (Russian, 1890–1977)

Linear Construction in Space No. 1 1945-49
Perspex with nylon filament. 61.3 x 61.3 x 13.0

By the mid-1930s Gabo's work was becoming well known on both sides of the Atlantic. He visited England in 1935 for the first time to discuss his participation in the forthcoming exhibition *Abstract and Concrete*, organized by Nicolette Gray. In 1936 Gabo was represented by seven works in Alfred Barr's pioneering exhibition *Cubism and Abstract Art* at the Museum of Modern Art, New York.

Gabo settled in London in 1936, where he lived in close proximity to Moore, Hepworth, Nicholson and the critic Herbert Read. In 1936-37 he made a number of constructions in Perspex onto which he incised lines suggestive of thin strings. This work is one of 17 variations on the same theme, which are entitled *Linear Construction in Space No. 1*. The first version may have been made as early as 1938, but it was not until 1942 that Gabo began to concentrate in earnest on this subject. Both Moore and Hepworth made stringed figure sculptures in the late 1930s, but it is difficult to determine if their work influenced Gabo.

In Gabo's work, the complex way in which the nylon filament fits into the numerous notches and becomes totally integrated with the transparent Perspex serves a totally different function from the strings in the work of Moore and Hepworth, which cut across open spaces and connect solid forms. In this superbly crafted work of great luminosity and purity, both the nylon filaments and the Perspex are transparent and reflective, resulting in a tense interplay between the two media.

Gift from the Volunteer Committee Fund, 1986   85/553

Henri Matisse (French, 1869–1954)

Ivy Branch 1941
Oil on canvas. 55.8 x 46.6

Matisse's early work was strongly influenced by the Impressionists, but through his
contact with paintings by van Gogh, Cézanne, Gauguin and Seurat, colour became of
prime importance in Matisse's art. During the summer of 1905, Matisse and Derain had
their work exhibited together at the *Salon d'Automne*, where it was labelled *fauve*
(wild) because of the emotionally charged explosion of pure colours that were free
from any descriptive function. The complex compositions of Matisse's work and the
use of flat, relatively unmodulated planes of luminous colour reflect his interest in
Oriental art, Persian miniatures and Japanese prints.

    Ivy Branch was executed in 1941, several months after the painter underwent an
operation for cancer. The stark composition is comprised of three parallel lines, with
a potted plant resting on the unmodulated pink table. The organic shapes of the ivy
leaves, set against an orange background, contrast with the severity of the setting. It
has been suggested that this seemingly straightforward still life may be charged with
personal significance for the artist. In Christian art, ivy is a symbol of everlasting life.
The black, ominous shadow – not in the least realistic – that looms behind the ivy may
represent death. The subtle, tonal nuances in this work justify yet again Matisse's
reputation as the greatest colourist of the 20th century.

Gift of Sam and Ayala Zacks, 1970   71/249

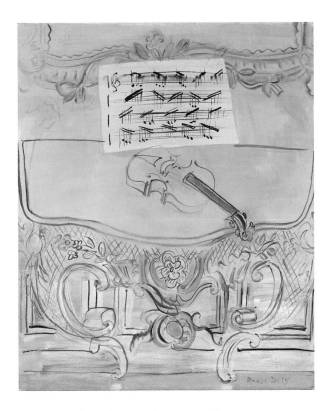

Raoul Dufy (French, 1877–1953)

The Yellow Violin 1949
Oil on canvas. 100.3 x 81.2

The Yellow Violin is one of the most important paintings from Dufy's last years. During wwii he began working on a series of paintings characterized by a monochromatic or restricted use of prismatic colours. The subjects of these works were often views of the artist's studio or apartment and the world of music.

    The massive Louis xiv console that occupies two thirds of this canvas was a piece of furniture in Dufy's apartment. The ornate, curvilinear legs contrast with the flat, monochromatic surface of the console, which has been tipped upwards into the picture plane, a feature found in the early still-life paintings of Picasso and Braque of 1908-09. The stark musical notation, like a Cubist *papier collé*, contrasts with the warmth of the surrounding yellow. By outlining and thus defining the various objects – console, violin and mirror – against the yellow ground, Dufy has created a charming still life whose decorative features are inseparable from the boldness and directness of the overall composition.

    Gift of Sam and Ayala Zacks, 1970   71/133

Georges Rouault (French, 1871–1958)

Autumn 1936-38
Colour aquatint and roulette on laid paper. 50.7 x 65.5 (impression);
57.1 x 78.2 (sheet)
Edition: 75/175

The theme of female bathers preoccupied avant-garde European artists in the late 19th and early 20th centuries. *Autumn* is Rouault's contribution to this popular theme, though the women he portrays are prostitutes rather than virtuous paragons of female beauty. The intent behind his choice of subject was to record and criticize the decadence and corruption that he saw permeating contemporary society. The heavy black outlines, the deep, luminous hues, the complex composition, and the distortions of female anatomy combine to create an image of great visual and emotional power.

Rouault first re-interpreted this image, based on his painting *Les Baigneuses (The Bathers)*, in a lithograph in 1927 and ten years later did so again in this brilliantly coloured intaglio print.

Gift of Walter Carsen, 1981   81/552

Henri Matisse (French, 1869–1954)

Icarus from *Jazz*, plate VIII   1947
Pochoir (stencil) print on wove paper. 40.5 x 27.7 (composition)

Despite a bedridden convalescence after a serious operation, Matisse produced some of his most exuberant works during the 1940s. His publisher, Efstratios Tériade, encouraged him to make an album of painted paper collages to be accompanied by some of the artist's handwritten thoughts. Matisse developed a stencil printing method based on the cut and collaged paper images he had begun in the early 1930s. The resulting 20 plates were published in an edition of 100 in 1947 under the title *Jazz*.

Matisse later described the *Jazz* series: "The images in vivid and violent tones have resulted from crystallizations of memories of the circus, popular tales, or of travel." By juxtaposing flat areas of colour, Matisse emphasized the two-dimensional surfaces of the works and created some of the strongest and brightest-coloured prints ever executed.

This print recalls the Greek myth of the boy Icarus, who flew too close to the sun, which melted the wax in his wings, causing him to plunge to his death. In Matisse's print a generalized black figure floats freely on a luminous blue background, which is punctuated by brilliant yellow stars. His Icarus becomes a metaphor for the artist, who has high aspirations but often finds himself isolated and tragically cast down.

Gift of Mr. Arthur Gelber, 1986   86/130

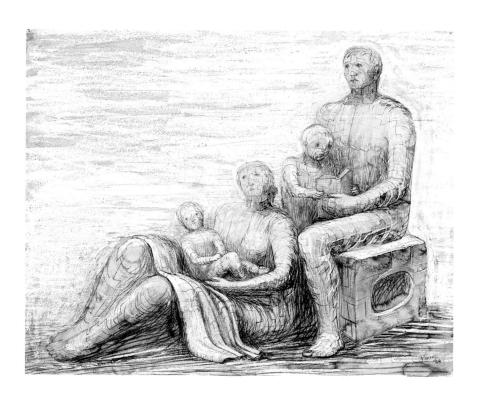

Henry Moore (British, 1898–1986)

Family Group 1948
Ink, crayon, wash on paper. 55.2 x 68.2 (sheet)

Moore's drawings and sculptures of the mother-and-child theme and of family groups
are undoubtedly his best-loved works. Whereas the former subject had been a constant obsession from the beginning of his career, his interest in family groups dates
from the shelter drawings of 1940-41 in which he depicted scenes of Londoners shel-
tering from the Blitz on the platforms of the London Underground.

Scenes of family life were the subjects of a number of large drawings of 1948-49.
They were intended to be what Moore called "pictorial drawings," that is, highly
finished works depicting figures in domestic settings, rather than the more spontaneous sketchbook studies of ideas for sculpture. In *Family Group* Moore has used traditional
light and shade modelling, as well as what he called the linear, two-way sectional line
method of drawing. He defined this stylistic innovation as drawing by the use of line in
two directions, "both down the form as well as around it," as is clearly visible on each
of the figures. This drawing no doubt reflects the happiness of Henry and Irina Moore's
own domestic life that followed the birth of Mary, their only child, in March 1946.

Purchase, 1974   74/338

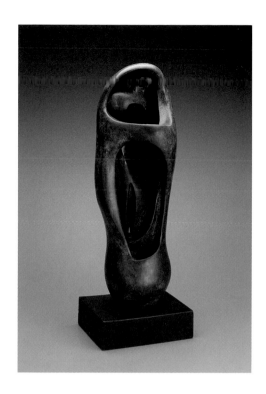

Henry Moore (British, 1898–1986)

Working Model for Upright Internal and External Forms 1951
Bronze. 64.0 x 21.6 x 20.3

This bronze, the first Moore sculpture to enter the AGO's collection, was acquired in 1951, the year it was made. Moore's initial development of the internal/external-form motif dates from a series of drawings of the mid-1930s that were based on a Malanggan carving from New Ireland, Oceania. Moore was greatly impressed by the inner and outer framework of such works and by the extraordinary craftsmanship required to create forms within forms. His first internal/external-form sculpture – *The Helmet* of 1939-40 – was not based on Oceanic art but on two prehistorical Greek utensils he had seen illustrated in *Cahiers d'art*.

This bronze, as were almost all Moore's sculptures from 1921 to the mid-1950s, was based on a preparatory drawing, *Ideas for Sculpture: Internal and External Forms*, 1948 (Smith College Museum of Art). It was also preceded by a small maquette. The artist has written about this sculpture: "I suppose in my mind was also the mother-and-child idea and of birth and the child in embryo. All these things are connected in this interior and exterior idea."

Gift from the Women's Committee Fund, 1951   51/14

Henry Moore (British, 1898–1986)

Upright Motive No. 1: Glenkiln Cross 1955-56
Original plaster. H. 334.8

Understandably, a number of writers on Moore's art see the totemic *Glenkiln Cross* as
one of his greatest achievements. The sculpture is named after Sir William Keswick's
Glenkiln Estate, Dumfries, Scotland, where the first cast was placed on a hillside.

 This work is made up of three distinct units. In the top section the small orifice
is suggestive of the mouth of some primeval creature. Below this, compressed, eroded
shoulders and truncated arms give the sculpture the shape of a crucifix. Below this is
the smooth, bonelike form of the torso, the central portion, upon which the head and
arms balance, not precariously, but with an organic inevitability. The swelling knob
at the bottom of this section resembles waist and hips. Moore has described the third
section – the rectangular front of the lower half of the sculpture – as "the column and
on it are little bits of drawing which don't matter sculpturally, which represent a
ladder and a few things connecting it with the Crucifixion."

 Other bronze casts of the *Glenkiln Cross* and two related upright motives are
grouped together, with this work at the centre, at the Amon Carter Museum, Fort
Worth, Texas; the Kröller-Müller Museum, Otterlo, the Netherlands; and at the Tate
Gallery, London, England.

 Gift of Henry Moore, 1974 73/78

Henry Moore (British, 1898–1986)

Warrior with Shield 1953-54
Bronze. H. 152.5

From the mid-1950s until the end of his working life, Moore relied increasingly on natural forms – bones, shells, pebbles – to generate ideas for sculpture. The idea for *Warrior with Shield*, according to Moore, "evolved from a pebble I found on the seashore...which reminded me of the stump of a leg, amputated at the hip.... First I added the body, leg, and one arm, and it became a wounded warrior, but at first the figure was reclining. A day or two later, I added a shield and altered its position and arrangement into a seated figure, and so it changed from an inactive pose into a figure which, though wounded, is still defiant. The head has a blunted and bull-like power but also a sort of dumb animal acceptance and a forebearance of pain."

The subject of most of the few single male figures in Moore's art is the fallen or wounded warrior. This bronze is also one of the few works that Moore specifically connected with an event in recent history, namely, the bombing of London by the German air force. He said that "the figure may be emotionally connected...with one's feelings and thoughts about England during the crucial and early part of the last war. The position of the shield and its angle gives protection from above."

Gift from the Junior Women's Committee Fund, 1955   54/12

Henry Moore (British, 1898–1986)

Draped Reclining Figure 1952-53
Original plaster. 100.4 x 160.4 x 68.6

Moore began work on this sculpture after a trip to Greece in 1951. It was the first of several draped figures of the 1950s with obvious affinities to classical Greek sculpture. And yet the pose is reminiscent of the Pre-Columbian *Chac Mool* reclining figure that had such a profound impact on his work of the late 1920s and early 1930s.

"Drapery can emphasize the tension in a figure," Moore has explained, "for where the form pushes outwards, such as on the shoulders, the thighs, the breasts, etc., it can be pulled tight across the form (almost like a bandage), and by contrast with the crumpled slackness of the drapery which lies between the salient points, the pressure from inside is intensified.... Also in my mind was to connect the contrast of the sizes of folds, here small, fine, and delicate, in other places big and heavy, with the form of mountains, which are the crinkled skin of the earth...."

However much the drapery may remind us of classical Greek sculpture, Moore uses it, as art critic John Russell has perceptively pointed out, "to romantic ends that would have been incomprehensible to the Greeks. The 'crinkled skin of the earth' was not something that they would have thought of as a metaphor for the folds of costume, but it was one of the quintessential metaphors for emotional states in the England of the 1940s and 1950s.... Drapery, for Moore, was another way, and a new one, of mediating between landscape and the human body."

Gift of Henry Moore, 1974   73/96

Henry Moore (British, 1898–1986)

Two Piece Reclining Figure No. 1 1959
Original plaster. W. 212.1

Moore first executed a series of divided figures in 1934. Twenty-five years later he returned to the theme of multipart sculptures in the magnificent series of two- or three-piece reclining figures of 1959-63, of which this was the first.

Moore saw this sculpture as a mixture of rock forms, mountains and imagery of the female figure. In some of his prewar sculpture, Moore related the human figure to landscape in which the body is like a landscape, that is, the figurative elements are dominant, with echoes of hills, hollows and ridges. In this work the simile is reversed; landscape features are dominant but have references to the human figure. The landscape is likened to the female reclining form; as a metaphor, the landscape becomes the human body.

The dynamic thrust of the leg may relate to the massive outcropping of rock that Moore saw as a child near his hometown of Castleford, Yorkshire. While working on this sculpture, Moore said he was reminded of the cliff formation in Seurat's 1885 painting *The Bec du Hoc, Grandcamp* that formerly belonged to his friend Kenneth Clark and is now in the Tate Gallery, London.

Gift of Henry Moore, 1973   73/66

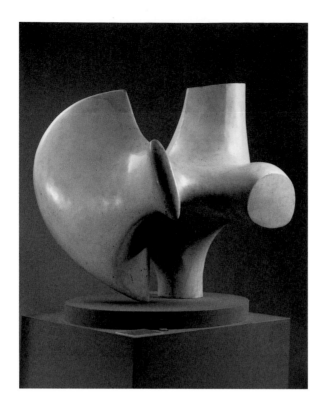

Henry Moore (British, 1898–1986)

Working Model for Three Way Piece No. 2: Archer 1964
Original plaster. H. 79.0

No single work of 20th-century sculpture has had such extraordinary and far-reaching consequences for a museum and for the cultural life of a city as *Archer* has had for the AGO and Toronto. This was the controversial sculpture that Moore and Viljo Revell, the architect of Toronto's new city hall, chose for the outdoor setting in Nathan Phillips Square, which ultimately led to the Art Gallery of Ontario building the Henry Moore Sculpture Centre to house its collection of Moore works, many of them donated by the artist himself.

Moore first made a small maquette that was followed by this working model. The work attests to his interest in full three-dimensional realization in sculpture.

As was customary with many of Moore's sculptures, the title was assigned after the work was completed. The curved end is taut like a tightly strung bow. The bridge between the two ends of the work can be seen as an arm, straining forward against the pressure of the bow. In a shape inspired by a natural form – one of the many flint stones that the sculptor collected from the fields near his studio – Moore had seen something of the controlled tension and pent-up energy of an archer about to release his charge.

Gift of Henry Moore, 1973   73/70

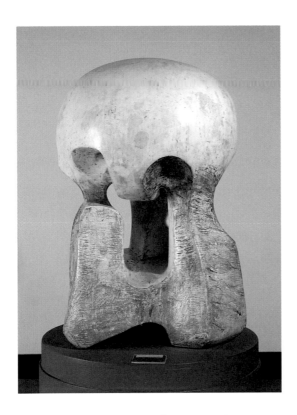

Henry Moore (British, 1898–1986)

Atom Piece (Working Model for Nuclear Energy) 1964-65
Original plaster. H. 120.7

In 1963 Moore was asked by the University of Chicago if he would consider doing a commemorative sculpture that would mark the 25th anniversary of the first controlled nuclear chain reaction, achieved in 1942 at the Chicago campus by Enrico Fermi and his colleagues. The sculpture, he was told, would be "a monument to man's triumphs, charged with high hope and profound fear, just as every triumphant breakthrough has always been."

During a visit from the Chicago committee to discuss the proposal, Moore remembered a maquette he had made that he thought might be a suitable image for the theme. Upon approval of this maquette he proceeded with this working model.

It is significant that the finished work, *Nuclear Energy* (based on this working model), did not originate in the artist's mind as an interpretation of atomic power. The domelike skull has obvious affinities to Moore's earlier helmet-head series, but seen in the context of the commission it becomes an ominous reminder of a mushroom cloud from an atmospheric atomic explosion.

Gift of Henry Moore, 1974   73/72

Henry Moore (British, 1898–1986)

Large Two Forms 1966 and 1969
Bronze. 386.0 x 610.0

In December 1969 when plans for the Moore gift were gathering momentum, this sculpture was chosen as the monumental bronze the Gallery would acquire at casting cost and would eventually place outdoors northeast of the Moore Centre. This work was one of Moore's largest sculptures to that date.

The forms of this bronze may well have been inspired by a flint stone. Whereas most flints are solid – like that on which Archer was probably based – some have holes through them, a feature more commonly found in sea-worn pebbles.

The subject of two forms in close proximity (but not touching) was not a new one for Moore. The small wood *Two Forms*, 1934 (Museum of Modern Art, New York), is a distant relative of this work. In the much earlier carving, the larger form arches forward and over the smaller, more vulnerable shape in what Moore has described as a mother-and-child relationship. Much of the fascination of Moore's late works stems from their obscurities, suggested meanings and powerful sexual overtones. In *Large Two Forms* there is, in the pelvic forms, a sense of the erotic – as critic John Russell has written, "a mating dance momentarily arrested."

Purchase from the artist, 1973   73/82

231

Historical Canadian Art

Unknown

Virgin and Child c.1750
Wood with traces of polychrome. 166.0 x 57.2 x 53.4

The origins of the Quebec school of ecclesiastical sculpture date back to the end of the 17th century, with the arrival in New France of French-trained artisans. These first sculptors brought with them an artistic tradition that incorporated Romanesque, Gothic, Renaissance and Baroque forms. Because of the lack of sophisticated casting facilities and the scarcity of suitable metals, their usual medium was wood and their idiom was that of carved, rather than modelled, volumes.

Unfortunately, fires, vandalism and changes in taste have made it difficult to study the history of the first two centuries of French Canadian sculpture. Furthermore, it was not customary for the artisans to sign their work. This Madonna and child – believed to have ornamented a side chapel in Montreal's old Notre-Dame Basilica – has been variously attributed to Paul Labrosse, *dit* Jourdain (1697–1769), Charles Chaboillez (1638?–1706), and Philippe Liébert (1732–1804). It is certainly by the hand of a carver who possessed a knowledge of European sculpture and a high level of technical virtuosity (especially evident in the handling of the drapery and in the faces) married to a rustic simplicity.

Shortly before entering the collection of the Art Gallery of Toronto in 1935, the statue appears to have been found in a ditch near the church of Saint-Laurent, a few miles north of Montreal, to which it was moved after Notre-Dame was demolished in 1840.

Gift of Walter C. Laidlaw, Toronto, 1935   2307

George Heriot (Canadian, 1759–1839)

Village of Chippawa near the Falls of Niagara c.1801
Watercolour on wove paper. 13.4 x 18.2

In 1800, George Heriot, who came to Quebec City in 1792 to serve in the army paymaster's department, was appointed deputy postmaster general of British North America. The following year he embarked on his first trip to the western frontiers of Upper Canada, to develop new postal services and also to make notes and sketches for his projected *Travels through the Canadas*, published in two volumes in 1807.

This watercolour includes most of the details mentioned in the artist's description of the scene in his *Travels*: "A wooden bridge is thrown across the stream, over which is the road leading to Fort Erie. The former fort consists only of a large blockhouse near the bridge, on the northern bank, surrounded by lofty pickets; it is usually the station of a subaltern officer and twenty-five men.... There are in the village some mercantile store-houses, and two or three taverns. The waters of the Chippawa are always of a deep brown colour...."

Heriot's training and aptitude as a topographical artist working within the British picturesque mode rendered him keenly susceptible to the pictorial possibilities of Niagara Falls and its environs. He probably paid another visit to the Chippawa district in 1804, and he returned in 1805. His later interpretations of such scenery were more fluid and less documentary in manner than this watercolour, which reveals the influence of Paul Sandby, the artist's drawing master at Royal Military College, England.

Purchased with the assistance of the Government of Canada through
the Cultural Property Export and Import Act, 1983   83/239

Robert Irvine (Canadian, active 1812-21)

View of York c.1815
Oil on canvas. 68.0 x 91.0

This view of the shoreline of York, the capital of Upper Canada, was one of four Irvine canvases that once hung in the house of the artist's cousin, the Hon. George Cruickshank. When the house was dismantled in 1862, these latter three works were sent to auction and have since eluded tracing.

An amateur artist born in Orkney, Scotland, Irvine (*né* Crookshank or Cruickshank) was employed by the North West Company and served with distinction in the War of 1812. Around 1816 he seems to have moved to Saint John, New Brunswick, and he later worked in the West Indies, where he is said to have died. This information may help to date the picture, which was ascribed to 1820 by Toronto historian John Ross Robertson. Sometime between 1810 and 1815, Irvine painted a small oil-on-paper view of the York shoreline between John and Peter Streets (now in a private collection). This canvas was completed no earlier than 1813, as the Parliament buildings, burned by the American invaders that year, are represented in their restored two-story state. In his *Landmarks of Toronto*, Robertson noted that the painting depicts the lighthouse, erected on Gibraltar Point (now Toronto Island) in 1808-09. He also remarked that "no views have been found of the entire town of York prior to 1821.... [The work] gives an absolutely correct and artistic view, with the locations of all the houses on Front Street from a hundred yards west of the Old Fort and Garrison to the second Parliament Buildings...."

Gift of the descendants of the late Mrs. Stephen Heward, a daughter of the Hon. George Crookshank and cousin of the artist who painted the picture, 1953   53/32

237

Robert Clow Todd (Canadian, 1809–c.1865)

The Ice Cone, Montmorency Falls, Quebec c.1845
Oil on canvas. 51.2 x 67.9

Following the British conquest of New France in 1760, a rich "garrison" culture developed in Quebec City, the new military and administrative centre of British North America. Fed by an expanding military presence and a steady stream of English-speaking immigrants, this flourishing society peaked at about the middle of the 19th century. While most of the artists within the anglophone community until then were amateurs, usually army officers, there were some professionals, and the most notable of these was Robert Todd.

Little is known of Todd's life. He settled in Quebec City in 1835, advertising himself as a "house, sign, carriage and ornamental painter," and stayed until 1853. Of the few paintings by Todd that have come to light, the majority depict British officers displaying their teams and sleighs on the ice before Montmorency Falls, a favourite winter resort of the garrison community just outside Quebec City. One of the largest and arguably the most beautiful of these, the AGO's version of the theme shows an officer, whose splendidly turned-out groom, Arabian team, and richly detailed sleigh, all meticulously described in a highly developed provincial neoclassical style, extend across the whole scene. Recent conservation has revealed that the landscape was completed first, then set aside to await a commission to fill it with figures, both of the stock variety, as in the lower right, and highly personalized.

Purchased with the assistance of the Government of Canada through the Cultural Property Export and Import Act, 1987   87/94

Joseph Légaré (Canadian, 1795–1855)

The Fire in the Saint-Jean Quarter, Seen Looking Westward c.1845
Oil on canvas. 151.1 x 220.3

To satisfy the need of the church for paintings of sacred subjects, Légaré began his career by producing large-scale copies based on the European masterpieces he became acquainted with through his work restoring canvases in the Desjardins Collection, which was brought to Quebec from France following the French Revolution. By 1833 Légaré was also a skilled painter of historical subjects, portraits, landscapes and cityscapes, but he is today best known for his romantically lit large-scale disaster scenes, beginning with his depiction of the Quebec cholera epidemic of 1832.

The Fire in the Saint-Jean Quarter is one of three large pictures he completed to record the disastrous fire that broke out in the Saint-Jean district of Quebec on the night of June 28, 1845. The artist has painted the fire at its height, as seen from the raised vantage point of the ramparts of Quebec, near the Saint-Jean Gate. The viewer's eye is drawn into the inferno by Saint-Jean Street, at the centre, and by Saint-Joachim and d'Aiguillon streets, to the left and right, respectively; all lead to the vanishing point on the horizon, which is obscured by a curtain of flames. Contrasting with the compositional movement, refugees are depicted fleeing the city with their possessions, while a detachment of soldiers with fixed bayonets maintains order.

Like that of its complementary piece showing the ruins left by the fire, which is also in the Gallery's permanent collection, this work reflects the impact of a collective trauma with a frightening historical basis.

Purchase, with assistance from Wintario, 1976   76/210

George Theodore Berthon (Canadian, 1806-92)

Portrait of William Henry Boulton 1846
Oil on canvas. 240.5 x 147.5

Born in Vienna, the son of a court painter to Napoleon I, Berthon unwittingly laid the
groundwork for his career as the foremost "court painter" in Canada West (renamed
Ontario in 1867) by accepting in 1827 the position of drawing instructor to the daugh-
ters of British statesman Sir Robert Peel. On immigrating to Toronto late in 1844, he
quickly established himself as the favourite portraitist of the ruling Family Compact,
specializing in the depiction of such clients as judges, chief justices, lieutenant gov-
ernors, physicians, military and naval officers, and their families. The most important
of these commissions was his commanding likeness of the Right Reverend John Strachan,
lord bishop of Toronto, painted soon after Berthon's arrival in Canada.

In 1845 Berthon received a commission from the Law Society of Upper Canada
to paint Chief Justice Sir John Beverley Robinson. This event led to his unofficial
appointment as chief delineator of the Robinsons and their relations by marriage, the
Boultons, whose residence, The Grange, was erected in a park at the head of John
Street by D'Arcy Boulton, Jr., in 1818; it is now part of the Art Gallery of Ontario.

William Henry Boulton, the subject of this canvas, married Harriette Mann Dixon
of Boston in 1846 — the same year that he became master of The Grange on the death
of his father, D'Arcy Boulton. William Henry Boulton, seated, is resplendent in his
official garb as mayor of Toronto (1845-7 and 1858). Less formal is Berthon's oval
portrait of Mrs. Boulton, also in the AGO's collection.

The Goldwin Smith Collection, 1911   GS111

Paul Kane (Canadian, 1810-71)

Indian Encampment on Lake Huron c.1845
Oil on canvas. 49.0 x 73.6

Galvanized by his experience of the American painter George Catlin's celebrated touring
Indian Gallery in London, England, in 1843, Kane returned to Toronto in 1845 determined to "devote whatever talents and proficiency I possess to painting a series of
pictures illustrative of the North American Indians and scenery."

Accordingly Kane set out in June 1845 on an expedition that would take him to
Coldwater and Penetanguishene on Georgian Bay, then south to Owen Sound and the
Ojibwa village of Saugeen, after which he travelled to Manitoulin Island, Sault Ste.
Marie, Mackinaw, Lake Michigan and the Fox River; by the end of November he had
returned to Toronto via Buffalo. This excursion served as a trial run for his more ambitious transcontinental trek of 1846-47, during which he made the sketches that would
serve as the basis of his own Indian Gallery and drafted the journal from which a
ghostwriter drew his *Wanderings of an Artist*, published in London in 1859. From this
book the reader learns that the sketch on which this canvas was based "represents an
Indian encampment among the islands of Lake Huron; the wigwams are made of birch-
bark, stripped from the trees in large pieces and sewed together with fibrous roots....
Their canoes are also made of birch-bark stretched over a very light frame of split cedar
laths; the greatest attention is paid to symmetry and form."

Kane painted two versions of this subject, the second of which is in the Royal
Ontario Museum, Toronto.

Purchase, 1932   2121

241

John O'Brien (Canadian, 1832-91)

The Ocean Bride, Leaving Halifax Harbour 1854
Oil on canvas. 51.1 x 76.5

The leading Maritime ship painter of his day, O'Brien recorded the golden age of sail during two separate eras in Halifax, Nova Scotia, the first of them dating from 1850, one year after the death of the city's reigning artist, William Valentine.

Essentially self-taught, O'Brien honed his skills in draughtsmanship by copying commercially distributed prints and engraved illustrations in contemporary periodicals, in addition to studying British and American instruction manuals in the Halifax Mechanics' Institute Library. He likely saw the 30-odd marine paintings – coastal scenes, sea pieces, and ship portraits – that were included among the 380 works in the exhibition mounted in 1848 at the Mechanics' Institute. His preoccupation with these three related genres would carry forward into his second phase, beginning in the 1880s, some years after he had virtually given up painting at the height of his powers.

This view shows the *Ocean Bride* – a brigantine – under full sail near Halifax Harbour. Running before the wind in the foreground is a schooner, *The Water Witch*, of Herring Cove, a fishing village at the mouth of the harbour. O'Brien's attention not only to the details of naval architecture but also to the ever-changing weather of the Atlantic coast reveals his familiarity with the marine paintings of the 17th-century Dutch masters and such British exemplars as J. M. W. Turner and Clarkson Stanfield.

Purchase, 1976   75/99

Antoine-Sébastien Plamondon (Canadian, 1802-95)

Passenger Pigeon Hunt 1853
Oil on canvas. 184.2 x 183.0

In this canvas the St-Roch-born but Paris-trained Plamondon reveals the continuing influence of his master from 1826 to 1830, Paul Guérin, court painter to Charles x and pupil of the leading French Neoclassicist Jacques-Louis David. From his teacher, wrote the Canadian art historian J. Russell Harper, Plamondon learned "the virtues of the classical painters' cool blue shadows, evenly distributed light, quiet poses, and carefully drawn contours" – qualities all present in his charming group portrait of three dandified young pigeon hunters posing with their prey on a rock overlooking the St. Lawrence River.

Plamondon's introduction of landscape elements in place of the dark backgrounds of his society portraits, his recently adopted tactic of positioning his figures at a slight distance from the picture plane so as better to convey the outdoor setting, and the seeming spontaneity of the hunters' gestures and expressions all suggest a tendency toward the naturalism of the Romantic painters who were challenging the conventions of the Neoclassicists at the time of his Parisian sojourn. On the other hand, the rigidly pyramidal composition, the statuelike solidity of the figures, and the posed feeling of the whole re-affirm Plamondon's stylistic and philosophical roots in the *ancien régime* of art.

Gift from the Albert H. Robson Memorial Subscription Fund, 1943   2601

Cornelius Krieghoff (Canadian, 1815-72)

Settler's Log House 1856
Oil on canvas. 62.4 x 92.7

In 1853 the Amsterdam-born, Düsseldorf-trained Krieghoff moved from Montreal, where he had settled in 1849, to Quebec City. Although Krieghoff painted his first major canvas of the Quebec vicinity (a view of Montmorency Falls) the year before he gave up his Montreal studio, he did not begin to search for subjects in the outlying country north of the St. Lawrence River until 1856. Among his favourite motifs were the farmsteads of *habitants* and settlers in winter, which also appealed to the writers, travellers and art patrons of the time.

As its title indicates, *Settler's Log House* records a phase in the history of the colonization of Quebec of which Krieghoff was an eyewitness; he filtered his impressions, however, through the 17th-century Dutch genre tradition in which he was steeped. His aim was to evoke the heroic nature of the pioneering endeavour, which he here treats with a seriousness and sobriety rare in his depictions of more domestic *habitant* subjects. In its impressive scale and in the romantic treatment of the evening sky, this painting seeks to elevate the land-clearing project to an epic plane and to inspire thoughts regarding the political economy of the emergent Lower Canada — the future province of Quebec — in the viewer.

Gift of the Reuben Wells Leonard Estate, Toronto, 1937   2413

Lucius Richard O'Brien (Canadian, 1832-99)

Lords of the Forest 1874
Watercolour on paper. 74.3 x 49.9 (sight)

A product of O'Brien's early maturity, this work reveals the level of technical skill he had acquired, which, abetted by his social position, made him perhaps the leading professional painter in Toronto. After gaining effective control of the Ontario Society of Artists (OSA) in 1874, he consolidated his position by campaigning to have the Ontario government establish a yearly purchase grant to acquire works from the annual exhibition of the society. One of the two such acquisitions from the OSA show of 1875 was O'Brien's own *Lords of the Forest*.

The popularity of the subject matter, which O'Brien exploited throughout the 1870s, in part derived from the success of the *Leatherstocking Tales* of the American novelist James Fenimore Cooper. The title may be an allusion to a well-known passage from Washington Irving's romance of the fur trade, *Astoria; or Anecdotes of an Enterprise Beyond the Rocky Mountains*: "The lords of the lakes and forests have passed away...." (Irving's lords were, admittedly, not Indians but the "mighty Northwesters," that is, the magnates and servants of the North West Company, which was absorbed by the Hudson's Bay Company in 1821.) In O'Brien's interpretation, "lords" might refer not only to the magnificent trees of the primeval forest – doomed to fall before the woodsman's axe – but also to the "noble savage" in their midst.

Gift of the Government of the Province of Ontario, 1972   72/19

Frederic Marlett Bell-Smith (Canadian, 1846–1923) and
James Inglis (Canadian, 1835–1904)

Loretto Convent 1871
Albumen (composite). 22.3 x 34.3 (sheet)

The vigorous and often idiosyncratic interrelationship between painting and photography in the 19th century became particularly complex with the popularity of combination and composite pictures. In order to gain aesthetic legitimacy for the medium, photographers employed the tools and theories of painting to take their art beyond the mere copying of nature. Similarly, painters used the properties of photography to achieve the degree of realism considered desirable in portraiture and narrative studies.

To compose the separate figures and groups in *Loretto Convent*, British-born painter Bell-Smith collaborated in the studio with the Montreal-based photographer Inglis. Photographs were skilfully composed on a painted background; the collaged composition was then retouched for pictorial unity and rephotographed. Although the responsibility for welding together the diverse elements of the composite was incumbent on the painter, the task of accomplishing gradual picture planes and integrating the figures was not easy. The qualities of collage are often evident in the anomaly of scale, in the ambiguous spatial relationships, and in the overlapping figures.

The figures in this composite, who are engaged in numerous activities, do not emerge as a seamless narrative, as they would in a painting, yet Bell-Smith and Inglis have combined 44 tiny "portraits" of reality to create the illusion of a playful summer day.

Purchase, 1988   87/178

Daniel Fowler (Canadian, 1810-94)

The Wheelbarrow 1871
Ink and watercolour on wove paper. 24.3 x 33.7 (sight)

After working as a topographical artist and illustrator in London, England, the Kentish-born Fowler immigrated to Canada in 1843. He purchased a farm on Amherst Island, in Lake Ontario, near Kingston, and laid down his brushes for several years. Visits to England in 1857 and 1859 introduced him to the work of the Pre-Raphaelites and re-acquainted him with his old teacher, J. D. Harding, who encouraged him to purchase drawing materials to take back with him to Canada. In 1860 he began to paint dead game and flower studies, and three years later he first exhibited publicly in Canada.

One of Fowler's discoveries on his return to England was that "contrasted with the dancing light and life of the Canadian atmosphere, the lights on the English landscape seemed all toned down, the shadows deep and obscure." Resolved to capture in watercolours the "light and life" of Amherst Island according to the tenets of renowned art critic John Ruskin (a pupil of Harding's) and the Pre-Raphaelites ("purity, simplicity, and above all . . . local and actual truth"), he set out to paint "from nature in *colour*, out of doors, at all possible seasons," his adopted home ground.

In *Wheelbarrow* Fowler reveals the influence of his friend and sketching companion from the 1830s, Edward Lear, from whom he adopted the practice of "making an outline of a sketch subject with a pen." His loose, energetic brushwork and bold use of undiluted pigment, however, were entirely his own, and Fowler is unquestionably the finest 19th-century Canadian watercolourist.

Bequest of Dr. John G. Lee, 1955   55/6

Homer Watson (Canadian, 1855–1936)

The Death of Elaine 1877
Oil on canvas. 78.5 x 106.5

Inclusion in the Art Gallery of Ontario's groundbreaking *The Sacred and Profane in Symbolist Art* exhibition in 1969 rescued this most atypical Watson canvas from the oblivion to which it had been consigned in the gallery vaults. Popular and respected in his day as a painter of pastoral Ontario landscapes, the Doon, Ontario-born Watson rarely strayed in later life into the visual interpretation of literary or allegorical subject matter. A two-year sojourn in New York in 1876-77, during which he visited the studio of George Inness and came under the influence of the Hudson River School, seems to have liberated his somewhat naive imagination, and *The Death of Elaine* was the unusual result.

The inspiration for this work was a passage from Lord Tennyson's poem "Elaine," part of the *Idylls of the King*, in which the dead maiden is borne to her burying place on a barge. The lines to which Watson's canvas directly allude begin: "Then rose the dumb old servitor, and the dead / steered by the dumb went upward with the flood...."

A more immediate source than the poem was the frontispiece to the Moxon edition of *Idylls* (1867) by the French illustrator Gustave Doré. From him Watson borrowed not only most of the salient details of the composition but also its romantic, moonlit mood; his variations include use of a horizontal rather than a vertical format and the reversal of the direction in which the barge is being steered (rather than rowed, as in Doré's version). Another likely model was the American painter Toby Rosenthal's celebrated *Elaine* (1874), which Watson could have seen during his visit to the Philadelphia Centennial Exhibition in 1876.

Gift of Mrs. Mary King, Toledo, Ohio, 1937   2434

249

Allan Edson (Canadian, 1846-88)

Landscape c.1875
Watercolour and gouache on paper. 66.0 x 50.2

Shortly after his marriage in 1871, Edson gave up his Montreal studio and moved across the St. Lawrence River to Longueuil. A few years before, he had embarked on a series of large, highly finished canvases depicting the Eastern Townships that in the early 1870s he augmented with a number of watercolours that explored similar subjects on a more intimate scale. These suggest an affinity with the American "New Path" painters, who sought to apply the theories of critic John Ruskin to the North American landscape, and in particular to the scientifically accurate rendering of wild flora and fauna. *Landscape*, however, is freer and more poetic and shows more feeling than much of this type of work; it has a breadth of attack suggestive of Constable, and its coloration and composition are reminiscent of the later landscapes of Samuel Palmer.

    The use of opaque gouache allowed the creation of multilayered textures through overpainting, the desired effect being somewhat like that achieved by oil on paper. The surprising brightness and freshness of the result testifies to Edson's preoccupation with conveying forms as well as atmosphere through the medium of reflected light.

Gift of Mrs. Kathleen D. Steiner, Ancaster, Ontario, 1979   79/47

Lucius Richard O'Brien (Canadian, 1832-99)

Northern Head of Grand Manan 1879
Oil on canvas. 60.2 x 121.9

In 1878 O'Brien travelled to St. Andrews, New Brunswick, and Grand Manan Island, in the Bay of Fundy, by way of the Grand Trunk route through New Hampshire. The island was a favourite resort of such influential American landscape painters of the Luminist School as Alfred Bricher and Frederick E. Church. Bricher's *Morning at Grand Manan* is compositionally close to this canvas – O'Brien's most important work to date.

Exhibited in the seventh annual show of the Ontario Society of Artists in 1879, the work was warmly praised by the Toronto *Globe*'s reviewer, who wrote, "The left of the foreground is closed in by towering cliffs, whose rugged outlines are softened by subdued light in which they are thrown, their dark sides showing an exquisite blending of dark-brown, purple and grey, here and there enlivened by the rich verdure of bright creepers straying over the sombre face of the precipice. Beyond this there is a break in the shoreline, and a bright belt of sunshine streaming through...."

Perhaps in response to this encomium, George Brown, the founder of the *Globe*, purchased the work from the exhibition. After Brown's death the painting was taken by its inheritor, John Gordon Brown, to his native Scotland, where it remained in family hands until its repatriation in 1981.

Purchased with the assistance of the Government of Canada through
the Cultural Property Export and Import Act, 1982   82/26

Homer Watson (Canadian, 1855–1936)

The Old Mill 1886
Oil on canvas. 97.2 x 147.3

Painted some four years after Watson was dubbed "the Canadian Constable" by Oscar Wilde, this canvas is the self-taught artist's second major interpretation of a subject that was close to his heart. From around 1858 to 1861 his father had owned and operated a wool mill at Doon, a village on the Grand River, in southwestern Ontario's Waterloo County. Young Watson's career was launched by the Governor General's purchase of *The Pioneer Mill* from the first Royal Canadian Academy exhibition, for the Royal Collection, Windsor. Queen Victoria ordered a second Watson oil, *The Day of Drouth* (also depicting a mill), in 1881.

There are at least two versions of *The Old Mill*; a smaller one is in a private collection. This canvas exhibits the artist's early grasp of the fundamentals of dynamic composition and vigorous paint handling within a relatively modest compass. Although certain parts of the canvas – the foreground in particular – betray Watson's lack of professional training, comparison with Constable is justified not only by his treatment of the mill itself, which calls to mind the British painter's depictions of Flatford Mill, on the river Stour in rural Suffolk, but also by the way in which the turbulent massing of the rain clouds echoes the tossing foliage of the trees.

Gift from the Fund of the T. Eaton Co. Ltd. for
Canadian Works of Art, 1948   48/10

William Blair Bruce (Canadian, 1859–1906)

Twilight 1882
Oil on canvas. 30.8 x 74.0

The exhibition label on the reverse of this canvas tells a tale. It reveals not only the title and the selling price, but also the artist's address at the time it was painted: "Hotel Siren, Barbizon, Seine-et-Marne, France." Bruce's own letters home to Hamilton, Ontario, from the artists' colony at Barbizon where he lived, reveal that he had high hopes for *Twilight*, when he successfully submitted it and a companion piece, *A Summer's Afternoon*, to the *Autumn Exhibition* of the Walker Art Gallery, Liverpool, in 1882.

Bruce was disappointed by the reaction of the *Liverpool Mercury*'s reviewer, who wrote, "There is a vigorous ideal purpose," in *A Summer's Afternoon* "which makes it more effective, and to sympathetic minds more felt than if it were sought after by the coarser processes of elaborate and painful precision of... *Twilight*...[which] is treated in a similar manner to the former, an evening effect being substituted." (Bruce's comment was "rot.") The "passing clouds" that the critic thought "leaden and somewhat over done" were, Bruce contended, "the very things that give the character to the whole composition – only it takes a man with nerve and 'independent impressions' to put four or five little dark gray clouds upon a very mellow evening sky...."

The huddled woman in the right foreground recalls similar figures by van Gogh, while the treatment of the farmyard reflects the influence of such French Barbizon painters as Millet, Troyon and Rousseau – artists Bruce would later throw over in favour of the Impressionist Monet and his American disciple, Theodore Robinson.

Purchase, 1984   83/335

Alexander Henderson (Canadian, 1831–1913)

Fall on Brook at Little Métis
Bonsecours Market Wharves – Montreal
(from album of photographs, assembled 1884)
24 albumen prints mounted. Cover: 37.3 x 29.4; Page: 35.7 x 26.5

The invention and rapid development of photography as a medium of picture-making ascended at a time of a heightened awareness of nature. This general consciousness and the desire to depict nature for its own sake appeared in Europe and North America from the 1830s to the 1880s, and found liberal expression in painting and poetry and perhaps most abundantly in photography.

Alexander Henderson became one of several early photographers attracted to the outdoors – to the wilderness and countryside of Quebec and eastern Ontario, and also to their architecture and industry. During the mid-1860s Henderson issued albums entitled *Canadian Views and Studies*; presumably they were made to order, as each one varied in size, format and content. The album in the AGO's collection would appear to have been assembled about 20 years later. More than half of the photographs in the album are harmonious picturesque compositions in which figures are placed outdoors in either expansive vistas or intimate settings that capture its atmosphere and natural beauty. These views show some influence of the early calotype photographs of Scottish and English scenes, which Henderson could have seen before immigrating to Canada from Scotland in 1855.

Henderson's camera explorations succeed most dramatically when he places emphasis on form, structure and detail in his subject matter. His waterfalls, river scenery and winter views reveal a natural grandeur that functions as a premise for truth rather than mere effect. Henderson's well-composed city views demonstrate carefully chosen points of view, a mastery of light and an ability to manipulate the image in order to create "painted-in" clouds in the sky.

Henderson's experimentation with a variety of processes (often in harsh environments) came to rely on wet collodion and glass plate – a technique that required dexterity and speed on the part of the photographer, but also permitted the production of multiple high-resolution prints. Henderson's toned album prints attest to his relentless dedication to capture both the poetic and documentary sensibilities of nature in a rich personal manner.

Purchase, 1980   80/90.1–80/90.24

Fall on Brook
AT LITTLE METIS
361.

C.B. HICKEY
UPPER CANADA
WOOD MERCHANT

4
Bonsécour Market Wharves Montreal

255

Robert Harris (Canadian, 1849–1919)

Self-portrait 1889
Oil on board. 40.7 x 31.8

Harris probably painted more self-portraits than any other Canadian artist, past or present. His periodic recordings of his visage fulfilled something of the same function that this activity did for Rembrandt, serving not only as registers of his artistic development over the decades but also as mirrors of his own evolving psychological and physical states. Few of his official portrait commissions display the probity and unflinching realism of these painterly explorations of the self and of his characteristic subtle self-withholding.

Harris preferred to work on an intimate scale in these self-portraits, concentrating on the head, usually presented in three-quarter view, the bespectacled eyes directly confronting the spectator. Of profound impact on his style was his visit in 1889 to the Low Countries, during which he renewed his acquaintance with the Dutch and Flemish masters with whom he had first studied in 1876-78. The experience confirmed his allegiance to the formative influences in evidence in all his essays in self-portraiture, notably Velázquez, whose works he had copied at the National Gallery, London; Alphonse Legros, Slade Professor at University College, under whom he studied in 1877; and Léon Bonnat, in whose Paris atelier he painted in 1878.

This tough, cogent, quietly emotive self-portrait reveals the confidence of an artist whose national pre-eminence had been recognized by the awarding of the commission to paint the ultimate Canadian group portrait, *The Fathers of Confederation*, in 1883.

Purchase, 1983   83/227

George Agnew Reid (Canadian, 1860–1947)

The Other Side of the Question 1890
Oil on canvas. 104.0 x 132.5

In 1886 Reid opened a studio in Toronto and conducted a private art class according to the methods of Thomas Eakins, his teacher at the Pennsylvania Academy, Philadelphia, where he had studied in 1883-84. This event coincided with the devising of a scheme to paint a sequence of semi-autobiographical depictions of Ontario farm life.

The first of these canvases, *The Call to Dinner* (McMaster University Art Gallery, Hamilton), was painted in 1886-87, inspired by a visit to the Reid homestead, near Wingham, Ontario. Over a dozen canvases exploring rural scenes and themes were completed, the best known of which is Reid's *Mortgaging the Homestead* of 1890 (National Gallery of Canada) and its companion piece, *The Foreclosure of the Mortgage* (1893; new version, 1934, Government of Ontario).

The Other Side of the Question represents either a rural school board or a township council in the process of debating some weighty issue. As was customary with Reid, the sitters included family members, friends, and neighbours. The older bearded man at the centre of the group is undoubtedly a portrait of his father, Adam Reid. The white-bearded patriarchs shown in profile and three-quarter views were based on a distant cousin by marriage of Adam Reid's named Joseph Shuter, a bibulous ex-employee of Gooderham and Worts in Toronto who worked on the Reid farm (he later became a clock cleaner). The younger figure seen in profile at the extreme right is probably a self-portrait.

Purchase, 1985   85/247

Paul Peel (Canadian, 1860-92)

After the Bath 1890
Oil on canvas. 147.3 x 110.5

Like many of his Canadian contemporaries of the late 19th century, Peel found it necessary to leave his country for artistic training in order to gain credibility at home. His three years of study with Thomas Eakins at the Pennsylvania Academy, Philadelphia, followed by a few months at the Royal Academy, London, and five years in the Parisian ateliers of Jean-Léon Gérôme and Benjamin Constant, enabled him to become a master at presenting the draped and nude figure in both interior and landscape settings.

    After the Bath is one of six known versions of this subject by Peel and his imitators. When first exhibited at the Paris Salon in 1890, it was awarded a third-class medal, a distinction no other Canadian artist had been accorded. Beating out a rival bidder in the person of the French actress Sarah Bernhardt, the Hungarian government purchased the painting for its national collection. It remained in Budapest for 31 years before being sold to a London, Ontario, art dealer to help pay off Hungary's war debt and subsequently was donated to the Government of Ontario by a later owner.

    In his tragically short career as a painter, Peel specialized in works involving children and their activities. This painting, reflecting the popular taste of the time for sentimental subjects, combines the artist's technical facility at rendering the nude human form with a subtle use of colour to convey the fire – the sole source of lighting – and its warmth. As was his custom from the late 1880s until his death, he worked from a photograph that established the pose of the figures and the composition.

    Gift of the Government of the Province of Ontario, 1972   72/24

William Cruikshank (Canadian, 1848–1922)

Anne Cruikshank c.1890
Oil on canvas. 98.4 x 90.2

This sensitive yet cogent portrait of the painter's unmarried sister Anne is a major contribution to a late 19th-century figurative genre. In this contemplative full-length private (as opposed to official) portrait, painted for the artist's satisfaction and to commemorate a family member rather than for any public or commercial purpose, the need to flatter or aggrandize the sitter was replaced by other, more aesthetic considerations.

The benefits of the Scottish-born Cruikshank's training at the Royal Academy Schools, London – where among his painting instructors were J. E. Millais, G. F. Watts, and George Richmond – can readily be seen in this portrait.

After settling permanently in Toronto in the mid-1870s, Cruikshank continued to augment his meagre income from painting with illustration and teaching. As painting instructor at the Central Ontario School of Art and Design and its successor, the Ontario College of Art, Cruikshank taught many of Canada's prominent artists.

Evidently painted as a fond tribute to the only other surviving member of his family in Toronto, *Anne Cruikshank* was among the works in the confirmed bachelor's possession at the time of his death in Kansas City, to which he had retired to live with his sister in 1919.

Gift of Mrs. Charles B. Norris, Madison, Wisconsin, 1958   58/14

Laura Muntz Lyall (Canadian, 1860–1930)

Interesting Story 1898
Oil on canvas. 81.3 x 100.3

Lyall is remembered as a skilled portraitist and painter of children and child life. One of six siblings, she was born in England, brought to Canada in 1869, and raised on a large farm at Alport, on Lake Muskoka. The artistic talent that she possessed at an early age was unfortunately deemed by her family to be indicative of "traits requiring discipline and correction." Despite such discouragement she went on to study art for a short period in Hamilton, Ontario, under the prominent portraitist J. W. L. Forster, before travelling to London to attend the South Kensington School of Art and then to Paris, where she became a student at the Académie Colarossi. In 1892 she had a canvas accepted at the Salon, and three years later she won an honourable mention there. Perhaps the recent success of her compatriot Paul Peel with sentimental child subjects induced her to explore such themes in her own work.

During the remainder of Lyall's stay in Paris, she exhibited regularly, and one of the last paintings she showed at the Salon, *Interesting Story*, was purchased by the Government of Ontario and exhibited for many years in the Legislature.

By the time of Lyall's death in 1930, her modified Pre-Raphaelite style, which she combined with touches of Impressionist brushwork, had long been out of fashion except among conservative collectors, but a revival of interest in the art of the Victorian and Edwardian eras in the 1960s and 1970s and the research of feminist art historians have brought renewed attention as an exemplar of the taste and values of her day.

Gift of the Government of the Province of Ontario, 1972   72/18

Emanuel Hahn (Canadian, 1881–1957)

Man and Woman 1905-10
Painted plaster. 61.0 x 26.0 x 20.0

This small but powerful sculpture, which the artist may have intended to enlarge for casting in bronze but which never advanced beyond its painted plaster state, is an early instance of the impact of international Symbolist tendencies on Canadian art. The sculptor, a native of Reutlingen, Germany, emigrated with his family to Canada in 1888, but returned with his father in 1903 to study in Stuttgart.

Hahn preferred working directly in clay and plaster to carving in stone, an activity he left to the master masons he assigned to work from his maquettes and scaled drawings. Following the example of one of the most potent influences on turn-of-the-century European sculpture, Auguste Rodin, Hahn here elected to abstract the draped, elongated bodies of his couple, detailing being reserved for their faces alone. By abstracting the intense emotion conveyed by the interlocking figures and by lending individual expression to their features, Hahn represents both the mutual dependency of man and woman and their eternal separateness.

Purchase, 1981   80/209

Maurice Cullen (Canadian, 1866–1934)

Moret, Winter 1895
Oil on canvas. 59.7 x 92.1

This canvas is often cited as the wellspring of Impressionist painting in Canada, although it is not the first instance of the use of this late 19th-century technique by a Canadian artist. Although Cullen entered the École des beaux-arts in Paris with the intention of furthering his studies in sculpture, the revelation of the work of Monet and his fellow Impressionists convinced him that his true métier was landscape painting in oils. *Moret, Winter* was completed in the year of his return to Canada in 1895.

      After working at the Académie Julian and being accepted into the atelier of Elie Delaunay, his teacher from 1889 to 1892, Cullen left Paris to paint *en plein air* at such popular haunts as Moret-sur-Loing, Gevery and Le Pouldu. It was not until he met the Norwegian painter Fritz Thaulow that he realized the possibilities of applying the broken colour, unmixed palette, and vigorous brushwork of the Impressionists to the depiction of Canadian winter scenes.

      As if in preparation for his St. Lawrence River and later Laurentian and Eastern Township snowscapes, Cullen executed a number of river views centred on the village of Moret, near Fontainebleau, southeast of Paris.

      In *Moret, Winter* Cullen expresses his love for the interplay of solid forms and their fluid reflections, and for the brilliant whites of snow contrasting with the blue-blacks of still and flowing water, which would move A.Y. Jackson to remark that "To us" – meaning the Group of Seven and its followers – "he was a hero."

Gift from J. S. McLean, Canadian Fund, 1957   56/29

Marc-Aurèle de Foy Suzor-Côté (Canadian, 1869–1937)

Stream in Winter c.1911
Oil on canvas. 60.8 x 74.0

Like his contemporary Maurice Cullen, Suzor-Côté was inducted into the prismatic methods of the Impressionists during his years of study at the École des beaux-arts, Paris. Unlike Cullen he did not begin to work seriously in this mode until re-establishing himself in his native Quebec, though he too was prepared for his rapprochement with the Canadian winter landscape by the example and encouragement of the Norwegian Impressionist Fritz Thaulow. Thaulow's specialty was the snow-bordered river, whether frozen or during spring breakup – these two states being interpreted as symbolic of time's arrest and passage.

Having set up a studio in his home town of Arthabaska in the Eastern Townships of Quebec, Suzor-Côté embarked on an ambitious series of canvases, drawings and bronzes illustrative of the life and landscape of the *habitants* who farmed along the shores of the Nicolet and Gosselin rivers, in the shadow of Mont St-Michel. He painted at least 20 variations on the snow-bordered-river theme, of which *Stream in Winter* is perhaps the most abstract and tonally subtle. The use of the spatula to flatten the thick impasto surface creates a softly textured pattern, admirably suggesting the mist that rises from the slowly flowing open water to mask the faded gold disc of the setting sun.

Gift of Moffatt Dunlap, from the estate of his mother,
Mrs. R. A. Dunlap, 1947   2884

James Wilson Morrice (Canadian, 1865–1924)

Return from School c.1901
Oil on canvas. 44.5 x 73.7

Although Morrice was a more or less permanent resident of France as early as 1890, he made periodic visits to his native city of Montreal, where he had family and where there was a growing market for his work. This charming canvas is identified as Canadian on the basis of the artist's notebooks in which he made frequent reference to it as "les enfants canadiens." Elsewhere it was exhibited and reproduced variously as *A Québec Pastorale, Ste. Anne de Beaupré, Winter, Retrait en hiver*, and *Effet de neige*.

   Another reason for Morrice's trips home was his love of Quebec winters, at least as a painting subject. As in Morrice's other winter scenes, the restricted tonal range causes the rare touches of brighter pigment, as in the clothing of the children, to stand out all the more vividly. The figures silhouetted against the olive-grey snow of the field and the darker ruts in the road assume a timeless quality that amounts almost to monumentality, despite their diminutive stature.

Gift from the Reuben and Kate Leonard Canadian Fund, 1948   47/1

James Wilson Morrice (Canadian, 1865–1924)

Beach Scene, Tangier c.1912
Oil and graphite on panel. 22.6 x 31.4

Although he appears to have first visited Marrakesh as early as 1910, Morrice painted the bulk of his Moroccan oils in 1912, having made a winter journey to Tangier in January that year and again the following December. On both trips Morrice's painting companion was his Parisian neighbour Henri Matisse, whose work the Canadian expatriate had first noticed and admired in 1905.

Morrice's headquarters in Tangier was a room with a balcony in the Hôtel de France. His Tangerine subjects included the view from his window, the fruit market, Moorish buildings, and the hilly environs of the town. His favourite view, judging from the number of times he returned to it, was of the beach, looking toward the brilliant blue waters of the Strait of Gibraltar. He revelled in the frothing white surf pounding on the tawny sand and in the shapes of billowing clouds over the sea, against which he several times posed the figures of colourfully robed Moors.

A comparison with Morrice's Parisian and Canadian works immediately preceding his discovery of the dazzling subtropical light of North Africa reveals the degree to which his palette was clarified and intensified by the eye-opening experience of such southern exposure.

Purchased with funds from the Laidlaw Foundation, 1981   81/162

Maurice Cullen (Canadian, 1866–1934)

The Last Loads 1916
Oil on canvas. 115.6 x 171.6

The Last Loads is one of the most memorable expressions of a particular Canadian time, place, and way of life ever captured in oils. That it evoked a disappearing premechanical past even as Canada was recklessly throwing her forces into the bloodiest campaigns of WWI no more relegates it to the category of the quaint and picturesque than does Cullen's modified impressionistic technique, which by this date could be criticized as *retardataire* rather than, as when he introduced it to Montreal painting circles in the mid-1890s, revolutionary.

The St. Lawrence River between Quebec City and Montreal had preoccupied Cullen since his return from France in 1895, and by 1916 he was ready to give himself fully to the subject from the vantage point of Longueuil, on the south shore opposite the island of Montreal.

The twin foci of the composition are, on the lower right, the blue-green blocks of ice on the lead sled of the procession, and, on the left horizon, the rising full moon. The static quality of the scene is undercut by the brisk assuredness of the paint handling, especially the treatment of the twilit sky and the snowy foreground. Still, Cullen's beloved draught horses never plodded with such slow deliberation as they do in this melancholy celebration of *l'heure bleue*.

Gift of Reuben Wells Leonard Estate, 1954   54/3

Charles William Jefferys (Canadian, 1869–1951)

Dark Woods 1913
Oil on canvas. 41.2 x 61.5

The artist's wife, Clara, posed for the figure in the foreground of this canvas. The Jefferys house, in the then-rural community of Hogg's Hollow, north of the Toronto city limits, was situated on a property adjacent to the pine woods forming the backdrop of this picture. These woods bore the name of Cornelius van Nostrand, a "late Loyalist" who had brought his family from Long Island to a farm on Yonge Street in 1800 and built a large gristmill and sawmill at York Mills in 1837. Jefferys, who moved to York Mills in 1910, explored the area in numerous oils and watercolours, concentrating on the pastoral valley of the Don River and steeping himself in local history.

Dark Woods suggests Jefferys's affinity to the modern Scandinavian school of painting, which applied Impressionist techniques and Symbolist imagery to the depiction of typical Nordic subjects. He had first seen such work in the World's Columbian Exposition at Chicago in 1893 and so was gratified to have his endorsement of it confirmed by J. E. H. MacDonald and Lawren Harris on their return from Buffalo, where they had taken in the landmark exhibition of Scandinavian art at the Albright-Knox Art Gallery in January 1913. The brooding, ominous character and sombre tonality of this canvas reveal a desire to give symbolic import to a distinctively Canadian subject.

Gift of Mrs. K. W. Helm, daughter of C. W. Jefferys,
Kneeland, California, 1980   80/168

Tom Thomson (Canadian, 1877–1917)

Northern River 1914-15
Gouache on paper. 30.4 x 26.7

Thomson first painted in Algonquin Park in May 1912 and returned every succeeding spring and summer until 1917, the year of his death by drowning in Canoe Lake. Clearly inspired by his solo canoe journeys in and out of the park, this densely patterned, decorative image was probably executed in the artist's Toronto studio, perhaps from on-site sketches. Although Thomson had resigned from the Toronto commercial art firm of Rous and Mann Ltd. in 1912, he still accepted the occasional commission. This gouache study for a 1914-15 canvas, also titled *Northern River* (National Gallery of Canada), may possibly have been completed for reproduction, perhaps in a travel brochure or advertisement. Certainly the pagelike vertical format was unusual for Thomson, who rarely resorted to it in his essays in "pure" painting; it was favoured, however, by the Symbolist- and Art Nouveau-influenced Scandinavian artists whose work Thomson knew through international art periodicals. Gouache was a preferred pigment for illustrators because of its brightness, fluidity, fast-drying properties, and ease of reproduction.

    Thomson's abilities as a graphic designer are in evidence here, especially in the balance of silhouetted foreground filigree and sunlit, undetailed background and in the interweaving of curvilinear motifs through the scrim of spindly fir trees screening the water and woods beyond. The result is far more than an illustration; its mood is imbued with a solitude and mystery that some commentators have suggested is that of a kind of wilderness cathedral.

Purchase, 1982   82/176

Lawren S. Harris (Canadian, 1885–1970)

Autumn Forest with Glaciated Bedrock, Georgian Bay
(Decorative Landscape) 1914-15
Oil on canvas. Centre section: 128.0 x 110.0; each wing: 128.0 x 36.0

This triptych – completed after a visit Harris and J. E. H. MacDonald made to Buffalo
in 1913 to view an exhibition of recent Scandinavian painting – is the most splendid
of Harris's canvases from the early period of the Group of Seven. The Scandinavian
influence is apparent in many features. There is the dramatic composition, in which
the foreground rises to fill more than two-thirds of the picture, blocking entry while
allowing the eye to soar up and out through a break in the trees. There is a celebration
of typically northern subject matter: granite outcropping, lichen, bright birches and
twisted conifer. There is the patterned colour, the Impressionistic brushwork, and the
dramatic contrast of tone. Above all there is a pervasive quality of spirituality, reinforced by the display of the image across three supports that form a triptych, a familiar
conformation in the religious traditions of northern European art.

Autumn Forest also reveals the highly experimental approach to painting favoured
by Harris during these years. The rich effect of the granite, for instance, has been
achieved by "scumbling," dragging one pigment over another that is still wet, combining the two in a manner that is partly optical, partly mechanical, and vitally organic.
And the impressive way that the central black crack of the granite has been worried
into life not only delights the eye with its sure design but touches a primal chord of
experience, uniting painterly mastery and resonant spirituality in a potent symbol
of man's sense of his place in this part of the world.

Purchase, 1989   89/14

Tom Thomson (Canadian, 1877–1917)

A Rapid 1916
Oil on panel. 21.6 x 26.7

In the early spring of 1916, when the snow was still on the ground, Thomson returned to Algonquin Park for what would be the last full painting season of his life; he stayed on long enough to witness the first flurries of the following autumn. To finance this extended stay in the north, he signed on as a fire ranger during the summer, as he had the previous year.

A Rapid is one of Thomson's most daring conceptions, incorporating an expressionistic treatment of moving water that is breathtaking in its economy and suggestiveness. The rushing white of the falls draws the eye upward, against the current, to the dark canyon wall occupying the background from far left to middle right, where a vivid gold splash of birch or poplar foliage hovers like a puff of spray. The flat, generalized treatment of the tree reflects the lingering influence on Thomson's style of art nouveau tapestry and stained-glass patterns.

One of Thomson's own favourites, this panel was acquired by his friend and supporter Lawren Harris, who allowed him to live and work rent-free in a wooden construction shack behind the famous Studio Building from late 1914 until his final departure for Algonquin Park in the spring of 1917.

Gift of Mr. and Mrs. Lawren Harris, Toronto, 1927   864

A.Y. Jackson (Canadian, 1882–1974)

Maple and Birches 1915
Oil on canvas. 81.6 x 99.7

According to Jackson's own dating, he painted this canvas in January 1915. The previous October had seen the formation of the so-called Algonquin School of artists – the future Group of Seven – when Jackson, Arthur Lismer, Tom Thomson and F. H. Varley camped around Algonquin Park's Canoe Lake.

In *Maple and Birches* Jackson sets a flat foreground scrim of sinuous tree trunks against rhythmically undulating hills retreating to the horizon – a compositional device that was already a Jackson signature.

The pensive, elegiac mood of this painting doubtless reflects the painter's worries about the European conflict into which Canada had been drawn in August 1914. In his autobiography, *A Painter's Country*, Jackson recalled that "The maple, the birch and the poplar ran their gamut of colour and finally the tamarac [sic] tinted to shimmering gold; falling leaves and snow flurries made us aware that the sketching season was over. There was a war on too; in Algonquin we heard little about it and hoped it would soon be over. When we reached Toronto, however, we realized that we had been unduly optimistic; that war was likely to be a long one, and that our relatively carefree days were over.... The war made me restless.... I left Toronto and returned to Montreal with the intention of joining the army."

Purchase, 1942   2704

Tom Thomson (Canadian, 1877–1917)

The West Wind 1917
Oil on canvas. 120.7 x 137.2

The West Wind (sketch) 1916
Oil on panel. 21.1 x 26.6

There are few more widely recognizable and frequently reproduced icons of Canadian art than *The West Wind*. One of its closest competitors is *The Jack Pine*, also painted during the winter of 1916-17 (National Gallery of Canada). A considerable amount of controversy surrounds the exact location within Algonquin Park of the subjects of both works.

Thomson's patron, Dr. MacCallum, who claimed that he had witnessed the execution of the sketch *in situ*, wrote in 1937 that "the *West Wind* was done at Lake Cauchon," and Lawren Harris recalled in 1954 that he and Thomson had painted together in "an old clearing at the south end of the Cauchon Lakes" – two long, narrow lakes, set among hills in the remote northeastern sector of Algonquin Park, that form part of the upper chain that drains into the Petawawa River system. Harris vividly described the violent spring thunderstorm that had whipped the dark blue-grey waters of the lake into sudden whitecaps: "Tom and I took shelter in an abandoned lumber shack. Then Tom looked out, became excited by the drama of the scene, grabbed his sketch box, ran out into the gale, squatted behind a big stump, and commenced to paint in a fury."

Despite such testimony as to the setting of both *The West Wind* and *The Jack Pine*, a convincing case has been made for Grand Lake, the head of the Barron River, near the eastern border of the park, where Thomson worked as a fire ranger in 1916 and 1917.

At any rate, a more interesting debate surrounds the relative success or failure of Thomson's translation of his wonderfully spontaneous sketch to the more laboured studio canvas. One can see Thomson's training as a designer coming into play in the easel painting – for instance, in his emphasizing the S-curve of the taller of the two foreground pines and in his flattening of the clumps of needles into heavily outlined patterns imposed against a more volumetrically rendered middle ground and background. In the sketch, the uneasy balance of realistic details and decorative or abstracted passages is avoided; here is the true experience, made ever-vivid by the painter who saw and felt it so tellingly.

Upper: Gift of the Canadian Club of Toronto, 1926   784
Lower: Gift from the J. S. McLean Collection, 1969; donated by
the Ontario Heritage Foundation, 1988   L69.49

J. E. H. MacDonald (Canadian, 1873–1932)

Falls, Montreal River 1920
Oil on canvas. 123.0 x 153.0

In search of renewal after the dispiriting experience of WWI, Lawren Harris organized the first of what would amount to four box-car trips to the Algoma district of Ontario, north of Sault Ste. Marie, in September 1918. MacDonald, the senior member of the "brotherhood" that began exhibiting under the name of the Group of Seven in 1920, accompanied Harris, Frank Johnston, and Dr. MacCallum on this epoch-making expedition.

So successful was this experiment in finding a substitute for Algonquin Park (rendered a painful memory for its former adepts by the drowning death of Tom Thomson in 1917) that MacDonald participated in three more Algoma trips in 1919 and 1920. Emboldened by the grandeur of the scenery, he produced sketch after sketch on boards – the freedom, vigour, and chromatic daring of which were unlike anything he had achieved before.

Back in his studio, MacDonald worked up one of his sketches into *Falls, Montreal River*, his largest canvas to date. The position he adopted in depicting the cataract places the viewer in the direct centre of the action, at the top of the falls and seemingly in the process of being swept inexorably into the canyon far below. The yellow-green of the poplar-clad hills forms the background and contrasts with the darker hues of the evergreens palisading the torrent.

Purchase, 1933   2109

Lawren S. Harris (Canadian, 1885–1970)

Above Lake Superior c.1922
Oil on canvas. 122.7 x 153.2

Following their painting trip in the fall of 1921 to Algoma, fellow Group of Seven members Harris and Jackson decided to stay on in order to explore the northeast Lake Superior coast. Although they remained only a few days and Harris completed only two known sketches, the experience was a turning point for both artists. The hulking islands in the bay, the glacier-stripped hills along the shoreline, and the fire-ravaged forests behind them revealed the Northern Ontario hinterland to Harris in its most primeval and essential state. He returned to Toronto resolved to purge his art of excess detail and to seek out the basic structures underlying natural forms.

In the Lake Superior canvases Harris executed between 1922 and 1928, he restricted himself to two major points of view: either looking out toward the lake, usually through a *repoussoir* of simplified tree shapes, or northward over the undulating Laurentian Shield. The Group's first historian, F. B. Housser, saw a spiritual dimension in this painting, declaring that Harris had "gathered to himself the oversoul of that wilderness which rolls from Superior's coast to the Hudson Bay.... The mood is static, lonely, eternal and austere.... It summarizes locality, yet is not locality. It is the North's being."

Gift from the Reuben and Kate Leonard Canadian Fund, 1929   1335

A.Y. Jackson (Canadian, 1882–1974)

Early Spring, Quebec 1927
Oil on canvas. 53.5 x 66.7

In his autobiography, *A Painter's Country*, Jackson confessed that he did not know how many Quebec canvases he had painted. In fact, his painting expeditions to the province, undertaken between 1921 and 1958, totalled at least 37; the results of this prolonged exposure to a well-loved and deeply understood landscape constitute perhaps his most characteristic work.

One of the most fruitful of his Quebec excursions, made with Dr. Frederick Banting along the south shore of the St. Lawrence River, east of Trois-Pistoles, took place in the early spring of 1927. As the artist's niece, Naomi Jackson Groves, noted in *A.Y.'s Canada*, "We can construct the sequence of events of that mild, lightly clouded early spring day.... The sketch in oils... was done to catch the play of veiled sunlight on sodden snow and half-dried shingle – quickly, before the light changed too much. Then out came the sketchbook and pencil to capture and keep the fine detail of the sharp angles of the little homes set offside against the series of rising ridges, each modelled by its pleated furrows, with the road telescoping wildly straight up the middle of the composition.... The next appearance of the drawing will be when it is tacked onto the top of the easel at home in the studio, in preparation for the canvas." The canvas closely follows the preparatory on-site drawing but exaggerates the incline of the hill up which the muddy road climbs.

Gift of the Canadian National Exhibition Association, 1965   135

Adrien Hébert (Canadian, 1890–1967)

Ship Loading in the Port of Montreal 1926
Oil on canvas. 86.5 x 91.4

As the son of the renowned French Canadian sculptor Louis-Philippe Hébert and the younger brother of sculptor Henri, the young Adrien was absorbed by art. Although born in Paris, he divided his time between that city and Montreal, where he set up a studio. While in Paris he was fascinated by the Seine, and he was often a passenger on the popular *bateaux mouches*.

Following his permanent return to Canada in 1924, Hébert turned his attention to Montreal's harbour, as he believed he could not find the true life and spirit of contemporary art in "wild forests" or "drowsy villages." A leading exponent of Modernism in Quebec painting, he departed from the rigid academic approaches of his immediate predecessors and modelled his compositions on those of the French Post-Impressionist Paul Cézanne. Like many younger painters of the day, and increasingly during the 1930s, he wished to record the social and environmental conditions by which he was surrounded and of which he was a part. Hence his interest in complementing views of his own studio and residence with depictions of his immediate environs, and of the industrial activity that took place alongside, and analogous to, his assiduous labours at his easel.

Typical of his harbour paintings, this canvas features a strong geometrical design, bold outlines, and broad applications of colour wedded to a subject in which machinery is forefronted and figurative components are treated as accents.

Gift of Mrs. Helen Karrel, Toronto, 1983   84/39

James Wilson Morrice (Canadian, 1865–1924)

Landscape, Trinidad c.1921
Oil on canvas. 74.6 x 92.7

Morrice's life of deliberate exile from his native Montreal began in 1890, when he headed for Europe, settling in Paris the following year. Much as he loved the City of Light, his innate restlessness drove him to travel. If Morocco represented the Mediterranean alternative to the rainy Île de France, he found in the West Indies a refuge from the snows of Canada, to which he now and then returned. The hot countries heated up and liberated his palette, but he needed the cooler, more muted tonalities of northern latitudes to balance the sunny hues of his subtropical canvases – hence his frequent shuttlings north and south in both the New World and the Old.

Morrice's second trip to the Caribbean (his first occurred in 1915) took place in 1921; he found it easier to work in watercolours and waited until he was back in his studio before working up several of his sketches into easel paintings. *Landscape, Trinidad* is one of the artist's last major works. As with its companion canvases, Morrice worked swiftly, diluting his pigments to give them a watercolourlike transparency and fluency. The thinness of the paint is more than compensated for by the brilliance of the pink wall of the house in the clearing and the greens and yellows of the trees, though these in turn appear relatively subdued in contrast to the deep cobalt blue of the sky.

Purchase, 1937   2417

David Milne (Canadian, 1882–1953)

Ripon, High Street 1919
Watercolour on paper. 50.7 x 35.4 (sheet)

Having left New York City in 1916 for the village of Boston Corners, New York, the
Ontario-born Milne devoted himself to the painting of landscapes and still lifes in
watercolours and oils using the dry-brush technique. This method was ideally suited to
the flat patterning, undiluted hues, lack of modelling, and emphatic outlines called
for by such painters as Henri Matisse and Maurice Prendergast, under whose influence
Milne came around the time of the Armory Show of 1913 in New York.

In 1917 he returned to Toronto to enlist in the Canadian army. While based in
North Wales, Milne heard about the fledgling Canadian War Memorials program,
launched to record Canada's participation in the conflict, and he successfully applied
for Official War Artist status. He completed 37 depictions of various bases before
being promoted to the rank of lance corporal and dispatched in 1919 to France and
Belgium to paint deserted battlefields, cemeteries, and repatriation camps.

Ripon, High Street, one of the artist's few war works not in the Canadian War
Memorials Collection (the Milnes are housed in the National Gallery of Canada), was
completed while he was visiting the military camp near the market town of Ripon,
Yorkshire. In painting this bird's-eye view of the busy street, Milne employed pure
watercolours squeezed directly from the tube onto his brush, the result being a depth
and brilliance suggestive of unthinned oil on paper.

Gift of the Frances E. Barwick Estate, 1985   85/127

David Milne (Canadian, 1882–1953)

The Camp c.1930
Oil on canvas. 40.6 x 50.8

Almost as much as he loved painting the lakes of mid-Northern Ontario, where he began to spend his summers after leaving the United States for good in 1928, Milne enjoyed depicting the paraphernalia of camp life and the outdoor studio. His art, more than that of most of his Canadian contemporaries, was always as concerned with the problems and pleasures of art-making – of observation and creation – as it was about the places that compelled his brush and burin into action. When in the wilds, he was as likely to concentrate on the mundane details of shelter and domestic comforts as to dwell on the outline of a headland or the contours of his canoe.

The Camp is a characteristic example of his mature style in which areas of unpainted canvas act as outlines defining basic forms. Severely restricted in its chromatic range (blacks prevail), it likewise makes no concessions to the niceties of balanced composition. The dating and locale of the work are uncertain; the announcement of the 1958 exhibition from which it was purchased by the Art Gallery of Toronto identified all the canvases in the show as being from 1929-36, during which period Milne painted at Lake Temagami, the village of Palgrave, and Six Mile Lake, on the Severn River near Georgian Bay. He in fact first camped at Temagami, northeast of Sudbury, in the summer of 1928, and lived at Six Mile Lake from 1933 to 1939.

Gift from the McLean Foundation, 1958   58/18

Lionel LeMoine FitzGerald (Canadian, 1890–1956)

At Silver Heights 1931
Oil on canvas on board. 35.8 x 40.2

With this painting, FitzGerald paid a temporary farewell to the medium of oils, preferring for the next few years to work in watercolours, charcoal, graphite, and coloured
pencils. In 1930 he had visited the Art Institute of Chicago and subsequently travelled
to various cities in the United States and eastern Canada with the object of familiarizing
himself with the Modernist international and American art in their museums. Among
the painters on whom he commented in his diary were Seurat, Cézanne, and Charles
Sheeler (an American Precisionist whose example induced FitzGerald to simplify his
style in order to bring out the significant forms of nature, the human figure, and
man-made objects and constructions).

On his return to his native Winnipeg, FitzGerald devoted himself to explorations
whose ultimate outcome would be the still lifes, portrait studies and nudes that in turn
would evolve into the pure abstracts that preoccupied him until his death. Although
At Silver Heights displays Precisionist elements, especially in the treatment of the
rhythmically positioned foreground trees and the female figure standing among them,
the composition harks back to FitzGerald's middle-period series of Winnipeg backyards
and parks. The presence of the curvaceous figure at the right emphasizes the summery
feeling of the work. The woman and the trees seem to sway together in a timeless
dance of forms and forces, figures and grounds.

Purchase, 1981   81/7

Melvin Ormond Hammond (Canadian, 1876–1934)

At Recess 1931
Chloro-bromide. 29.8 x 26.3 (sheet)

One of the most gifted amateur photographers in Canada, Hammond distinguished himself equally through his political writings as a magazine editor for the *Globe* and as a
champion of Canadian artists.

The pictorial movement flourished in Canada from the turn of the century
until the late 1930s, lasting two decades longer than in Britain and the United States.
Hammond, perhaps best known for his highly accomplished portraits of Canadian
artists, musicians, and men and women of letters, was an active participant in
photography salons for more than twenty years.

For this photograph, Hammond extracted theoretical ideas of aesthetic excellence
advocated by the Pictorialists in their struggle to have photography accepted as a
medium of artistic expression. By emphasizing the printing process, Hammond achieved
control of his subject matter by the use of dark and light to emphasize atmospheric
effect and to create an animated mood. A horizontal zigzag composition creates a geometric relationship between the room and the articulated groups of young women.
The flickering highlights, which Hammond carefully achieved by working on the
negative, play on the folds of the clothing and contrast with the denser forms in the
shadows. Patterns of light, geometry of space and arrangement of lines are the true
subjects of this picture; the group at recess at the Ontario College of Art has only made
it possible for Hammond to synthesize an idea and an effective technique.

Gift of Skip Gillham, 1985   85/166

Elizabeth Wyn Wood (Canadian, 1903-66)

Reef and Rainbow 1927–c.1935
Cast tin on black marble base. 25.0 x 96.5 x 24.8

Wood and her husband, the sculptor Emanuel Hahn, spent their honeymoon in 1926 on Hahn's island in the Pickerel River, near Parry Sound. She was struck by the muscular forms of the bare, windswept, "whalebacked" granite rocks that are this region's principal feature and returned to them again and again in her work. Although this sculpture could have been prompted by similar islands and shorelines in Georgian Bay and along the west coast of Lake Superior, where she and Hahn canoed during their summer vacations, *Reef and Rainbow* may well have been inspired by the Pickerel River scenery that had been her introduction to the Laurentian Shield country of Northern Ontario.

The streamlined Art Deco simplicity and gracefulness of this work owe as much to the glacier-sculpted character of the primal landforms themselves as to the influence of the modernist sculptors and designers Wood admired: notably, Henri Gaudier-Brzeska, Aristide Maillol, László Moholy-Nagy, Alexander Archipenko, and the Group of Seven painters who were her friends. Wood was unique in applying their functionalist principles to organic and geological subject matter.

Gift from the Albert H. Robson Memorial
Subscription Fund, 1950   49/54

Emily Carr (Canadian, 1871–1945)

Guyasdoms D'Sonoqua 1928-30
Oil on canvas. 100.3 x 65.4

Not long after her return to her native British Columbia, from two years of study in France (1910-11), Carr struck out for new painting terrain along the west coast of Vancouver Island. Among her preferred subjects were the dilapidated but still awe-inspiring Indian villages facing the Pacific, with their weathered cedar-plank housefronts and teetering totem poles. Carr intensively explored the often disturbing imagery of these places until 1913 and returned to it in a less programmatic way in the mid-1920s.

In 1912 Carr paid her first visit to the Kwakiutl village of Gwayasdums, on Gilford Island, which she described as "off the beaten track...one of the old-time original villages, unchanged by fashion and civilization...." A hiatus of 16 years intervened between the date of this seminal sketching trip and Carr's return to the subject in this late-1920s canvas.

In her autobiography, *Klee Wyck* (1941), Carr recalled how, upon disembarking on the deserted island, she landed by misadventure at the feet of "the great wooden image towering above me," the appearance of which "was indeed terrifying." She continued: "Her head and trunk were carved out of, or rather into, the bole of a great red cedar. She seemed to be part of the tree itself, as if she had grown there at its heart, and the carver had only chipped away the outer wood so that you could see her.... I stood looking at her for a long, long time."

Gift from the Albert H. Robson Memorial Subscription Fund, 1942   2705

Arthur Lismer (Canadian, 1885–1969)

Sunlight in a Wood 1930
Oil on canvas. 91.4 x 101.6

For several decades, from the 1920s to the 1950s, Lismer spent his summer holidays on
Georgian Bay – a domain he described as "a paradise for painters." These escapes from
his duties as vice-principal of the Ontario College of Art (1919-27) and subsequently
as educational supervisor at the Art Gallery of Ontario (1927-38) and the Montreal
Museum of Fine Arts (1941-67) renewed his artistic and physical energies.

    Sunlight in a Wood likely represents a tract of dense coniferous forest in back of
the Lismer cottage at McGregor Bay, in the northeast corner of Georgian Bay. The
artistic possibilities of this area had been discovered by Lismer as early as 1922 and by
his fellow Group of Seven member A.Y. Jackson in 1928. Most of Lismer's McGregor
Bay oils and drawings depict shoreline and island vistas or studies of tangled under-
growth rather than woodland interiors to which genre this oil belongs. Throughout
the 1930s and 1940s, he thoroughly explored the challenges of this tricky subject,
though never more successfully than he did here.

    Bequest of John M. Lyle, Toronto, 1946   2847

Emily Carr (Canadian, 1871–1945)

Stumps and Sky c.1935
Oil on paper. 58.4 x 90.2

The year 1935 was a watershed date in the career of Emily Carr. Her work up to that time had undergone a steady evolution, as she had become more focused on her twin obsessions, the B.C. woodland interior and the totemic imagery of its native inhabitants. But, just as by 1930-31 she had shifted her attention from Northwest Coast Indian themes to those of the forest, by mid-decade she had begun to emerge from the dark, Gothic solitudes of the deep underwood to a more open range, where the thickets thinned and the "jungle" gave way to clearings, from shade to light. Ironically, this new, less confined vantage was as much attributable to the clear-cutting caused by lumber companies as to the increased elevation Carr sought in her restless quest for the "bigger something" that lay beyond the timberline and the peak's cold shoulder.

As if to complement Carr's liberation, the range of her media expanded to encompass the portable, fast-drying alternative to her former preference for oil on canvas: gasoline-thinned oil on manila paper. She handled this highly fluid medium like watercolour, painting with broad, rhythmic strokes in the hypnotic presence of those natural forms that captured her vision of nature as a living, breathing entity.

In the 19 September 1935 entry of her journal, she described the method by which she captured the churning movement of the clouds revolving across the sky: "It is done in swirly rings. Why? Not for affectation any more than the cubists squared for affectation. Like them I was trying to get planes but used disks instead of cubes."

Gift from the Douglas M. Duncan Collection, 1970   70/31

A.Y. Jackson (Canadian, 1882-1974)

South from Great Bear Lake c.1939
Oil on canvas. 81.5 x 101.8

Jackson had more sustained and fruitful contact with the sub-Arctic and Arctic regions of Canada than any other artist of his generation. His far-northern journeys, extending from 1927 to 1965, established him as an explorer in his own right, and the role he played in visualizing these little-known regions for his compatriots was unexampled. As he remarked toward the end of his life, "I guess I'm like the compass, always heading north. I really do belong to the caribou country, not the cow country."

Jackson first sketched at Great Slave Lake in the Northwest Territories with Dr. Frederick Banting in 1928 and ten years later fulfilled his desire to fly to Great Bear Lake and the Barren Lands astride the Arctic Circle. On this occasion his six-week August-September stay was made at the invitation of the prospector Gilbert LaBine, discoverer of the Great Bear Lake pitchblende deposit, who wished Jackson to view his famous Eldorado silver and radium mine.

Jackson was entranced by the rugged, rolling, sombrely hued scenery around Great Bear Lake, the southern shores of which he described as being "surrounded by big rocky hills, open patches of spruce in places...." In a letter to his niece, Naomi Jackson Groves, he observed that "the country seemed monotonous at first, but gets better all the time. You don't get effects as you do down south.... The skies are far away, and everything that takes place does it over a thousand square miles."

Gift from the J. S. McLean Collection, 1969; donated by
the Ontario Heritage Foundation, 1988   L69.21

Frederick Horsman Varley (Canadian, 1881–1969)

Liberation 1936
Oil on canvas. 213.7 x 134.3

While virtually penniless, Varley launched into this largest and most ambitious of his canvases in the confines of his Ottawa studio in 1936, convinced that this was to be the masterpiece by which he would make his reputation in Europe – it being his intention to return in triumph to his native England. By his account, *Liberation* had the power to act as a catalyst on other witnesses besides himself: "No one sees paint, they only see a six-and-a-half-foot figure coming out of strange colour lights, an evanescent something which in a moment more will be solid matter – molten metal and jewels – I can scarcely believe I have something impossible for me to lose or wreck...."

Alas, Varley did "lose or wreck" the elusive "creative period" he dreamed would be ushered in by this work. He never again approached the intensity of vision whereby his own inner and outer image (for the Christ-like figure emerging from the threshold of the tomb appears to be a self-portrait) could be elevated from the physicality of paint into the realm of light through the transformative agency of art. This essay in the application of colour complementaries to religious autobiographical subject matter was rejected by the jury of the Royal Academy in 1937; unable to afford the cost of shipping the canvas back to Canada, Varley had it placed in storage in a London warehouse, where it remained, forgotten, until 1975.

Gift of John B. Ridley, 1977; donated by the
Ontario Heritage Foundation, 1988   L77.131

Frederick Horsman Varley (Canadian, 1881–1969)

Dhârâna 1932
Oil on canvas. 86.5 x 101.6

Varley's move from Toronto to Vancouver in 1926 coincided with his discovery of
Oriental art and Buddhist philosophy and his growing interest in colour theories, both
scientific and esoteric. His own intuitive theory derived from the five basic qualities
of tantric energy, each colour having either good or bad connotations according to
personal and karmic interpretation.

For Varley, green, the prevailing hue of the interior of British Columbia, was
"spiritual," an attribute he also found in his beautiful young former student and frequent
model, Vera Weatherbie. Posing Vera against the mountainous landscape, he tended
to restrict himself to the blue-and-green palette that she herself preferred. In painting
Dhârâna he varied this combination with iridescent green-mauves and gold.

The work's title refers to the Buddhist concept of oneness with nature, otherwise defined as the concentration of the mind and senses on a single thought. The
background is Lynn Valley, on Vancouver's North Shore, to which Varley and Weatherbie
started to make weekend sketching trips in 1932. The original preparatory drawing of
Vera's raptly expressive head is also in the AGO's collection.

Gift from the Albert H. Robson Memorial Subscription Fund, 1942   2593

Edwin H. Holgate (Canadian, 1892–1977)

Interior c.1933
Oil on canvas. 76.8 x 63.5

Holgate was one of the few Canadian artists of his day to excel in a wide range of media
and genres, from landscapes and portraits in oils to murals and woodcuts. Perhaps his
most signal achievement is his small but forceful series of monumental nudes, begun in
1930 – the same year that this Paris-trained, Montreal-based artist first exhibited with
the Group of Seven as an official member.

    While the northern landscape backgrounds of several of these compositions sug-
gest the lingering influence of the Group, the figures themselves, whether in outdoor
or indoor settings, are indicative of Holgate's Cézanne-derived theory that "the basic
structure was what was most important...." Furthermore, they reflect the interest in
the human element that was to lead to the formation of the Canadian Group of Painters
in 1933, the year *Interior* was acquired by the Art Gallery of Toronto and the year
Holgate's first one-man show was mounted at the Art Association of Montreal.

    The confidence of the firm, rounded modelling and the bold yet subtle colour
balance in this canvas reveal an artist at the height of his powers. Holgate never again
combined the elements of a figural masterpiece so effectively as he did in *Interior*.

Purchase, 1933   2155

Bertram Brooker (Canadian, 1888–1955)

Phyllis (Piano! Piano!) 1934
Oil on canvas. 101.8 x 76.2

Although he began and ended his painting career as a dedicated abstractionist, Brooker was also a passionate interpreter of the human figure in both indoor and outdoor settings. During the 1930s he executed a number of striking portraits and nudes, many of them in vertical formats that give equal emphasis to the head and body of the sitter.

In this instance, the subject is the artist's daughter, Phyllis, then aged ten and a reluctant piano student. Her father encouraged her to persevere with her studies, despite her opposition, as he believed she had a natural talent. Phyllis's melancholic countenance betrays the sense of futility and frustration of a child who performs solely to please a parent or teacher. The title – which in musical parlance means "*Quiet!*" – could be an ironic echo of the nagging parent's demand that the daughter attend to her lessons: "*Piano! Piano!*" also could be the command to stop whatever else the child is doing and sit down at the instrument.

The sitter recalls that her father painted her in another part of the house than that in which the upright piano stood and then positioned her figure in front of the keyboard, which forms the backdrop of the composition. Typically, Brooker placed as much as he could in the foreground and middle ground, so that both the girl and the piano to which she (symbolically?) turns her back exist in a relatively shallow space – an indication of his attempt to adapt the tenets of abstraction to the field of figure painting. The main title, *Phyllis*, was added only after Brooker's death in 1955.

Purchase, with assistance from Wintario, 1979   79/59

Frances Loring (Canadian, 1887–1968)

Sir Frederick Banting c.1934
Bronze. 62.5 x 30.0 x 31.0

Frances Loring and her lifelong companion, Florence Wyle, have been described as being "to Canadian sculpture what the Group of Seven is to Canadian painting." As the daughter of a mining engineer, Loring lived and studied for extended periods in Europe and the United States before settling permanently in Toronto in 1912. Determined to excel in all areas of sculpture, from direct carving to cast bronze, she developed a facility for sympathetic rendering of the human figure in both intimate and monumental formats. Her ambition was to make her figures as anatomically accurate as possible, while also conveying the emotive, expressive qualities of the body and face in captured movement and in thoughtful repose. Her commissions ranged from large architectural decorations and war memorials to commemorative portrait busts.

In Loring's opinion, the strongest of these latter works was her bust of Sir Frederick Banting, a close friend and patron not only of "The Girls," as Loring and Wyle were affectionately known, but also of the Group of Seven. Banting, who was awarded the Nobel Prize for medicine in 1923 for his co-discovery of insulin, was also a collector of art and a proficient landscape painter in oils, and often accompanied A. Y. Jackson on sketching trips. That Loring considered Banting to be more than just an ordinary sitter is evinced in the sensitivity of modelling and attention to character displayed in this brooding, heroic head.

Gift from the Fund of the T. Eaton Co. Ltd. for
Canadian Works of Art, 1950   49/59

Paraskeva Clark (Canadian, 1898–1986)

Portrait of Philip 1933
Oil on canvas. 127.7 x 128.3

While studying art in her native St. Petersburg, Clark (*née* Plistik) received evening
instruction at the Petrograd Academy of Fine Arts; during the day she worked at a factory. After the Revolution in 1917, the Academy was transformed into a "free studio,"
open to all persons interested in art. She studied with Kuzma Petrov-Vodkin, a follower
of Cézanne. Following the death of her first husband, she went to Paris, where she
eventually met a young Canadian lawyer and art lover, Philip Clark, whom she married
in June 1931. Shortly thereafter they sailed for Canada, settling in Toronto.

Philip Clark encouraged his wife to return to her painting and provided her
with an entrée into local art circles, notably the Canadian Group of Painters (CGP) to
which she contributed an international flavour. Her preference for figural compositions
and still lifes over the wilderness-landscape aesthetic of the Group of Seven was in
accordance with the CGP's collective program of broadening and humanizing modern
Canadian art in both subject matter and style.

This portrait of her husband shows the artist's debt to Cézanne. The complex
structure of strong diagonal and perpendicular lines, with the point of view from
above the figure, create a visually dynamic painting. In contrast, the sitter is shown in
calm repose. Clark admirably balances formal considerations of composition, palette
and paint handling with an insightful – perhaps somewhat satirical – exploration of
lawyerly, as well as husbandly, character.

Purchase, 1984   84/89

Miller Brittain (Canadian, 1912-68)

Two Waitresses on a Streetcar Crossing the Reversing Falls c.1939
Oil on masonite. 55.8 x 45.7

As Brittain's interest lay in representing the people of his native Saint John, New
Brunswick, in routine working and domestic situations, he was described in the late
1930s as "having more right [than anyone] since Krieghoff to be called the Canadian
Brueghel."

    During his studies in New York, he came under the influence of the contempo-
rary American Regionalists and the artists of the Ash Can School, who were popular
chiefly because of their facility at realistically rendering the figure and the social comment that their work contained. Brittain was most influenced by Raphael Soyer, who
depicted New York office girls and their shoddy urban environs, and by Reginald
Marsh, noted for his gritty views of the Bowery and its residents. From the examples
of these painters and draughtsmen, Brittain not only developed an ability to convey
individual mannerisms of people in a crowd, he also affirmed that the "hang" of clothes
identified the character of the wearer as much as the expression on their faces.

    In this painting, a confident closed-contour line silhouettes the figures. The
relationship of the women to each other reveals a sensitivity to figural placement to
create a rhythmical, unified composition, while the portraits embody a pathos expertly
suggested through an economy of line and colour. Although ostensibly static, the
picture, as the title suggests, is as much about implied movement and change in life
itself, as well as in physical space, as it is about repose.

Purchase, 1982   82/35

Carl Schaefer (Canadian, b. 1903)

Storm over the Fields 1937
Oil on canvas. 68.7 x 94.0

Schaefer's rediscovery of his own home ground, the rolling farm country around the rural
Ontario town of Hanover, coincided with his adoption of the watercolour medium
(ideally suited to pictorial treatment, in addition to being both economical and portable). In 1934 he began to use watercolours exclusively in the painting of landscapes,
having been introduced to them by an older painter and teacher, Franklin Carmichael.
The masterpiece of his so-called Hanover series, *Storm over the Fields*, had its genesis
in a large watercolour of the same title and date (also in the AGO's collection).

In the mid-1930s, Schaefer's early mentors, the Group of Seven, were supplanted
by the British landscape painter Paul Nash and the American Regionalist Charles
Burchfield. Like Nash and Burchfield, and also like van Gogh, he sought to evoke the
expressive qualities of particular times and places through the emotive handling of colour and line, but Schaefer's personal vision was more austere and less anthropomorphic.

This canvas, with its stark contrasts of light and dark and its overwhelming sense
of foreboding, has been read as a symbolic warning of the ultimate outcome of the
Depression, namely WWII. Undoubtedly, the painter's own response to his past, present, and future in the context of his ancestral surroundings – rather than the global
zeitgeist – constitutes the true subject matter of this dramatic statement of combined
identification with and alienation from the land.

Gift from J. S. McLean, Canadian Fund, 1954   53/51

Jean-Paul Lemieux (Canadian, b. 1904)

Lazarus 1941
Oil on masonite. 101.0 x 83.5

Lemieux's early interest in art was developed under the tutelage of Suzor-Côté and through his studies at Montreal's École des beaux-arts. Further instruction in Paris in the early 1930s brought him into contact with Clarence Gagnon. Like him, Lemieux was unaffected by the Parisian avant-garde, preferring to comment on conditions in his native province. On his return to Canada, he became part of a small group of painters who concentrated on depicting traditional *québécois* ways of life.

In *Lazarus* Lemieux combines his keen sense of irony with an allegorical representation of rural Quebec society faced with the reality of WWII. *Lazarus*'s tripartite composition is dominated by a church opened at the roof to reveal a service in progress, while, outside, paratroopers and civilians are firing at each other and a funeral procession is marching to a cemetery, where Christ, in contemporary dress, is raising Lazarus. All three episodes are unified by the road, which draws the viewer's eye into the painting. The aerial perspective attests to the continuing influence of Lemieux's childhood practice of drawing pictures of battles where characters were shown inside cutaway houses. The separate but related scenes of synchronous action reflect the artist's familiarity with the religious and narrative genre painting of the Northern Renaissance. Described as a "good-natured parody," *Lazarus* challenges a complacent society to confront the violent presence of war and find renewed life in the midst of catastrophic events.

Purchase, 1941   2574

Goodridge Roberts (Canadian, 1904-74)

Pleasant Island, Georgian Bay 1952
Oil on masonite. 81.4 x 122.0

Not every Canadian painter has been able to adapt to the seasons so happily as
Goodridge Roberts. Instead of allowing the vagaries of this country's weather to limit
him to particular themes, he took advantage of its changes to explore a variety of genres
in regular sequence: landscapes painted outdoors in spring and summer, then still lifes
and figures in the studio during the fall and winter. This practice made Roberts not
only one of the most versatile of our artists, but also one of the most consistent in his
painterly approach.

Although most closely identified with the pastoral Eastern Townships and the
more rugged Laurentians, the Montreal-based Roberts also favoured a small selection
of landscapes farther afield, one of which is the eastern shore of Ontario's Georgian Bay.
During a sojourn in August 1952, he painted Pleasant Island, the largest and most
heavily wooded island in the stretch of rocky coast between Parry Sound and Byng
Inlet. It commands a panoramic view of which Roberts took full advantage, positioning
his easel at the top of a knoll in order to look out across wind-bowed pines to the
choppy open water below. Nowhere more effectively than in this oil, the product of
a single session, does Roberts demonstrate his tactic of direct engagement with his
expressionistic medium and his elemental subject matter.

Gift from the Fund of the T. Eaton Co. Ltd. for
Canadian Works of Art, 1952   52/15

Lawren S. Harris (Canadian, 1885-1970)

Painting No. 4 c.1939
Oil on canvas. 129.3 x 93.2

F. B. Housser, first chronicler of the Group of Seven, referred to Harris in 1926 as "a modern mystic who has attempted to express through painting, moods reached through mystical experience." Profoundly influenced by the doctrines of theosophy, Harris sought to convey in oils an understanding of the eternal unity and common truth in all things. For Harris, art provided a bridge between the confusing, temporal diversity of the material world and the harmony of the spiritual realm.

Throughout the Teens and early 1920s, Harris had been preoccupied with his chosen subject matter of Toronto urban scenes and Northern Ontario landscapes. A change can be seen in his approach by 1923, the year he joined the Toronto branch of the International Theosophical Society, when he increasingly simplified his compositions, introducing starkly minimal elements bearing symbolic purport. By 1938, having moved to the U.S. four years earlier, Harris was experimenting intensively with abstraction. He became a member of the Transcendental Painting Group in Santa Fe, New Mexico.

Painting No. 4 demonstrates Harris's somewhat formalized approach to abstraction, using as a point of departure the landscape, namely, the Sangre de Cristo mountain range in New Mexico. The painting's series of overlapping planes folding inward and the large mandala at the centre of the composition reveal his debt to the American abstract painter Emil Bisttram.

Purchase, 1984   84/864

298

Alfred Pellan (Canadian, 1906-88)

Thought of Bowls (Pensée de boules) 1936
Oil on panel. 161.3 x 90.2

Throughout his life, Pellan subscribed to a nondoctrinaire approach to art. At any one time he was working in several different modes of representation or abstraction. His work reflects an eclecticism born of a continual interest in exploring the problems of subject matter and media and the challenges posed by working within many artistic conventions. He formed this attitude at the École des beaux-arts in Quebec City, where Pellan was considered a prodigy. His talent netted him the first bursary of the Province of Quebec in 1926, and with it the opportunity to study in Paris.

The rigorous discipline of the studio exercises in a Parisian art school was balanced by the education Pellan received by visiting galleries. Consequently, he saw at first hand the latest developments in Cubism and Surrealism, elements of which found their way into his own paintings and drawings. This painting shows his knowledge of the spatial organization seen in Léger's and Braque's work, of Matisse's and Derain's palette, and of the theatricality and inventiveness of Picasso and Ernst.

Pensée de boules is a good example of his work of the mid-1930s, which was considered too radical by the examining board of his alma mater, when in 1936 he briefly returned to Quebec to apply (unsuccessfully) for a teaching post. Pellan's influence was pervasive in his home province following his departure from Paris in 1940, and it was chiefly through his example that European Modernism was introduced into this country.

Gift of Sam and Ayala Zacks, Toronto, 1970   71/289

Contemporary Art

Arshile Gorky (Armenian, 1904-48)

They Will Take My Island 1944
Oil on canvas. 96.6 x 122.0

Gorky left Soviet Armenia for the United States in 1920, where he studied at the Rhode Island School of Design. He was the last important artist with close ties to the Surrealist movement. This work was one of nine paintings exhibited at the Julien Levy Gallery in New York. By this time Gorky had fully assimilated the work of Picasso and Miró and had also been deeply influenced by the biomorphic fantasy of the Chilean-born Surrealist Matta. Gorky's imagery was based on a unique combination of organic forms inspired by nature and the human body.

They Will Take My Island, which is thinly painted, gives the impression of having been done spontaneously, even automatically, but it was in fact based on a large drawing. Gorky seems to have drawn the thinnest, and also the most deliberate, lines first. The heavier black lines appear more dynamic and almost impulsive, as do the applications of red, yellow and green washes. Gorky worked from nature and calculated drawings to a partly abstract imagery. "Gorky is," Breton wrote, "of all the Surrealist artists, the only one who maintains direct contact with nature – sits down to paint before her."

Purchase, with assistance from the Volunteer Committee Fund, 1980   80/71

Jackson Pollock (American, 1912-56)

Untitled 1946
Spatter, pen and black and coloured inks, gouache, wash,
sgraffito on paper. 56.2 x 76.8

In their spontaneity, abstraction and scale, Pollock's all-over drip paintings of the late
1940s and 1950s initiated and epitomized the liberation of the painting process that
many of his generation participated in. The path that led him to this breakthrough is
rich with contradictory influences and psychological drama.

    This untitled drawing illuminates Pollock's wide-ranging imagination and his
readiness to experiment with media and techniques along with pictorial conventions
and to some extent summarizes the iconographic and stylistic concerns in his art to the
mid-1940s. The Jungian approach to the image – in which psyche and image are one
and the same – is coupled with a positivist emphasis on immediate sensation, demon-
strating the tension Pollock felt between his need for symbolic figuration and his
ambition for a total visual effect. Dripping, pouring and spattering are superimposed
on the kind of totemic figuration that dominated Pollock's work till that time. Automatism – the one crucial Surrealist influence that survived Pollock's progression from
fantasy imagery to total abstraction – became an ideal technique for the fusion of
remnants of earlier painting styles.

    Gift from the Volunteer Committee Fund, 1976   76/199

Robert Motherwell (American, b. 1915)

In Grey with Parasol 1947
Collage, oil on paper board. 121.2 x 91.5

Motherwell's unique contribution to American art of the midcentury was a determined theoretical emphasis on internationalism, which assimilated modern European aesthetic values into American painting. His collages, which he first experimented with in 1943, bear witness to his European influences, Picasso and the Cubists. By 1947 he began to separate the expressive power of oil from collage's emphasis on construction and composition. Collage enabled him to work out complicated rectangular relationships within the shape of the work.

In Grey with Parasol is part of a series begun in 1943. Key to the series is the figure itself. Composed within a structure that allows a shallow location of the planes, the figure fits the centre, its surfaces parallel to the picture's, and thus forms a triangle, its base parallel to the picture's bottom edge. It is in this figural series, where a more interpretive format allows a greater degree of interplay between pure textural delight and the necessities of positioning a figure, that the freely painted and the tightly composed aspects of Motherwell's art are totally integrated.

Gift from the Women's Committee Fund, 1962   61/75

Willem de Kooning (Dutch, b. 1904)

Two Women on a Wharf 1949
Oil, enamel, graphite, collage on paper. 62.1 x 62.4

As a leader among the first generation of Abstract Expressionists, Dutch-born de Kooning stands as one of the most innovative and vigorous of midcentury American painters. From 1947 to 1949 de Kooning painted a number of significant images, all of them of women. Generally his women were painted singly; when they appear in pairs, as in this work, their bodies often intertwine, producing a complex mélange of forms and colours. In depicting the ambivalent relationship between the figures and the purely abstract structures, de Kooning has the figures remain part of the densely packed picture plane, without differentiating between the solidly situated internal planes. Seemingly random, nonobjective elements group into configurations that can be read as figures. Contradiction and ambiguity remain.

     Although here, as in other works, he patterned certain features of the female anatomy after Surrealist prototypes, de Kooning's figures fit comfortably within the tradition of demimondaines as Manet's *Olympia* or Picasso's *Les Demoiselles d'Avignon*. But they are also rooted in popular fantasies of smiling females in magazine ads and Hollywood sex goddesses such as Marilyn Monroe.

Purchase, Membership Endowment Fund, 1977   77/68

Franz Kline (American, 1910-62)

Cupola 1958-60
Oil on canvas. 198.1 x 269.9

Kline's work belongs to the "action" or "gestural" side of Abstract Expressionism.
His mature style began in 1949 when he saw his small sketches projected onto a wall
and magnified into monumental linear strokes. The new approach he developed also
required new means, and Kline soon adopted wide house-painter's brushes and quick-
flowing enamel.

If Kline's loose grids of broad black and white swaths derive from Cubist
structure, they are also new because of their spontaneity and violent energy. And if
the paintings allude to skeletal urban structures, they resist traditional figure-ground
readings, their black and white gestures acting as equal forces held in taut equilibrium.
Only in the late 1950s did Kline introduce colour into his work.

Cupola was completely repainted between 1958 to 1960. Dissatisfied with the
first version, a small sketch enlarged onto the wall-size canvas, Kline superimposed on
it the composition of a second sketch, breaking up the original ominous central black
field with textural modulations and energetic, interpenetrating shafts of white.

Gift from the Women's Committee Fund, 1962   61/55

Mark Rothko (American, 1903-70)

No. 1, White and Red 1962
Oil on canvas. 259.1 x 228.6

Rothko is among the most solemn and mystical of the Abstract Expressionists. Living
and working in New York from 1925, he developed artistically under the influences
of social realism, Surrealism, and an involvement with the mythic, organic forms of
tribal art. This work gave way, in the postwar years, to the colourfield painting of his
mature style. In these large stained canvasses Rothko's concern was to eliminate all
representational and literary references from the painted surface in order to remove, as
he said, "all obstacles between the painter and the idea, and between the idea and the
observer." He believed that the true subjects of art must be tragic and timeless and
that art must be an act of revelation, exaltation, and an embodiment of universal truth.
In pictures such as *No. 1, White and Red*, painting is reduced to an essence: colour alone
becomes volume, form, space and light. In their simplicity and regularity these paintings carry an immense conviction of the sublime as expressed in basic emotional tones.
In them, the absence of gesture, the spatial suggestiveness, the breathing intensity of
surface all offer the opportunity for the meditative attitude that Rothko demanded
for his art.

Gift from the Women's Committee Fund, 1962   62/7

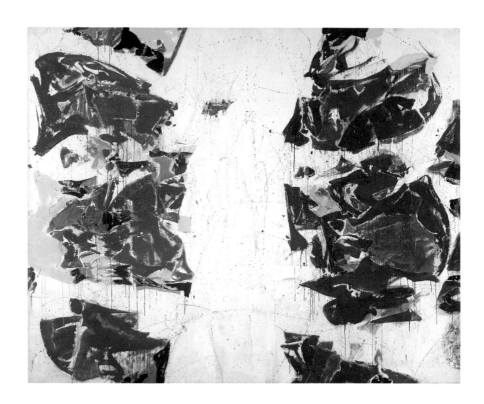

Sam Francis (American, b. 1923)

Untitled 1959
Oil and acrylic on canvas. 243.8 x 295.9

Francis began to paint during an extended stay in a military hospital. While he was lying flat on his back, the sky and the quality of light itself deeply impressed him and continued to inspire him throughout his career. He abandoned his studies in medicine to study art. After graduating from the University of California at Berkeley in 1950, he went to Paris, where he was influential in bringing an appreciation of the new American painting to an European milieu.

Travels throughout Europe and Asia, and extended visits in Japan, were instrumental in the development of Francis's art. Time spent in Aix-en-Provence familiarized him with the light and colour of Cézanne's painting and country. The subsequent influence of Japanese aesthetics is evident as his compositions grew more austere and compressed.

The paintings from 1957 and 1959 are his best-known works and *Untitled* is exemplary of their style. In these paintings the white ground covers more and more of the surface, animated by drips and spatters of colour, which progressively become more metallic, colder and saturated.

Gift from the Women's Committee Fund, 1960   60/3

Hans Hofmann (American, 1880–1966)

Obeah 1961
Oil on canvas. 152.4 x 132.1

Known as the dean of American painting for most of his long career, Hofmann has not
only been acclaimed as the most important 20th-century teacher of art, but also as one
of its most significant painters. As a teacher Hofmann encouraged experimentation
and artistic independence. His own willingness to experiment, and the variety of styles
in which he worked, often deprived him of sympathetic critical attention.

   Hofmann's principle of creating form through colour alone, without modelling
or perspective, as well as his conception of the illusionistic spatial relationships between
one colour and another, were formulated during a ten-year stay in Paris amidst the
creative fervour of the Fauves and Cubists. As early as 1939, he experimented with the
technique of spattering and pouring paint and with the principle of allowing the picture
to develop while painting it. For this, Hofmann is acknowledged as pre-eminent
among the originators of gestural abstraction and action painting.

   By 1956 Hofmann had arrived at a mature style characterized by paintings
composed of rectangular planes with dense paint surfaces in warm opulent colours.
Obeah is an example of this mature style.

   Gift from J. S. McLean, American Fund, 1962   62/6

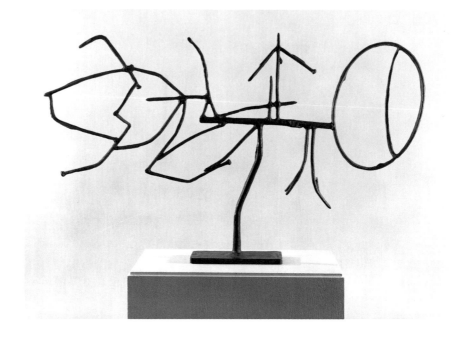

David Smith (American, 1906-65)

O Drawing 1957
Bronze. 78.7 x 128.2 x 22.8

When Smith was killed in an auto accident in 1965, he left behind a prodigious body
of work of immense complexity and stylistic diversity.

Smith's characteristic way of working was to use a single idea and develop it
through a series of closely related sculptures, often working simultaneously with two
or three distinct styles. He used drawing throughout his career as the principal means
of catching the immediacy and fluidity of imagery from the subconscious. He sought
to reach a similar kind of flexibility of handling in sculptural form. Throughout the
1950s he produced a number of line-drawing sculptures, the outstanding example of
which is *O Drawing*. It is based on a slightly smaller, almost identical work of 1954; the
principal change from the first idea was the addition of a loop bisecting the *O* that
bulges in a semicircular curve into space, thus intensifying the interplay of surface and
depth. As a linear articulation of three-dimensional space, the tense staccato character of this "linescape" has all the lightness and immediacy of drawing despite the
unwieldiness of the material and technique.

Gift of Mr. and Mrs. Roger Davidson, Harris Davidson, Matthew Davidson,
in honour of Mrs. Harry Davidson, 1985   85/305

Irving Penn (American, b. 1917)

David Smith, Bolton Landing 1964
Platinum-palladium, Rives paper on aluminum. 60.6 x 50.8 (sheet)

Since 1943 Penn has paralleled his celebrated work for *Vogue* with formal portraits,
studies of tradespeople, found objects, and a series of close-cropped nudes. Penn's
portrait of sculptor David Smith is a faithful rendering of the way the camera framed
the subject and bluntly captured its directness and austerity, suggesting a timeless
quality. For Penn this timelessness is most brilliantly expressed by recreating 19th-century
studio photography, which required complicity with and isolation of subject matter as
compared with the limitless freedom of the modern camera. Penn's deliberation of
exact description is further intensified by his preferred printing process – contact
exposure of enlarged negatives on hand-sensitized platinum-palladium paper, which
recalls the luminosity and long tonal range of earlier photographers.

This study of Smith commands a sense of sculptural illusion by the sheer solidity
of the subject. Its physicality is emphasized by the cropping of the head that force-
fully fills the frame and by the veracity of detail: texture of skin, deformed nail and the
reflective glint in the eyes. These features do not necessarily reveal the life or personality of Smith as much as they accentuate the considered probity that Penn's
photography has achieved.

Purchase, with assistance from the Junior Committee Fund, 1981   81/16

Paul-Émile Borduas (Canadian, 1905-60)

Abstraction 1942
Gouache and charcoal on wove paper. 59.2 x 43.5

The completion of a series of 45 paintings in gouache – a medium chosen for its inexpensiveness and fluidity – marked a pivotal stage in the advancement of Borduas's career, since up to the early 1940s he had worked primarily as a church decorator and art teacher. Any nonfigurative work he produced was measured in relation to that of his contemporary Alfred Pellan, the prodigious French Canadian artist who, on his return from Paris in 1940, introduced Modernism to Quebec painting. In 1942 Borduas's gouaches received important critical attention upon being exhibited in his first solo show; he then found himself moving to the forefront of the Quebec avant-garde.

The basis of works such as *Abstraction* is the Surrealist principle of Automatism, a process that seeks to allow the free expression of the unconscious and deliberately exploits the element of chance in the realizing of an artwork. Borduas turned to this method after reading André Breton's paraphrase of Leonardo da Vinci's idea about basing a painting on what one would perceive "on an old wall, after having contemplated it for some time." In his gouaches Borduas substituted paper for the wall and randomly drew on it with charcoal. He then emphasized arbitrary outlines or forms before applying colour to strengthen shapes or to alter the composition.

Gift from the Junior Committee Fund, 1977   77/18

Paul-Émile Borduas (Canadian, 1905-60)

Woman with Jewel (La femme au bijou) 1945
Oil on canvas. 109.1 x 81.2

This canvas marks Borduas's return to the use of oil paint, following his *automatiste* experiments with gouache, which began in the early 1940s. Although the Surrealist principle of Automatism is still the basis of these oils, the transition was not easy. While gouache on paper allowed spontaneity and ease of execution, with oil on canvas Borduas was compelled to follow a more deliberate process, beginning with a background screen of colour and then situating objects and figures within this colour field once it had dried.

In *Woman with Jewel* the foreground image takes on a suggestive figural analogy. The work shows a vigorous, gestural, almost expressionist application of pigment and a bold colour sense to depict a masked, centrally positioned femme fatale wearing a dazzling jewel, which some commentators see as a sexual metaphor.

When Borduas first displayed this painting in Toronto at Eaton's Fine Arts Gallery during the Contemporary Art Society exhibition of November 1945, a local critic hailed it as "a good example of modernism which does not smack of being 'anti' anything, just a creation of something visually gratifying." Since then, this canvas has been one of the most frequently exhibited and reproduced of Borduas's paintings.

Bequest of Charles S. Band, Toronto, 1970   69/50

Paul-Émile Borduas (Canadian, 1905-60)

3 + 3 + 2 1956
Oil on canvas. 129.4 x 88.7

After Borduas left Montreal in 1953, he lived in New York City, then departed for Paris in September 1955. Despite his feelings of loneliness and his longing to return to Canada, he produced some of his best work in the series of black-and-white paintings he completed there.

Borduas's concern in these works is with activating the entire surface of the painting through the most economical means. Spatial depth is reduced to a minimum. Looking to Piet Mondrian's example in structuring a composition with the use of a grid, Borduas laid on with a palette knife a skin of thick white pigment over a black underpainting, areas of which are allowed to show through, with tints of warm pink barely discernible at the outer edges.

The numerical title suggests the order in which the black areas are to be "read": the viewer's eye is immediately drawn to the C-shaped black central area, which is nearly divided into three smaller squares. Above this shape is an arc described by three black patches, while the two black shapes in the lower corners keep the eye within the format and redirect it to the central motif. The cycle begins again, with the gaze being continually guided around and through the surface, while the pink touches further reinforce the movement around the painting's outer edges. The fact that the equation is incomplete – the implied total is not part of the title – confirms that within the apparently static image is perpetual perceptual motion.

Bequest of Charles S. Band, Toronto, 1970   69/49

Jean-Paul Riopelle (Canadian, b. 1923)

Composition 1952
Oil on canvas. 194.5 x 130.0

As a young art student in Montreal in 1942, Riopelle attended the classes conducted by Paul-Émile Borduas at the École du Meuble. Inspired by his teacher, he experimented with *automatiste* processes, and in 1946 he exhibited his paintings in the first "Surrealist" group exhibition to be held in Montreal. Later that year he left for Paris, where he became closely involved with the French Surrealists and in 1947 was included in the vast *Exposition Internationale du Surréalisme* organized by André Breton and Marcel Duchamp.

Riopelle's canvases are complex investigations of the spatial tensions of colours, textures and lines. In *Composition*, through what initially seems to be an impenetrable screen of elements, a central area of deep space emerges. The eye is drawn into the heavily textured surface and is held within its perimeters by strongly articulated vertical and horizontal lines at the edges. The movement of the eye toward the centre of the composition and into the heavily impastoed surface is reinforced by diagonals and a bold red accent at the visual focus of the painting. Out of the apparent randomness of paint application emerges the reality of a controlled exploration of space and colour. This resolution is illustrative of the *automatiste* principle underlying the work, which seeks to liberate the unconscious from the forces that repress imagination and free association.

Purchase, with assistance from Wintario, 1977   77/28

Jean Dubuffet (French, 1901-85)

Texturologie XXVIII 1958
Oil on canvas. 97.4 x 130.4

Inspired by the drawings of children and lunatics, Dubuffet sought for his art a condition of unselfconscious subjectivity. Every picture of Dubuffet's is of something: often common objects of little significance, fragments borrowed from within the framework of unconscious regard, or undeliberate traces that inscribe themselves spontaneously in the memory of ordinary human beings.

The *Texturologies*, begun in 1957, are a series of paintings in celebration of the ground. They are descriptive views of the ground, seen from above, free of all figurative subject matter, anecdote or narrative. They reject any centre of interest or other compositional devices and move toward an apprehension of the unbroken phenomena of continuity. Always innovative technically, Dubuffet splattered and dripped paint on the canvas spread on the floor, scattered sand over the painting, applied material or paper to the fresh paint surface and then peeled it away, and scratched it with the tines of a fork. By painting surfaces that are both continuous and endless, he evokes a vision of infinity. "These pictures provide me with peace," he wrote, "great peace of rugs and naked and empty plains, silently uninterrupted distances whose homogeneity and continuity cannot be altered."

Gift of Sam and Ayala Zacks, 1970   71/130

David Hockney (British, b. 1937)

I saw in Louisiana a live-oak growing 1963
Oil, india ink, graphite, newsprint offset on canvas.
122.0 X 122.0

Hockney first came to prominence in the early 1960s while a student at the Royal
College of Art in London. His was a narrative art that incorporated the pictorial language of contemporary abstraction while giving full value to an insistently autobiographical subject matter. He made use of a range of styles derived from children's art,
Egyptian figuration, graffiti, and other seemingly anonymous styles in order to depict
personal events, experiences with friends, his travels. The poetry of Whitman and
Cavafy inspired numerous paintings. In reference to this work, Hockney has said, "*I saw
in Louisiana a live-oak growing* is from the Whitman poem about the tree that's 'utter-
ing joyous leaves of dark green all its life without a friend or lover near.' I thought,
what marvellous lines about a man looking at a tree. The tree is painted upside down
to make it look more alone; it was just so simple as that, really."

Gift from the Volunteer Committee Fund, 1984   84/83

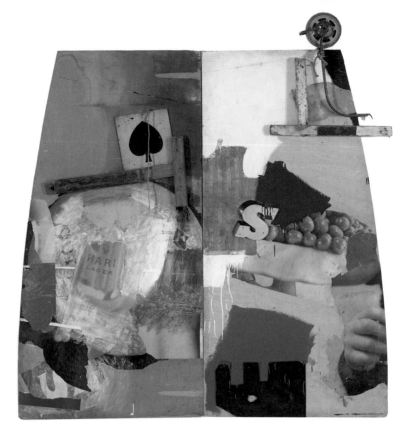

Robert Rauschenberg (American, b. 1925)

Story 1964
Mixed media on panel. 106.0 x 97.0

Since the mid-1950s there has not been much antiformalist American art that was not either anticipated or provoked by the work of Robert Rauschenberg. To him is owed much of the assumption, now taken for granted, that a work of art can exist for any length of time, in any material, anywhere and for any purpose.

For ten years Rauschenberg designed costumes and sets for most of the new dances of the Merce Cunningham Dance Company and from 1961 to 1964 he travelled with the group as lighting designer and stage manager. *Story*, first performed in Los Angeles, was an indeterminate work for which Rauschenberg devised costumes and props out of whatever he found backstage on the day of the performance. The *Story* combine-painting was realized with the same means, on stage, during performance of the dance work. Rauschenberg's aesthetic of heterogeneity and multiplicity results from the recontextualizing of all sorts of extra-art objects and images that remain more-or-less intact, life-sized. These modest things are then reconciled by the patina of paint and wear and by their non-hierarchic order of associations.

Purchased with assistance from the Women's Committee Fund, 1970   69/246

black bathroom #2

Jim Dine (American, b. 1935)

Black Bathroom #2 1962
Oil, porcelain, steel, canvas. 183.0 x 183.0

Pop Art dominated the New York art scene in the early 1960s and for a time Jim Dine was allied to it. Though his subjects were fetishes of the time and much of the work maintains a cool humour typical of Pop, Dine's feeling for the paint itself and the emotional foundation for the work reveal his continued links with Abstract Expressionism. His earliest paintings were outstanding examples of the new realism of the early 1960s. By the end of 1961 he had moved from representing objects to affixing real objects to the canvas. *Black Bathroom #2*, when it appeared in 1963, was a shocking piece because it violated all the traditional standards of painting and ignored the impossibility of preserving the work in the traditional way. It was also a confusing piece because it mixed paint with real fact, presenting an actual object in an evoked environment. Dine uses the painted canvas like a backdrop, creating an undeniably theatrical effect. The rich black painted shadow, reminiscent of Franz Kline, and the pale shadow cast by gallery light give the object a dramatic emphasis. Yet the result is graphic, not sculptural.

Gift of Mr. and Mrs. M. H. Rapp, 1966   66/19

Andy Warhol (American, 1930-87)

Elvis I and II 1964
Left panel: screenprint on acrylic paint on canvas; right panel: screenprint
on aluminum paint on canvas. Each panel: 208.3 x 208.3

Warhol's first Pop paintings of 1960 were enlarged single panels of *Dick Tracy* and
Superman comic strips, popular press ads and Coca-Cola bottles. Warhol's adaptation
of the look and techniques of advertising art, especially after his introduction to silk-
screen printing, became the foundation of his style.

From the outset Warhol was obsessed with the idea of celebrity and his portraits
of Marilyn Monroe, Elizabeth Taylor and Elvis Presley suggest the idea of a market-
place where fame, glamour, even personality are just so many commodities. In this
image of Elvis, probably culled from a fan magazine, the eclipsed hero stands firm,
six-shooter in hand. But this is not Elvis at the peak of his fame, this is Elvis as a fading
star, already a cliché. Graphically, the figure is isolated from the chroma-key blue and
movie-screen silver backgrounds, compressed by the top and bottom edges of the picture
frame, and repeated as a flat static image, seemingly available for endless repetition
in any context. By these devices the painting obtains the strange intensity of a ritual
object, at once familiar and cold, useless and necessary.

Gift from the Women's Committee Fund, 1966   65/35

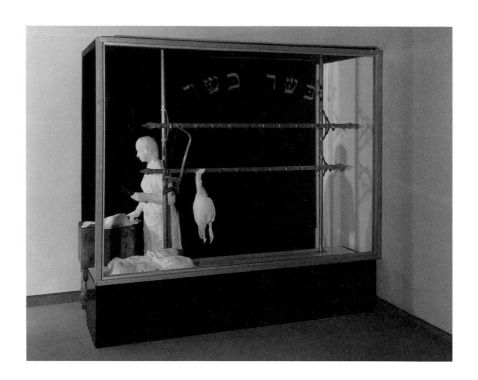

George Segal (American, b. 1924)

The Butcher Shop 1965
Plaster, wood, vinyl, metal, acrylic sheet, glass. 238.8 x 252.1 x 124.5

Though first identified with Pop Art because of the gritty urban character of his tab-
leaux, Segal's art bears closer ties to an older American realist tradition, which also
developed in the early 1960s through avant-garde impulses similar to those that fostered
"happenings" and performance. His sculptural environments aspire toward a reconcil-
iation of a moral or Utopian vision with matter-of-fact descriptions of everyday life.

    Both the psychological and formal power of Segal's work is evident in *The Butcher
Shop*. The piece was conceived as a memorial to Segal's father, a kosher butcher. His
mother posed for the female figure who is in the act of cutting off the head of a
chicken. All the equipment is authentic, purchased from a Third Avenue (New York)
wholesale supplier. The shop window carries Hebrew letters spelling "kosher meats."
For orthodox Jews the killing and preparation of animals for food is a religiously controlled ritual. Repetition of the ritual finds its formal equivalent in the multiple
reflections of forms in the black plastic mirror that comprises the back of the sculpture.

    Gift from the Women's Committee Fund, 1966   65/36

Claes Oldenburg (American, b. 1929)

Giant Hamburger 1962
Painted sailcloth stuffed with foam rubber. H. 132.1 x D. 213.4 (approx.)

Oldenburg's soft sculptures of food, appliances, giant baseball gloves and so on emerged as both type and token of American Pop Art in the early 1960s. They began as giant sewn props for "happenings" at Oldenburg's New York studio, where he first mounted *The Store*, a multimedia installation and performance. Invited to mount another version at the Green Gallery in 1962 (a large space on 57th Street), he produced a 10-foot ice cream cone, a 9-foot slice of cake and the *Giant Hamburger*.

On a formal level, the representational aspect of Oldenburg's soft sculptures of the 1960s can be understood as a challenge to the abstract art of the preceding decade. In their soft forms and giant scale, in their emphasis on the physical, they question the notion that "significant form" is only possible in abstract art. Their success lies with their visceral presence: the appeal of surface, shape and colour.

Purchase, 1967   66/29

Jock (J. W. G.) Macdonald (Canadian, 1897–1960)

Heroic Mould 1959
Oil and Lucite 44 on canvas. 182.9 x 121.5

More than any of his contemporaries, Macdonald participated in the major 20th-century movements that changed the face of Canadian art, from the Group of Seven landscape tradition, to the 1930s Regionalist concerns of the Canadian Group of Painters, to his experimentation with automatism in the early 1940s, and finally to his involvement with the first anglophone abstractionist collective, Painters Eleven, founded in Toronto in 1953.

By the late 1950s Macdonald had moved from his gridded watercolour abstractions, which reveal the influence of such Modern European masters as Kandinsky, Klee and Miró, to large nonobjective images in which ambiguous central forms rise from the base of the canvas to float in the shallow space of the picture plane. Among the inspirations for this late series were microscopic slides of cells and crystals that Macdonald translated into full-scale paintings suggestive of the elemental forces of growth and decay, using the fluid, translucent new medium of Lucite 44.

The biological origins of *Heroic Mould* conflict with the shieldlike appearance of the central form, the "mould" being interpretable as rust or patina on steel or bronze. On the other hand, the "shield" also resembles a door opening onto a snowy landscape. Completed a year before Macdonald's death, this majestic painting seems to prophesy either the fresh direction that his work would have taken had he lived or else a foreshadowing of his passage to the spiritual plane for which he quested all his life.

Bequest of Charles S. Band, 1970   69/54

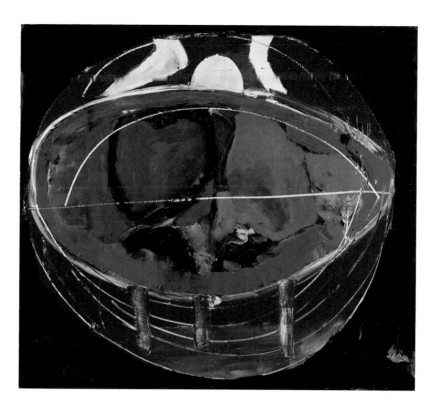

William Ronald (Canadian, b. 1926)

Exodus I 1958
Oil on canvas. 121.3 x 131.8

Ronald's place in the history of modern Canadian art is assured by virtue of his efforts
in forming Painters Eleven and in pursuing its goal of awakening the public to the
possibilities of Abstract Expressionism. As a reaction to the rigid jurying practices of
the conservative art societies of the early 1950s, Ronald approached his employer, the
Robert Simpson Co. Ltd., with the proposition that he be allowed to exhibit abstract
paintings in a furniture-display promotion entitled *Abstracts at Home* at its Toronto
department-store headquarters. After the company agreed, Ronald invited seven fellow
artists to contribute work to the exhibition following which this loose coalition
increased its ranks to eleven and resolved to exhibit as a group. As a result Painters
Eleven successfully presented the most advanced painting in English-speaking Canada
and achieved international recognition.

Characteristic of Ronald's painting of the late 1950s, *Exodus I* is composed of a
mandala shape, which may be viewed as set either within a dense colour field or against
a patterned background. A red field has been overpainted with black around the
perimeter of the canvas, thereby defining the central image as two crescents touching
at the tips. At the centre, thin washes of colour are juxtaposed with areas of thick
impasto. White paint applied directly from the tube describes the diameter of the
mandala and further defines the edges of the crescent.

Purchase, with assistance from Wintario, 1976   76/207

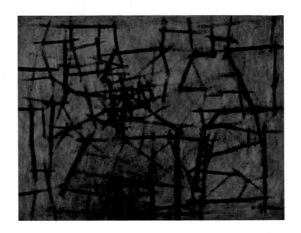

Kazuo Nakamura (Canadian, b. 1926)

Inner Structure 1956
Oil on masonite. 60.8 x 78.4

Nakamura was one of the original members of Painters Eleven, a group of Toronto-based abstract artists who banded together as an exhibiting unit in 1953. Nakamura's concern with the representation in abstract form of the fundamental structure of matter and the universal patterns found in nature sprang from his interest in the physical sciences and his belief that "scientists and artists are doing the same thing. This world of pattern is the world we are discovering together." Nakamura shared this desire to link the two apparently antithetical disciplines with a senior member of Painters Eleven, Jock Macdonald.

Nakamura's personal style, which evolved through at least four different representational modes, is not easy to classify. His constant experimentation with technique, media, tools, and processes is always subordinated to an intellectual analysis of the abstract forms found within the landscape. *Inner Structure* is a tightly composed investigation of the spatial relationships between calligraphic brush strokes of deep ultramarine and a modulated blue colour field. An unresolved visual tension exists between the painting's references to a landscape source and the artist's abstractions from it, while the title impels us to question the nature and location of that "inner structure" of which the image is an outward manifestation.

Gift of Mr. Charles McFaddin, Toronto, 1985   85/115

Harold Town (Canadian, b. 1924)

Great Seal No. 3 1961
Oil and acrylic on canvas. 188.0 x 208.9

Throughout the 1950s Town was an active member of Painters Eleven, a group of Toronto artists who, although they abided by no collective manifesto, were to challenge the status quo of Canadian art. Town has continued to take a fiercely independent approach to his work and has sought his own brand of Abstract Expressionism. A personal response to his art, as it is largely dependent on the viewer's imagination and recollection of past experiences, is encouraged by Town.

Town considers painting a mythic activity, and he layers rich iconographic associations over a modernist formal structure. About his *Great Seal* series Town explains, "I make up a set of rules and play with them until I win." In *Great Seal No. 3* Town uses circular forms filled with calligraphic patterns as images of historical and contemporary significance. Town believes that symbols are still important in the "cultural compost heap" of 20th-century life. Of the abstract "dabs and splashes" of this canvas Town claims, "If you look through a telescope you see patterns like this in nature."

Gift of Jessie and Percy Waxer, 1974; donated by the
Ontario Heritage Foundation, 1988   L74/10

329

Jack Bush (Canadian, 1909-77)

Hanging Figure 1959
Oil on canvas. 190.0 x 251.5

Although he was a respected member of all the major Canadian exhibiting societies and
an accomplished commercial illustrator in Toronto, Bush did not rest comfortably on his
successes, but continued to grow as an artist. His introduction to abstraction occurred
in 1947, when a psychologist urged him to experiment with Automatism in order to
express his feelings. On becoming a founding member of Painters Eleven in 1953, he
began more fully to experiment with abstraction and adopted the vocabulary of the New
York Abstract Expressionists. But not until 1958, when the influential New York critic
Clement Greenberg commented favourably on his work, did Bush feel that a significant
breakthrough had occurred in his artistic development. Greenberg encouraged him to
abandon the thick, gestural painting of the Abstract Expressionists for a simplified
palette and to apply his pigments in thin, transparent washes that would emphasize the
two-dimensional picture plane rather than attempt to create the illusion of depth.

While in *Hanging Figure* Bush seems to be following Greenberg's advice in his
application of thinned oil washed over unprimed canvas, the figurative allusions,
created by the combination of paint squeezed directly from the tube, applied with a
palette knife, or brushed on with broad, gestural sweeps, still provide "subject
matter." Subsequently, Bush would completely embrace nonfiguration, concentrating
on the visual "movement" caused by juxtapositions of bright primary colours and on
the eternal dance of abstract motif and abstract ground.

Gift from the Volunteer Committee Fund, 1986   86/182

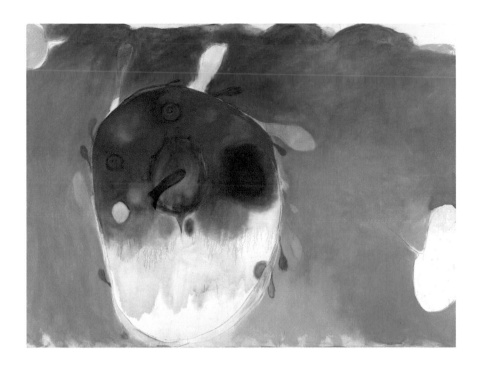

Joyce Wieland (Canadian, b. 1931)

Time Machine Series 1961
Oil on canvas. 203.2 x 269.9

At the beginning of the 1960s, Wieland's figurative work began to reflect the prevailing influence of Abstract Expressionism in Toronto. This canvas is characteristic of Wieland's mixture of abstraction and figuration. One of the few large stain paintings Wieland produced in the early 1960s, this canvas has been described as the purest female imagery painted in Canada to that time. While male and female reproductive organs may be identified within the work, the circular central form brings to mind the continuous cycle of ovulation. Representing the female viewpoint, Wieland focuses on the physical role of women in generation. Like a biological clock marking time, the glowing mass rotates in a kind of transformative play that exemplifies an extraordinary sense of life. *Time Machine Series* shares an intimate view of self and body that is both a microscopic vision of fertility and a macroscopic symbol of the cyclic forces of creation in life – and in art.

Gift from the McLean Foundation, 1966   65/25

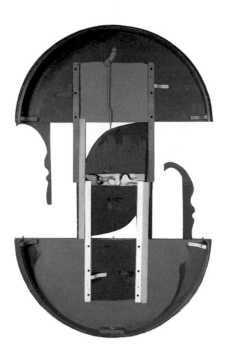

Gordon Rayner (Canadian, b. 1935)

Homage to the French Revolution 1963
Oil and acrylic on wood. 179.1 x 114.3

The process of discovery and improvisation is the basis for painter Rayner's creative impulse. Together with the closely knit group of artists associated with the Toronto-based Isaacs Gallery, Rayner was influenced by the American avant-garde artists Robert Rauschenberg and Jasper Johns. Returning to Dadaist issues of anti-art and non-sense, the neo-Dadaists of the 1960s welcomed the accidental as a valuable component in the exploration of material possibility. While refusing to follow any one school exclusively, Rayner allowed the idiosyncratic nature of materials at hand to suggest an attitude and an approach to working. Each work, complete in itself, is without reference to those preceding it.

Rayner's assemblages often utilize waste materials and manufactured or found objects brought together in ironic and unusual arrangements. In this work, a familiar piece of household furniture is presented in an unfamiliar context; the apparatus on the underside of a kitchen table, peculiar in itself, becomes the armature on which to hang the visual pun. This ordinary table, when placed on end, becomes the terrible instrument of revolution: the guillotine. Born out of a spontaneous and uninhibited investigation into the nature of material, *Homage to the French Revolution* becomes a powerful expression of the potentiality of the relationship between matter and meaning.

Purchase, 1964   63/40

Michael Snow (Canadian, b. 1929)

Venus Simultaneous 1962
Oil on canvas and wood. 200.7 x 299.7 x 15.2

Snow based all his work from 1961 to 1967 on the same image of the walking woman, which marked an important return to figurative art. Convinced of women's role as "*THE* subject . . . the classic theme in Art," Snow began to experiment with the walking-woman image, drawn from popular North American culture, as "a huge theme-and-variations composition." Caught in motion and cropped by an imaginary frame, she became a formal device with which Snow could explore spatial and temporal pictorial relationships.

Combining both painting and sculpture, Snow utilizes complex figure-ground relationships within this work. The walking woman, a Venus in contemporary guise, exists simultaneously in real and pictorial space, as she appears to enter the painting on the left and exit on the right. In between, she emerges as a three-dimensional form leaving behind her negative stencil, which is surrounded by two-dimensional line-drawing and collage versions.

Purchase, 1964   63/47

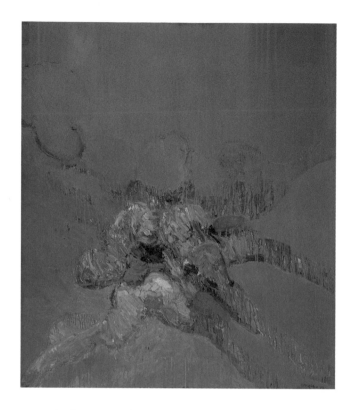

Graham Coughtry (Canadian, b. 1931)

Two Figures XII 1963
Oil and acrylic on canvas. 213.4 x 182.9

This painting is one variation in a series of figurative abstractions executed by Coughtry in the early 1960s. Along with his contemporaries Michael Snow, Gordon Rayner, Robert Markle and Dennis Burton, Coughtry was concerned with the spontaneous and subjective expression of experience. Coughtry's painterly interpretations descend from the Surrealist idea of automatism and the gestural power of the New York-based Abstract Expressionists and the French Canadian Automatistes. The most influential figure of the Abstract Expressionist school was painter Willem de Kooning, whose energetic brushwork built up the surface of the canvas in increasingly dense layers while retaining traces of the figurative subject.

At a time when formalist criteria dismissed the figure as an inappropriate artistic concern, Coughtry sought to synthesize the sensual nature of painting with that of the image. He allowed the fluidity of the figure in motion to become the subject and method of the composition. The surface of the canvas, built up through thick layers of paint alternating with thin washes, becomes at once the material from which the figures are made and the substance from which they emerge. Through an image of sexual encounter, Coughtry explores the sensual qualities of pigment and colour.

Gift of Reuben Wells Leonard Estate, 1964   63/43

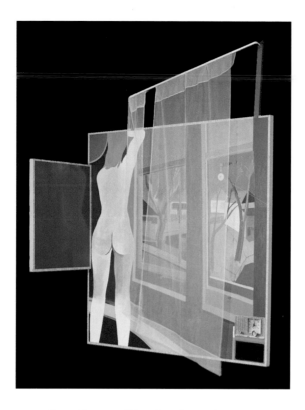

Greg Curnoe (Canadian, b. 1936)

Spring on the Ridgeway 1964
Oil on plywood, rayon/nylon, metal, wood, paper, string. 187.0 x 187.0

In the early 1960s Curnoe's life in his home town of London, Ontario, was the subject
of his art. Curnoe chose to investigate his roots in the cultural milieu of his childhood
rather than follow the general trend of the decade by moving to New York. Curnoe
defines Canada as a country made up of distinct regional cultures. Works such as this
one, which record a specific time and place in his London environment, are the artist's
quasi-anthropological documents of Canada.

    Spring on the Ridgeway is a representational version of Curnoe's 1961-62 "stamped-
letter" descriptions of views from his London studio. Here, limited to the perimeter
and largely composed of yo-yo terminology, the text intensifies the complex image of
the woman looking out the window. The viewer's traditional position before the work
is parodied by the figure, who stands before the window as before a picture.

Purchase, 1965   65/24

Dennis Burton (Canadian, b. 1933)

Mother, Earth, Love 1965
Oil and acrylic copolymer on canvas. 152.4 x 203.2

In the early 1960s, Toronto's storefront displays of women's undergarments convinced Burton that "the 20th-century woman is a packaged commodity. She is presented in advertisements, the entertainment field, and men's mags as an inanimate object divested of her humanity, leaving her only as a sex symbol." Burton was fascinated by what he describes as "the peculiarly significant individuality that underclothes give us all, especially women." "I am interested in their difference from me," he explains, "and I am interested in teaching...converting people to confronting reality (as I see it)." By clothing the traditional Old Master nude in modern underwear and by focusing on the torso, seen as if viewed through a keyhole, Burton mocks middle-class values.

The earth mother/goddess is rendered in flat line and colour, and in her reclining position she symbolizes a "landscape of love." As Burton explains, "At the same time, since I've always been deeply interested in astronomy, I made the breast areas suggestive of circular planetary orbits." *Mother, Earth, Love* thus becomes a tantric image of "Mother Universe."

Gift from the Junior Women's Committee Fund, 1965   64/83

N. E. THING CO. (Canadian, b. 1936)

Bagged Landscape with Water 1966
Inflated plastic, air, water, food colouring, metal. 198.1 x 137.2

With the development of conceptual art in the 1960s, Iain Baxter formed the N. E. THING CO. in 1966 around the question "What is art?" Describing himself as a "visual informer," Baxter sees the world as being made up of "pieces of information of all kinds, visual or sensory...and if you can get beyond the label attitude, you are able to see and experience all they contain." In his art Baxter aims to "alert the senses and open the mind" to the "visual richness" of the environment, so that culture may become a part of daily life.

According to Baxter, "plastic is the common stuff that we use every day" and the definitive product of modern technology. In this work the artist attempts to bridge the gap between art and life by combining the historically venerated landscape subject with the plastic packaging of everyday things. The inflatable landscape-in-a-bag, produced by the industrial method of heat-sealing vinyl, is part of Baxter's exploration of new media and the innovative ways of using them that "elucidate their processes and their functions because they're part of our lives and our culture."

Gift of Mr. and Mrs. H. A. Malcolmson, 1985   85/616

John Meredith (Canadian, b. 1933)

Seeker 1966
Oil on canvas. Triptych, overall: 177.8 x 366.4

The enigmatic paintings of Meredith developed in comparative isolation from the artistic trends of the 1960s. He pursued a more introspective approach to spontaneous expression; by turning to Far Eastern forms, he sought to concretize the mystical relationship of the self to the world. The circular mandala became the starting point for the development of a subjective mythology. Regarding the act of drawing as a form of intensely personal scrutiny, Meredith generated a vocabulary of psychic markings and calligraphic forms based on vegetal and anthropomorphic motifs.

Meredith's intuitive approach to colour and form led him to develop the expressive possibilities of line. By smudging the wet ink of the drawings, he electrified the line with its own potential rhythms. From these emotive drawings, the hieratic forms of the paintings emerged. This triptych is the first painting Meredith produced using the ink drawings as the source for the finished work. He literally transferred the energy of the drawings onto canvas, sustaining their impulse under formal consideration. Bright, flat colour bounded by the pulsating line operates on a primary level to support the complex personal imagery. Spontaneous and free of association, these painted drawings become the vehicle by which Meredith explores his own relationship with a changing world.

Purchase, 1967   66/23

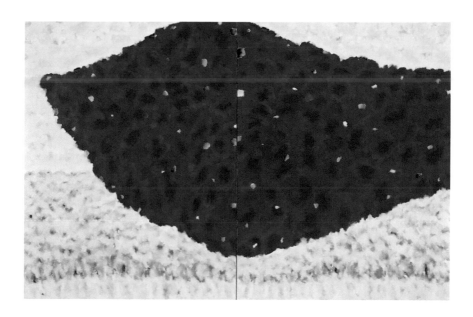

Gershon Iskowitz (Canadian, 1921-88)

Uplands H 1972
Oil on canvas. Diptych, each panel: 241.3 x 182.9

Turning to landscape for the subject of his paintings in the early 1950s, Iskowitz increasingly downplayed representational imagery in his work in favour of the expressive potential of colour and form. As a result the artist's works began to function on two levels: as personal recollections of his experiences with landscape and as formal investigations of colour harmonies, surface patterns, and layers of pictorial space.

The *Uplands* series includes one triptych and ten diptychs titled from *A* to *K* (without *I*), painted between 1969 and 1972. They represent what Iskowitz saw during helicopter trips made over northern Manitoba. The *Uplands* works recall the pulling up of the helicopter and the looking down over a panoramic landscape that is hidden and then revealed through several levels of space. The large, abstract central shape, by its intensity and definition of colour, appears to hover in front of the distant horizon. But this form, along with the division separating the two panels of the diptych, also reaffirms the presence of the picture plane and the artist's manipulation of layered colour harmonies and textures over its surface.

Purchase, with assistance from Wintario, 1977   77/26

Alex Colville (Canadian, b. 1920)

Woman in Bathtub 1973
Acrylic on hardboard. 87.8 x 87.6

As one of Canada's most celebrated Realist artists, Colville presents a sharply focused
look at the intimate subjects of his paintings. Remarking on the potential of the
smallest action, Colville contemplates human behavior and records his insights with
a meticulous precision.

     In this painting Colville represents a commonplace scene of domestic life. Using
the lines of perspective as a means of entry, the artist invites the viewer to examine
the nature of the relationship within. A nude woman bathes, quietly detached from the
figure behind her. Clothed and cut off from view, this unknown person injects the
scene with a disquieting tension, thereby increasing the woman's vulnerability. The
cold, clinical lighting enhances the precarious nature of their relationship. Elements
that are simplified and placed according to a mathematical system of proportion fix
the scene in time. Through the careful arrangement of pictorial elements, Colville
contrives the dissociation of the figures and presents for the viewer's scrutiny this
intimate tableau.

Purchase, with assistance from Wintario, 1978   78/124

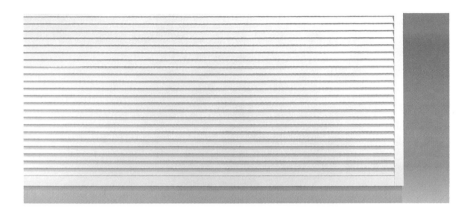

Christopher Pratt (Canadian, b. 1935)

March Night 1976
Oil on hardboard. 101.4 x 228.6

Throughout his career, the clapboard houses of Pratt's native Newfoundland have been
a recurrent theme in his paintings. Pratt argues that "There is a common human preoccupation with the places we inhabit." But, while he often returns to the same
architectural subjects, Pratt insists that his work proceeds from memory and imagination, rather than from actual things.

    Pratt's precise, linear technique and simplified, ideal forms remove any sense of
a specific time or place and allow the architectural imagery of *March Night* to stand for
the "archetypal house." Influenced by the Precisionist tradition in American art and
attracted to mathematical exactitude, he strives for "a quality of order." By contrasting
the solid wall with the open space of the landscape, Pratt creates a visual dialogue
between the linear and the painterly, the finite and the infinite and, ultimately, the
known and the unknown. "I like," Pratt states, "the immediacy, the sense of confrontation between the wall of my house . . . and the indeterminate space, the darkness
and mist and wild country." The image of the house reverberates with meaning and
memory, which act as a powerful means by which the artist explores the nature of
human existence.

    Purchase, with assistance from Wintario, 1977   76/226

John (Jack) Chambers (Canadian, 1931-78)

401 Towards London No. 1 1968-69
Oil on plywood. 183.0 x 243.5

Chambers's analytic approach to representational painting developed from acute observations of his personal experiences. As an artist living in London, Ontario, during the 1960s, he was impelled toward an increasing awareness of regional identity. In this painting, he presents a bird's-eye view of Ontario's contemporary landscape. This familiar stretch of highway, which the commuter quickly passes through, is stopped by Chambers for a detailed examination.

Chambers's desire to give truthful representation to experience led him to experiment with photography as a source for his painting. The camera brought him to a new understanding of reality through the objectivity of its mechanical "eye." This creative impulse to capture and render perceptions of reality objectively in a concrete expression of the "eternal present" he called Perceptual Realism. The sharply defined image presents the moment of sudden clarity when the senses apprehend the external world. For Chambers this affirmation of life in the concrete world forms the true basis for art.

Gift of Norcen Energy Resources Limited, 1986   86/47

Ivan Eyre (Canadian, b. 1935)

Highwater 1978
Acrylic on canvas. 178.0 x 167.7

Since the early 1970s landscape has become an increasingly powerful subject in Eyre's paintings. Having grown up in rural Saskatchewan and later settled in Winnipeg, Eyre has focused on the terrain of midwestern Canada. He began to paint large-scale landscape panoramas with no human or animal presence. But, as *Highwater* demonstrates, Eyre's deserted landscapes are far from lifeless. His precise and detailed drawing, his choice of radiating and contrasting colours, and the subtly shifting viewpoints combine to create a disquieting vision of a landscape with a life of its own.

As an artist Eyre has sought to minimize the influence of specific trends on his work. He argues that he is not a Realist, and describes his paintings as "geographies of the spirit." Eyre's landscapes are his response to his perception of "the unfolding of life," with all its "viciousness and beauty." "My efforts in painting," he confirms, "have always been with an eye to the eternal – the great mysteries – life, death, love, fate."

Gift of Norcen Energy Resources Limited, 1986   86/52

Chuck Close (American, b. 1940)

Kent 1970-71
Acrylic on canvas. 254.0 x 228.6

Close began to achieve prominence in the late 1960s for his huge, photographically exact, black and white portraits of himself and his friends. He worked in black and white to escape learned colour relations, but in 1970 he introduced colour in this portrait of Kent. Technique becomes the overt content of these paintings of photographs of subjects; their subject is perception.

By using colour transparencies Close began to experiment with a technique similar to photomechanical printing. For "working drawings" he obtained three continuous tone transparencies – one each of red, blue and yellow – and five dye transfer prints from which he produced two coloured pencil studies and a watercolour, which he then used as a colour-key guide to overlaying the three hues in sequence to produce full colour. Placing the dye transfer prints alongside the canvas, he proceeded to paint three one-colour paintings, one on top of the other, first red, then blue, then yellow. He worked from the top down and, staying within the boundaries defined by wrinkles or scars, painted small areas of the face. While painting *Kent*, Close wore tinted filters over his glasses so that he could see only the colour he was applying, in order to maintain constant colour values throughout the work.

Purchase, 1971   70/376

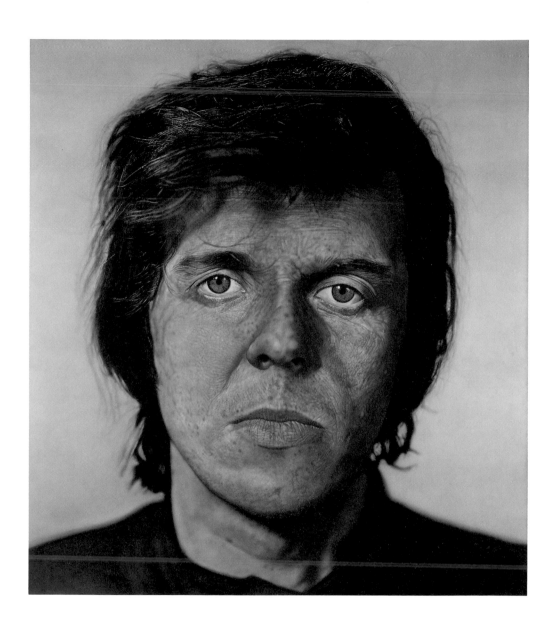

Morris Louis (American, 1912-62)

Lambda 1960-61
Acrylic on canvas. 266.7 x 391.2

After 20 years of conventional, Surrealist-inspired painting, Morris Louis accompanied friend Kenneth Noland on a visit to the New York studio of Helen Frankenthaler. Her free use of materials and techniques and her pictorial eclecticism were a flash of revelation to Louis, inspiring him to develop a style that produced some of the most radical and sensuously beautiful paintings of the 1950s. All of Louis's hundreds of canvases fall within one of four sequential series of works: veils, florals, unfurleds and stripes. *Lambda* is one of the unfurleds, works that allowed colour to speak directly as hue, in natural automatically generated configurations.

Louis's technique consisted of staining acrylic paint directly into lengths of unprimed canvas. With the unfurleds, he poured thinned Magna diagonally from the sides of the canvas and directed it inward, toward the centre and bottom. The unpainted canvas at the centre may have been gathered and folded to prevent accidental marring from spills. And the edges must have been folded in some way for the rivulets are roughly parallel in their flow and could hardly have been manually directed into the configurations that result.

Gift from the Women's Committee Fund, 1965   64/31

Kenneth Noland (American, b. 1924)

C 1964
Acrylic on canvas. Each side: 177.2; diagonal: 250.2

The visit to Frankenthaler's studio also had a profound effect on the career of Kenneth Noland (see opposite page). Shortly afterward both artists developed new techniques of staining raw canvas, which became fundamental to the growth of their respective styles. For Noland it led to a form of impersonal and anonymous abstraction (dubbed by Greenberg as "post-painterly"), whose aim was a fusion of colour, composition, shape, dimension, and surface into a single instantaneous whole. Working always in series both of format and colour, Noland used neutral geometric motifs to explore one group of related hues and then another. Staining served to identify the colour with the surface at the same time that it softened the hard-edged geometrical designs.

Noland first began to work with chevron-shaped images after moving to New York City in 1962. The first of these diamond-shaped pictures were merely squares turned on end, as is *C*, but their particular significance is in the way the design and the picture support are co-extensive, allowing Noland to organize the entire surface of the canvas into zones of colour related to the shape of the picture support and to one another by an explicitly deductive structural logic.

Gift from the Corporation's Subscription Fund, 1965   64/36

Ellsworth Kelly (American, b. 1923)

Blue White 1960
Oil on canvas. 215.9 x 172.7

Kelly's artistic identity was formed while living in Paris from 1948 to 1954, where he encountered the biomorphic abstractions of Arp and the paper cut-outs of Matisse. His best-known works are the bold two-colour compositions of the 1960s of which *Blue White* is a classic example. On first impression they seem impersonal, formal investigations of simple geometric shapes and colours. In fact, Kelly sought to erase all evidence of the artist's personality from his work in order to repudiate the prevailing thesis that art is primarily meaningful as a document of personal experience. He wanted to find a way of composing in which a depiction and its receptacle were one, so as to make visible the pattern of relations in the seemingly random environment. Many of the simple forms he used were developed from studies of plants and *Blue White* is among these. Two closely related works on paper, the ink drawing *Study for "Blue White"* and a collage *Study for "White Blue"*, derived from the drawing of an apple and its stem turned on its side.

Gift from the Women's Committee Fund, 1963   62/63

Kenneth Lochhead (Canadian, b. 1926)

Dark Green Centre 1963
Acrylic on canvas. 212.7 x 208.3

In 1955 Lochhead organized the Emma Lake Artists' Workshops, which brought internationally acclaimed modernist artists and theorists to an otherwise isolated Saskatchewan. Painter Barnett Newman's presence in 1959 and critic Clement Greenberg's lectures in 1962 were particularly crucial for the development of Lochhead and the other members of the Regina Five. This canvas, one of a series, is an experiment in the relationships of hues in geometric configurations and reflects his understanding of Greenberg's formalist aesthetic. The critic included this work in his landmark exhibition *Post-Painterly Abstraction*.

In this canvas Lochhead anchors a cluster of rectangular colour forms, positioned in the middle of an open expanse of canvas, to its bottom edge with a rectangular stem. The solid rectangles touch along subtly modulated edges to hold the design together and to echo the framing shape of the painting. By staining the colours directly into the canvas, Lochhead heightened the effect of shallow pictorial space and created an ambiguous relationship between the luminous forms and the uncoloured ground.

Gift from the McLean Foundation, 1965   64/20

Jack Bush (Canadian, 1909-77)

Dazzle Red 1965
Oil on canvas. 205.7 x 264.2

Bush, a founding member of the Toronto-based Painters Eleven, was one of the pioneers
of abstract painting in this country. Influenced by the brilliantly coloured landscapes
of the Group of Seven and postwar European and American abstraction, Bush used the
perceptual and emotional value of colour in a purely abstract way. Likening the effects
of colour to jazz music, Bush composed paintings using the concordant rhythms of
colour. Brought to the attention of New York critic Clement Greenberg in 1957, Bush
was encouraged to discard the "hot jazz licks" of his imitative abstract expressionist
painting. The subsequent work of Bush and his American contemporaries – Kenneth
Noland, Morris Louis and Jules Olitski – became known under the term coined by
Greenberg, Post-Painterly Abstraction.

    Dazzle Red is part of the *Sash* series, which was begun in the early 1960s and was
said to have been inspired by a mannequin wearing a brightly coloured blouse and
skirt belted with a broad green sash. The *Sash* paintings were explorations into the
formal arrangement of pure flat colour that eliminated the distinction between figure
and ground to emphasize the two-dimensionality of the picture plane. Instead of
making a vigorous expressionist statement, Bush developed a method of staining the
unprimed canvas to achieve a luminescent dialogue between adjacent hues.

Purchase, Corporations' Subscription Endowment, 1966   65/38

Jack Bush (Canadian, 1909-77)

Dipper 1974
Acrylic on canvas. 192.4 x 308.2

In the mature work of the 1970s, Bush returned to an exploration of artistic concerns that had preoccupied him early in his career. Following the abstract expressionist period of the early 1950s, Bush worked on a series known as the *Thrust* paintings, in which he explored opposing forces of varying textures and the interaction between figure and ground. In the work of the 1970s he again explored the nature of contrasting relationships through nonrepresentational compositions.

In *Dipper* the application of unmixed pigment onto the canvas through the use of a sponge or roller created a mottled surface over which was laid the flat, opaque colour bar. Colours abut in hard-edged and soft-edged contrasts, in directional and broken movements, in advancing and receding planes, to create a harmony. The relationship of colour to its environment constitutes the expressive power of the painting rather than one that is created through the association of colour with an image.

Purchase, 1986   86/126

Jules Olitski (American, b. 1922)

Patutsky in Paradise 1966
Acrylic on canvas. 292.0 x 409.0

Within American abstract painting of the 1960s, a major development was the colour field, executed in an impersonal manner and characterized by flatness and optical colour. In 1965 Olitski began spraying paint onto an unsized and unprimed canvas with electrically powered spray guns, which allowed him to reconceive the expansive field of Pollock's drip paintings with colours chosen from an eclectic and expressive palette that in this work is especially sweet and sensuous.

While Olitski's surfaces often achieve considerable illusions of deep and extended space, they cannot be read as infinite visions arbitrarily contained within neutral limits. In *Patutsky* the ethereal mist of pink that seems to float in front of the surface as much as it extends behind it is at second glance securely anchored in a palpable texture of paint often diaphanous enough to reveal the weave of the canvas support. The consciously proportioned shape of the picture and the specificity of its size is underscored by the reiteration of the frame, on both sides and the bottom, with edges drawn by maskings between spray applications. These second frames, with their irregularities and odd slants, add drama and dynamic ambiguity to the singleness of the dominant image.

Purchase, 1982   82/169

Robert Murray (Canadian, b. 1936)

To 1963
Painted aluminum. Tubular column: H. 271.1; planar column: H. 275.0

Murray's career as a painter was radically altered after he met American painter Barnett
Newman in 1959 at a workshop held in Emma Lake, Saskatchewan. Newman, recognizing a shared interest in the effects of large fields of colour on surrounding space,
encouraged Murray to break out of the two-dimensional confines of painting and explore
colour on a large, three-dimensional scale. Murray initiated this new sculptural direction with the production of large, nonreferential colour configurations.

Concerned with monumental scale and purity of structural form, Murray adopted
a reductive approach to sculpture. *To* asserts its verticality through minimal means.
The title, which serves to identify the work rather than to clarify meaning, refers to the
cross-section of the parts that form the letters *T* and *O*. The tubular and planar columns, unified by colour, are played against each other to activate the space between
and around them. By dominating the surrounding area, *To* transforms the perception
of colour into an experience of space.

Gift from the Junior Women's Committee Fund, 1966   65/60

Anthony Caro (British, b. 1924)

Titan 1964
Painted steel. 105.5 x 366.0 x 290.0

Though Caro was working in sculpture from the age of 15, he did not arrive at the methods of his renowned welded constructions until the beginning of the 1960s. Caro's originality sprang from his search for a low centre of gravity, a sort of weightlessness achieved through placing his constructions directly on the ground and expanding them laterally. High-key colour was applied to offset the inertial connotations of the steel and to impose a syntactical precision upon the configurations of disparate forms.

    In 1963 when Caro came to America to teach for a year, he made a series of sculptures of which *Titan* is the pre-eminent example. Each of the seven sculptures utilizes a manufactured piece of steel in the shape of the letter *Z* with right angles. In *Titan* the foot-high, L-shaped wall, though strictly vertical, articulates the ground clearly. The intersecting Z-shapes, at a 45° angle, and the I-beam, at an angle somewhere between the two, seem casually leaned against the *L*. The work achieves a balance and openness and reveals a coherence of the interior relationships that seems spontaneous, almost inevitable.

Gift from the Volunteer Committee Fund, 1983   83/248

André Fauteux (Canadian, b. 1946)

Stairway to Heaven 1978
Painted steel. 25.7 x 338.5

In the late 1960s Fauteux turned to sculpture as a means of breaking the traditional boundaries between media. Blurring the differences between drawing and sculpture, the artist used an open steel frame to create linear, geometric, space-defining shapes. Since the mid-1970s these shapes have grown more complex to increase the number of viewpoints. "In carving or modelling," Fauteux explains, "there are limits to the extension of solid forms in space. You can only cantilever outward within mathematically predicatable limits. I'm fascinated by the possibilities of extension by other means." The artist maintains simply that the work "comes to terms with gravity" and is stable.

    Stairway to Heaven demonstrates Fauteux's conception of "space calling out to be animated" through three-dimensional drawing. Since it is painted in a flat, neutral brown, any distraction from the steel structure is eliminated, and the artist allows the viewer's perception to move freely between negative space and outline.

Purchase, with assistance from Wintario, 1979   79/69

Frank Stella (American, b. 1936)

Ossipee II 1965
Epoxy on canvas. 241.3 x 350.5

Like many of his contemporaries, Stella rejected the emotional and gestural approach
of Abstract Expressionism, emphasizing instead an awareness of the painting as a
palpable object. The features marked out in the infamous *Black Paintings* – utter flatness with a predetermined regularity of design and surface treatment and with the
framing edge as an integral source of the internal design – have been resolutely pursued
and developed by Stella ever since.

    In the mid-1960s Stella began a series of eccentrically shaped polygonal canvases
to which *Ossipee II* belongs. The series consisted of eleven variations on the basic
theme of interpenetrating geometrical shapes and of four differently coloured versions
of each variation. These paintings exploit the spatial ambiguities between the actual
shape of the canvas and the depicted shapes of the surface pattern. The shape on the left
side of *Ossipee II*, for example, can be read either as a parallelogram or as a rectangle
in perspective. The mitred end of the dark green band at the bottom right enhances
the illusion further. Each variation in this series is named after a different town in
New Hampshire.

    Gift from the McLean Foundation, 1966   66/11

357

Guido Molinari (Canadian, b. 1933)

Serial Mutation Green-Red 1966
Acrylic on canvas. 205.7 x 248.9

As Molinari himself states, since the early 1960s his work has been concerned with "the elaboration of a rhythmic structure implying a new definition of space" in his paintings. Inspired by Mondrian's example of a "dynamic plane on which colour rediscovers all its potential energy," Molinari experimented with the spatial character of colour. Between 1964 and 1968 he juxtaposed coloured stripes in a serial pattern to create a variety of spatial structures. According to the artist, "in scanning the vibrant, undulating field of colour bands... the viewer becomes involved in a visual experience of constantly evolving complexity." As the painting is read horizontally, the stripes appear to breathe. The effect of each stripe, however, is modified by the artist's serialized chromatic mutations. "Perception of rhythmic structure," he elaborates, "implies that the perception of chromatic qualities is always evolving and changing in time, and also that it is modified by the perception of chromatic intensities surrounding them." "Painting," Molinari states, "should neither represent nor deal with the object." Rather, it occurs "where energy events take place... which determine a new spatiality and express the new relationships we are establishing with the world." The artist obliterates the distinction between figure and ground to attain "a unity between man and his surroundings," to correspond to "the emotional reality of the internal world" through the subjective interpretation of his colour-time-space continuum.

Purchase, Corporations' Subscription Endowment, 1967   66/32

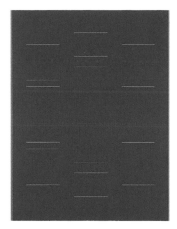

Yves Gaucher (Canadian, b. 1934)

Triptych 1966
Acrylic on canvas. Three panels, each 203.2 x 152.7

After a prolonged period of experimentation with printmaking, Gaucher returned to painting in 1964. *Triptych* represents a specific stage in his evolution as a painter, during which he completed the *Signals, Silences* series. In each monochromatic panel, Gaucher has created a subtle pattern of horizontal lines or "signals." The viewer perceives a change in these signal patterns over time, with the progression from the first red panel, *Signals, Another Summer*, to the less intense ochre panel, *Signals, very softly*, and the tranquil blue panel, *Silences, Silence*.

In 1961 Gaucher first heard the music of Anton Webern and first experienced the mesmerizing effect of Mark Rothko's paintings. In *Triptych* the phenomenon of pulsating signal patterns on evocative colour fields is analogous to Webern's "little darts of sound [sent] out into space." "I don't think rhythm is a musical term," Gaucher explains, "I think it is a term of life.... Rhythm is basically a recurrence of elements in time.... Then it envelops the whole cyclic thought – night and day...the four seasons...the heartbeat. The cycle of life and death is also a rhythmic cycle." *Triptych* comes alive with a slow revelation of the rhythmic expansion and contraction of signals through each stage of the cycle of panels. Gaucher believes that the viewer must "mentally establish this unity" with the work to achieve communion with the "rhythmic dance of creation."

Purchase, with the assistance of the Canada Council Special Purchase Assistance Program and Wintario, 1977   77/62

Claude Tousignant (Canadian, b. 1932)

Gong-88 1967
Acrylic on canvas. 223.5 diameter

As a member of the Plasticiens and L'Association des artistes non-figuratifs de Montréal, Tousignant has been concerned with hard-edge painting since the 1950s. By experimenting with formal structure and colour sequences, he created paintings that, once freed from figural allusion, became "pure sensation."

In 1965 Tousignant broke with the traditional rectilinear canvas shape to interlock formally concentric circles of contrasting colour with the exterior geometry of the work. In each of the *Gongs* of 1966-68, Tousignant uses optical effects "to express the different qualities of chromatic vibrations so that each painting has its own respiration." The viewer actively participates in the optical play between expanding and contracting rings that successively build toward their optimal intensity.

In *Gong-88* Tousignant suggests a certain similarity with the musical instrument, not only in its general appearance, but also in the feeling that one would experience when hitting a gong. The artist visually translates his impression of many particles of sound at different levels, which gradually "decompose" so that "you can perceive more and more separately the high and low sounds." The evenly spaced chromatic changes, chosen and positioned intuitively, coincide with the pattern and movement of sound waves in space. "You first read it as many different coloured circular bands," Tousignant explains, "but as you look at the painting there is established a series of relations and permutations that create movements that can be centrifugal or centripetal."

Gift from the McLean Foundation, 1968   67/18

Yves Gaucher (Canadian, b. 1934)

Green, Brown, Blue and Ochre #3 1974
Acrylic on canvas. 274.3 x 304.8

During the early 1970s, Gaucher rallied his increasingly intense colours into bold, contrasting stripes. This canvas belongs to Gaucher's *Colour Band* series of 1971-77. An energetic yet delicately balanced dialogue between the formal elements of the work is established by Gaucher's juxtaposition of symmetrically structured and finely tuned colour bands. The independence of each colour threatens the unity of the whole, thereby creating an emotionally suspenseful work that is further enhanced by Gaucher's choice of a horizontal format. The left-to-right thrust of each band plays against the vertical dynamism of their interrelationship to create a "complex, multidirectional network" of structural and colourfield tensions. Equal strain is placed on all four edges of the picture plane, and Gaucher has avoided any illusion of depth or three-dimensional form to ensure that the painting functions totally within the shallow space of its surface.

In this work Gaucher has achieved a taut equilibrium of forces and a precise synthesis of intellect, sensibility and emotion in an essential pictorial language.

Purchase, with assistance from Wintario, 1979   78/748

Guido Molinari (Canadian, b. 1933)

Blue Triptych 1973
Acrylic on canvas. 3 panels, each 292.1 x 229.2

In place of the vertical coloured stripes of his earlier work, Molinari experimented with
a variety of hard-edge formal structures, including the triangle, from the end of the
1960s to the mid-1970s. In his bi-triangle paintings, such as this one, Molinari continued
to create a time/space continuum that exists between the viewer and the canvas, but
the aggressiveness of his stripes has yielded to a more contemplative sensory experience.
Inspired by Barnett Newman's broader and more limited colour forms, this work
depends on colour relationships for its subjective emotional effect. "The new paintings,"
Molinari explains, "are part of a logical evolution.... It re-introduced the problem of
gravity into my paintings...using the triangle with its quality of top up, top down...
in a continually growing number of abstract nonassociative possibilities [of colour]."

Purchase, with assistance from Wintario, 1977   77/27

Jean McEwen (Canadian, b. 1923)

Loop-hole Crossing Yellow 1962
Oil on canvas. 190.5 x 152.4

This painting is one of a series of works that investigates the properties of colour in the restructuring of pictorial space. In this canvas McEwen widened the plumb line from an earlier series into a solid binary division. Besides emphasizing the verticality of the work, the central black band creates a spatial tension between the foreground and background and exposes the ground beneath the superimposed layers of colour. By playing upon the opaque and transparent qualities of his colours in a constant permutation of boundaries and planes, McEwen sets the work in motion, thereby creating the appearance of space. The influence of colour upon imagination and mood is also explored in this canvas. "A painting," McEwen states, "is created from rhythm, form, space, light, shade and colour – but it is the feeling, the poetry of the painter, that produces the harmony."

Gift from the McLean Foundation, 1962   61/64

Charles Gagnon (Canadian, b. 1934)

Cassation/Dark/Sombre 1976
Oil on canvas. 228.9 x 203.0

Like the works that precede them – the *Marker* and *Screenspace* series – Gagnon's
Cassation paintings explore the relationship between a two-dimensional canvas that figures a frame within a frame and the rapid brushwork that threatens to override them.
The internal frame in this painting functions as a window through which the viewer may
enter the three levels of the work's existence: the literal, the formal and the semantic.

On the literal level, the activity of making art objects is questioned. Gagnon uses
the frame within the frame, open to the viewer at the bottom, to establish a dialectic
between what is real and what is pictorial, and between art and perception. The frame,
like the camera's aperture, selects only a segment of a larger reality.

On the formal level, the gestural and heavy application of paint in this work
recalls the work of the Abstract Expressionists, who were influential during Gagnon's
stay in New York in the 1950s. By organizing the painting around an internal rectangle,
Gagnon investigates the "temporal and spatial dislocations" created when the painting
is scanned. "I always had a need to work with a structure in mind," adds Gagnon,
"with an intention extremely well-defined in both mental and physical terms."

Gagnon has not provided this canvas with a "directed message," but instead
has established a tension between the art object and its formal structure in order to
reveal the ways by which the viewer knows things and the means by which he or she
transforms them into art in the observing and interpreting mind.

Purchase, with assistance from Wintario, 1978   78/128

Editor's note: Technical limitations prohibit reproduction of The Rose.

Agnes Martin (Canadian, b. 1912)

The Rose 1964
Coloured pencil, graphite on acrylic on canvas. 182.6 x 182.7

Agnes Martin's devotion to the oceanic experience of nature no doubt began during her upbringing on a Saskatchewan wheat farm. She completed an MFA in New York, then travelled between there, Oregon and New Mexico for several years. In New York she met younger artists such as Ellsworth Kelly and Jack Youngerman and witnessed the movement toward pure abstraction that followed Abstract Expressionism. The first wave of her late work coincides with this period and was an evolution from earlier abstract-surrealist, biomorphic modes. From 1961 to 1967 Martin used measured systems of horizontal and vertical lines. In *The Rose*, delicate, irregular, red and black pencil lines inscribe a tremulous grid over an ivory ground – a use of earth colours typical of this period. Paradoxical tensions are created by opposing rectangular units against the square format and the grid's geometric order against its subtly chaotic execution.

Purchase with assistance from Wintario, 1979 78/751

Robert Ryman (American, b. 1930)

Untitled (Basel) 1969
Acrylic, plastic, matboard mounted on honeycomb hardboard.
5 units, each 63.4 x 63.4

Admiring Matisse's economy of means and Malevich's constructivist *White on White* series, Ryman developed a spartan vocabulary typified by square formats, white paint surface, and priority of method over content. Opposing Abstract Expressionism's concern with figure-ground relations and spatial depth, Ryman's approach became more radically reductive in 1965, when his works were simplified to a more modular activity. He concentrated interest in "paint as paint," with no references outside itself, and every physical visual element came to be of aesthetic concern: the sides of the stretcher, scale, method of attachment, wall, and site.

Untitled (Basel) was executed in the year Ryman began experimenting with plastic supports. The modulated surface is achieved by superimposing a horizontally brushed layer of white polymer over a vertical one. Tape marks, the exposed plastic grounds, honeycomb edges, and the intricate play of variation within similarity lend credence to Ryman's belief that "nothing which is visible is indifferent." Although he evades categorization, Ryman's interest in reducing art to basic forms with no ties to representation is shared by Minimalism.

Purchase, 1985   85/394 A-E

Ron Martin (Canadian, b. 1943)

The Heart's Rebellion #18 1975
Acrylic on canvas. 213.4 x 167.6

This canvas belongs to a series of black paintings produced between 1974 and 1981, after the artist underwent a brief but intense period of re-evaluation of his painting activity. To execute this work Martin totally engaged himself physically in the production of his work by placing the canvas on the floor, pouring litres of black paint on the canvas and working it with his hands. A great sense of physicality emerges from the highly turbulent, shiny surface.

This painting breaks away from the minimalist mode by engaging the viewer beyond the sole authority of its "factness." As Martin explains, by grappling with the paint in such a way he is "involved in a perpetual connection of attention" that makes it necessary for the viewer to react immediately "with a continuous connection of impressions."

Purchase, 1975   75/45

Garry Neill Kennedy (Canadian, b. 1935)

Untitled 1977
Acrylic on canvas on hardboard. 76.2 x 76.2

In the mid-1970s Kennedy attempted to "re-invent" painting as a "viable craft." Like
many other artists since the late 1960s who have questioned the traditions of painting, Kennedy went through a period of conceptual experimentation. He decided to
"deconstruct" painting and return to "point zero" in order to free his work from
the confines of representation and expression.

Kennedy turned to the material components and artistic processes of painting,
and as a result works such as this one are about "painting painting itself." Building
only upon irrefutable facts, the artist reasoned: "a painting...is paint on a support";
the most obvious paint material and support is acrylic on canvas, and the most straightforward brush strokes follow the characteristics of the canvas. In this painting the artist
has the brush strokes follow one of the two 60° diagonals in the weave of the canvas
fabric. One of the threads, the first to the right of the red oxide zone, has been left
unpainted, enabling the bare canvas to remain evident. To the right of the bare thread,
however, Kennedy has randomly selected colours to demarcate each subsequent thread
and to cover the remaining canvas. While the left-hand side of the canvas is of a constant thickness, by the time the last diagonal thread in the top right corner is reached,
the slow buildup of 0 to about 680 coats of paint is evident. The meticulousness of
the detailed execution reveals all traces of the time and process of its making and
re-invigorates the craft of painting.

Purchase, with assistance from Wintario, 1978   78/127

369

Robert Morris (American, b. 1931)

Wheels 1963
Painted wood and metal. 121.0 x 92.5 x 121.0

In the early 1960s Morris was one of the most severe of the Minimalist sculptors, contributing some of the movement's most uncompromising objects. *Wheels*, included in
his first one-man show at the Green Gallery, New York, in 1963, illustrates a central
principle of Minimalism in that it signals not so much a radical shift in formal style as a
change in the aesthetic perception demanded of the viewer, which is accompanied
not by a loss in quality or quantity of content but a displacement of the source of
the content away from the object per se and toward the spectator.

   If Modernist sculpture presents itself pictorially for visual confrontation, Minimal
objects shift the emphasis from passive "seeing" to more active "doing," in the way
that Morris's wheels come to life through the impulse to grasp them physically and play
with them. *Wheels* was constructed for use in a performance. It was never so used, but
Morris tells of wrapping himself around the sculpture's axle and rolling with it across
the length of his studio (an experience that in a museum must at best be recreated
imaginatively). *Wheels* is the least static of Morris's Minimalist objects and the most
prophetic in projecting the extended behavioural space of much American sculpture
of the 1970s.

   Gift from the Volunteer Committee Fund, 1977   77/179

370

Carl Andre (American, b. 1935)

Redan original 1964 (destroyed), reconstruction 1970
27 fir timbers, each 30.5 x 30.5 x 91.4;
installation: 91.4 x 106.7 x 622.3

Andre describes the development of his own and 20th-century sculpture as a change of interest from "sculpture as form" to "sculpture as structure" and finally "sculpture as place." With regard to structure, Andre's work is constructed (rather than molded or carved), hence, his use of materials to occupy or carve space.

    Redan is from a group of wood-timber works made from 1960 to 1965 in which Andre abandons the idea of cutting into material in favour of using the material itself as a cut into space. It consists of 27 identical units of timber in a mathematically derived configuration placed directly on the ground and unjoined. Each of the units is interchangeable with the others and when disassembled would be indistinguishable from any other fir timber of similar dimensions. The use of ordinary standardized forms and materials enables the viewer to focus on the way they have been ordered and on their setting. It is with regard to his conception of place and his site-oriented approach that Andre's work takes up its most persistent theme. By reducing art to its simplest terms – standardized units in rigid configurations – Andre became a leading exponent of Minimalism.

Purchased with assistance from the Women's Committee Fund, 1971   71/33

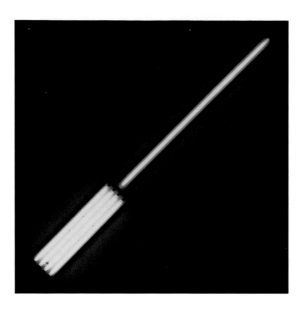

Dan Flavin (American, b. 1933)

The Alternate Diagonals of March 2, 1964 (to Don Judd) 1964
Daylight fluorescent lamps and ballasts. 366.0 x 30.5 x 7.6

Flavin's work was quickly identified with that of Robert Morris, Donald Judd and others. These artists shared the belief that art should be stripped of all associative and illusionistic properties. Their strategies included the use of industrial materials or standardized manufactured objects, geometrically derived configurations, and a preoccupation with the phenomena of perception. Flavin's interest is not only in the space that an object occupies but also the transformations that the object imposes on that space. Using fluorescent light, the works illuminate their surrounding space and create patterns of light and shadow. These pieces find their focus in the interaction between architectural and perceptual elements.

This work went through several transformations before arriving in its present state. When it was first exhibited the 4-foot tubes were red, and it was angled down from a ceiling corner. Later, all the tubes were cool white, and it was placed on the floor on a diagonal from the baseboard. The work is dedicated to Don Judd, Flavin's friend and critic for many years.

Gift from the Women's Committee Fund, 1969   69/63

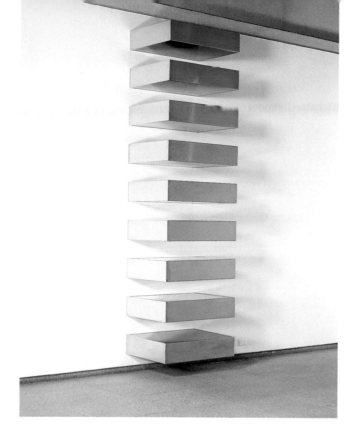

Donald Judd (American, b. 1928)

Untitled 1968
Stainless steel and acrylic sheet. 10 units, each 23.0 x 101.6 x 78.7

Preferring to call his works "specific objects," Judd has attempted to replace conventional notions of composition with a notion of order that arises out of the artist's incremental decisions about scale, colour, materials and so on.

Untitled is an early example of a group of works known as "stacks." It is meant to be comprised of the maximum number of boxes that can be hung vertically from floor to ceiling, the distance between each unit being equal to the height of a single box. While repetition of the units defines the scale of the piece, its containment by the space causes the vertical series to register as a single unit. Nevertheless, each part remains distinct, not subordinated to the whole. Translucent acrylic sheets, forming the top and bottom of each unit, define the interior volume while allowing it to remain visible, creating a visual continuity with the space it occupies. Identical forms repeated in this way give the viewer the same visual experience as seeing that form from different points of view. The viewer is squarely confronted with the differences between what is seen and what is known about the forms used.

Gift of Mr. and Mrs. Roger Davidson, 1970; donated by the
Ontario Heritage Foundation   L70.6

Sol Lewitt (American, b. 1928)

Open Modular Cube 1966
Painted aluminum. 152.4 x 152.4 x 152.4

Lewitt's paintings of the early 1960s were constructivist-derived grids that gradually assumed three-dimensional form. In 1965-66 he made his first modular cube, which he subsequently developed through a series of systematic permutations. Lewitt referred to his work as conceptual art, qualifying it in statements published in 1967: "In conceptual art the idea or concept is the most important aspect of the work.... When an artist uses a conceptual form of art, it means that all the planning and decisions are made beforehand, and the execution is a perfunctory affair. The idea becomes a machine that makes the art."

 The cubes emphasized the spatial intervals within the skeletal grid, the interplay of light and shadow, and the changing perspectival effects, all within the serial repetition of modular forms. This cube was originally exhibited 12 feet away from another one that had slightly smaller dimensions, thus making a playful statement about similarity and difference and directing the viewer to the multiplicity of relationships within the work. In all of Lewitt's work there is a paradoxical tension between the emphasis on the material *presence* of the work and the sought-after immateriality of the art object.

Purchase, 1969 69/62

375

Richard Serra (American, b. 1939)

Untitled (Steel Corner Prop) 1970
Hot rolled steel. Plate: 137.2 x 137.2 x 0.95; bar: 15.2 x 213.4 x 7.6

Stemming from a need to rethink and rename the properties and functions of art, all of Serra's sculptures are concerned with what can actually be experienced and observed. Some reveal the process of their making, some clarify aspects of their physical properties, and others redefine the nature of the space they occupy.

With the series *Prop Pieces* begun in the late 1960s, Serra focused his attention on the physical properties of sculpture, its weight and materials, and the principles of the work's construction. Weighted and cantilevered against each other, the floor and the wall, the steel plate and pole of this untitled corner prop are joined to effect not an *illusion* of balance but an *actual* balance. The work's structure reflects the dichotomy between the seeming stability of the material and its potential for disorder. Held together solely by weight and the force of gravity, the work's precariousness alludes to the potential for change and movement, thus suggesting the temporal conditions of perceptual experience.

Purchase, 1970   70/174

Royden Rabinowitch (Canadian, b. 1943)

Medium Grease Cone 1969
Steel and grease. 178.0 x 184.0

In the early 1960s Royden Rabinowitch began to develop a sculpture that was a "fully articulated internally determined body." Completed in 1964, his first major series, entitled *Barrel Constructions*, led him to this conclusion. This series also revealed to him the notion of duration, which was determined by the methods of construction, which in turn defined the internal nature of the piece and the temporal process by which it is internalized through an accumulation of experiences as the work is apprehended by the viewer. Articulation was lacking, and in order to achieve his aim he proceeded to examine closely "internal physical conditions."

The series of *Grease Cones* is such an attempt. In *Medium Grease Cone* the surface of the steel cone is obscured by grease that is thickly laid on in broken horizontal strokes. Through an awareness of both the materials and what constitutes the limits of acting in space, the viewer knows the internal nature of the cone is other than what is perceived optically. Such considerations, and the contrasting inherent qualities of hollow/solid, static/fluid, and soft/hard in the piece, demand the implication of the whole body. Consequently the artist concluded that the somatic properties were to be foremost in the conception of any sculptural body. Although this cone represents a specific investigation on the part of its maker, it nevertheless exemplifies the above concern and becomes for the viewer an exercise in experiencing total space.

Gift of Sandra and Joseph Rotman, 1987   86/205

378

David Rabinowitch (Canadian, b. 1943)

Metrical (Romanesque) Construction in 5 Masses and 3 Scales #2 1978
Mild steel. 15.2 x 457.2 x 457.2

On his first trip to Cologne, in 1971, David Rabinowitch began studying Romanesque
churches. That same year he incorporated various 'vertical scale' constructions in
his sculpture.

No ideal form or particular law of composition is sought in this work; instead,
it questions the relationship of part to whole and whole to part (Romanesque architecture offers many considerations in that respect). Literality of presence confronts the
viewer in the extensive horizontal mass. The vertical holes introduce light into the
mass, working as "reference standard for location." From every viewpoint there arise a
complexity in perception, a variety of contours, a new interplay of different axes, and a
constellation of extended surfaces. This work resists and escapes unification. According to the sculptor, we thus become "discoverers of the structure of our own judge-
ment with a world we experience as external and fully achieved desire." *Metrical
(Romanesque) Construction* acquires its meaning through the viewer's vision; his or her
relationship to it is strictly empirical. The sculpture thus confronts the spectator
with his or her individual modes of cognition.

Purchase, with assistance from Wintario, 1978   78/130

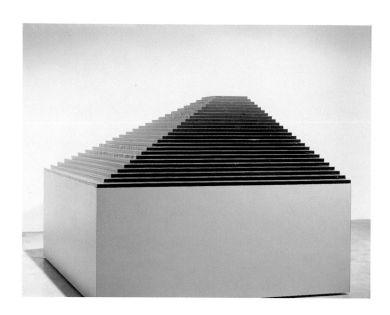

Robert Smithson (American, 1938-73)

Glass Strata 1969
Glass. 25 sheets, each square 2.5 cm thick; length and width range in 5.08 cm increments from 25.4 to 147.5

As the pre-eminent exponent of Earth Art, Smithson created such extraordinary works as *Spiral Jetty* in Great Salt Lake, Utah, and *Amarillo Ramp* in Texas. They embodied some of the most revolutionary thinking about sculpture to emerge from a generation that included Morris, Judd and Serra. In common with those of his Minimalist colleagues, his earliest sculptures are lean, geometric pieces made of such industrial materials as steel and aluminum. His goal was to straddle formalist and conceptual approaches so that historical and symbolic references, which had been excised from formalist art, could be reclaimed.

From the mid-1960s forward Smithson's work begins to reflect his growing interest in geology and landscape. While making his first *Glass Stratas*, his research was focused on the geologic processes of crystallization and stratification. In these works the sheets of glass look rational and precise, like the regularly layered planes that occur in such crystals as mica, but on the molecular level, glass is amorphous, a disordered and random structure. This dichotomy between appearance and reality was a central issue for Smithson's work.

Purchased with assistance from the Junior Committee Fund, 1981   80/210

Michael Snow (Canadian, b. 1929)

Atlantic 1967
Metal, wood, photographs, arborite. 171.1 x 245.1 x 39.9

Reproducing thirty times one photograph of the final scene from his film *Wavelength*, Snow created this photo-sculptural piece. When viewed as a whole, the box construction housing the photographs forms a grid that frames the repeated image of rolling waves as cinematic stills. "Film," he explains, is simply an agglomeration of "fast stills." In *Atlantic*, by freezing a single moment of rolling waves, Snow fixes "something which has stopped within the flux of what's going on." By the multiplication of the image, this moment is then extended over time and space to emphasize "the cosmic continuity, which is beautiful but tragic: it goes on without us."

Since 1964 Snow has been interested in the frame as a means to qualify an image as art. "Art is often a limitation, a focusing-in on things," he explains. "When you narrow down your range and are looking through just that small aperture of the lens, the intensity of what you see is so much greater." Within each of the reflective metal boxes the two-dimensional photograph in *Atlantic* is magnified into a three-dimensional illusion – an encapsulated reality.

Purchase, 1980   79/339

Dennis Oppenheim (American, b. 1938)

Condensed 220 Yard Dash 1969
Plaster casts and b/w photographs. 1 photo: 43.0 x 60.7;
6 photos, each 43.0 x 61.6; installation: 61.0 x 457.2 x 45.7

Oppenheim abandoned conventional sculpture in 1967 and in keeping with his focus on the idea and the processes of transformation, he took up a variety of means for applying his ideas about the circulation and transfer of energy. He first became known for his earthworks in which he superimposed symbols with social and political meaning onto a specific geographical site. Not long after, he introduced his body into his work, first merely as substance and material energy, later as persona and mental and psychological energy.

This installation marks Oppenheim's transition from land to body as his principal material. In the fall of 1969, Oppenheim ran 220 yards in a lot behind the Edmonton Art Gallery. Each footprint was carefully cast in plaster, using a one-foot square wooden frame. The dash was also recorded in photographs and on video. Consistent with Oppenheim, involvement with time, energy and location, the casts and photographs seek to transform a specific activity into a concrete material. By removing the distance between each footprint, he compresses the space and the impression of condensed time alludes to that very physical, energetic moment. That each block is numbered, dated and signed by Oppenheim further establishes his claim on that moment.

Gift from the Volunteer Committee Fund, 1978   78/112

Richard Long (British, b. 1945)

Sandstone Circles 1981
Credit Valley sandstone (about 205 stones). D. 8.84 m

Throughout the 1970s every boundary of form and medium was stretched. Words and gestures, performance, environmental interventions – all were accepted as appropriate artistic devices. The device that Long has developed is walking. Bound by rules of time or distance, he sometimes leaves traces of his passage – groups of twigs or stones displaced from his path and arranged in basic geometric shapes such as a line, a circle, cross or spiral. All that remains is the photographic record.

Long sees the earth as a surface of traces – those of passage, habitation, history and memory. His sculptures in the landscape, impermanent and without witness, are traces of his own fleeting presence in that place.

The sculptures that Long devises for public museums are independent of his walks but use similar geometric forms. They are sometimes composed of materials gathered on walks but more often are made of materials at hand. *Sandstone Circles* is made from Credit Valley sandstone obtained in Toronto and constituted part of Long's first exhibition in Canada. It is meant to complement the memory of the exterior works, but unlike photographic or written documentation the sculpture is "real," present in time and space, and thus constitutes a direct evocation of the experience of the landscape.

Purchase, 1981   81/157

Joyce Wieland (Canadian, b. 1931)

The Water Quilt 1970-71
Fabric, embroidery thread, thread, metal grommets, braided rope,
ink, painted wood. 121.9 x 121.9

Wieland's experience of the highly competitive art scene in New York, where she
lived from 1962 to 1971, polarized her view of life. She began to equate discrimina-
tion against women with the exploitation of Canada by other nations. By the mid-
1960s Wieland was using quilts to convey her political message, since the collaborative
nature of a quilt functioned symbolically of the way a country may be drawn to work
together. The quilt allowed Wieland "to elevate and honour craft, to join women
together and make them proud of what they had done." She also combined her feminist
and nationalist interests with ecological issues in "an art [form] that could embrace
these concerns and also retain beauty, texture, humour." Each of the 64 pillows making
up the quilt is covered by a flap on which an arctic flower has been embroidered.
Under each of these symbols of Canada's virgin northland is ironically hidden an
excerpt from James Laxer's book *The Energy Poker Game*, which details an American
plot to expropriate Canada's water supply.

    Wieland believes that her work should speak to and express the people's con-
science, "to give the people of Canada a sense of themselves."

Purchase, with assistance from Wintario, 1977   76/221

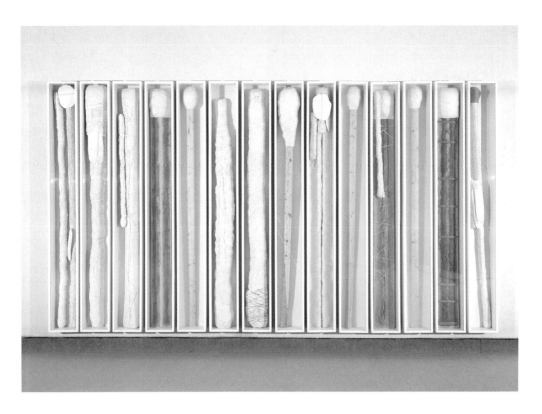

Irene F. Whittome (Canadian, b. 1942)

The White Museum II 1975
Mixed media. Each box: 220.0 x 361.0 x 16.0

An underlying concern in Whittome's work is the relationship that exists between museum, art object, artist and viewer. This dialectic is elaborated not so much by rejecting the museum structure as by creating a parallel one.

Notions of collecting, preserving and exhibiting works of art that result in a conditioning of the viewer's participation are inherent in all museums. *The White Museum II* recreates similar conditions. The setting apart of the forms against a white background in glass-covered boxes that are then neatly lined up against the wall transforms each piece into an archetypal museum object. The viewer is also faced with works that are easily assimilated to objects collected in anthropological museums, and readily endows them with an aura of fetishism. Their anthropomorphic configurations and the use of organic materials stir a collective memory of a primitive, archetypal past.

For Whittome repetition is process, as is evidenced in the formal structure of the pieces and in the continuous act of binding the wooden poles with string. This process is a somewhat obsessive attempt to arrive at the natural structure of things. In the same way, repetition is to be found in the classificatory devices used in museums, which constitute the process around which these institutions evolve.

Purchase, 1988   88/139

Jackie Winsor (American, b. 1941)

Glass Piece 1978-79
Wood, glass, tar. 79.7 x 79.7 x 79.7

Winsor matured as an artist in the late 1960s and early 1970s, which is apparent in her use of regular geometric forms and structures. Unlike the output of many of her Minimalist colleagues, evidence of craftsmanship and painstaking methods of working remain obvious in her work. The contradiction between her simplified forms and the complexity and deliberation with which they are put together provides a tension to the work that is echoed in other dualities: solid versus hollow, smooth versus rough.

This principle of contradiction can be seen at work in *Glass Piece*. Panes of glass are affixed with putty in all but the central square of each face. An oily film from the putty clouds the glass, imparting a sense of opacity to the glass and the space it encloses. Yet the glass allows the viewer's gaze to penetrate to the work's interior and at the same time prevents physical access. The open squares at the centre of each face allow a hand to be inserted into the interior space, again contradicting the impression made by the glass. This balancing of opposites continues to characterize Winsor's work in the 1980s, while the process by which the materials and structures reveal themselves has grown more powerful and dramatic.

Purchase, with assistance from Wintario, 1979   78/758

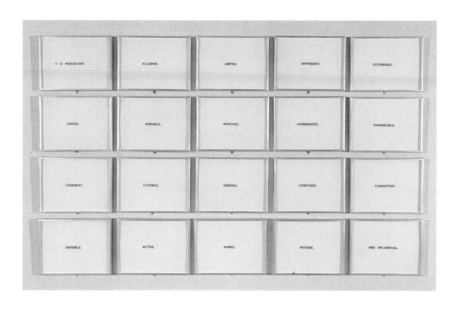

Robert Barry (American, b. 1936)

An Artwork with 20 Qualities 1970
Ink stencil on wove paper. 20 units, each 22.8 x 30.5

Beginning in the mid-1960s a number of artists undertook a fundamental re-examination of the function of art and the artist within a rapidly changing social and cultural context. For these artists the creation of an art object was strictly subservient to the creation of a concept in the mind of the viewer. This position offered an idealistic challenge to the privileged status of art objects and in the process admitted all manner of "extra-art" materials, procedures and content to the production of art. Like Weiner, Kosuth and others, Barry adopted words as his principal medium.

Around 1969-70 Barry made a group of word pieces that present series of short, descriptive words or phrases typed singly or in columns on standard sheets of paper. Many of these works, such as this one, were directed against assumptions about art and its institutions. *An Artwork with 20 Qualities* consists of a list of words indicating a number of qualities that may be imagined, specified and connected by the viewer. The work demonstrates the infinite possibilities of linguistic recontextualization. It depends on a viewer who is prepared to trust experience over expectations and to accept the myriad connotations that the artist evokes.

Purchase, 1984   84/768.1-.20

UTTERANCE   /MEH/
GLOSS   THAT IS A 'MAN'
FUNCTION   EXISTENCE
AGE   17.16   FEB 11 1975

UTTERANCE   /MEH/
GLOSS   THAT IS A 'MAN'
FUNCTION   EXISTENCE
AGE   17.16   FEB 11 1975

T2 2.11.75

      CONTEXT: M(mother) getting K(son) ready for bed. 20.00 HRS.
      SPEECH EVENT(S)   /meh/R8
8.1 M. Where's Kelly going, on Mommy's desk? (climbing up to get
     a screwdriver)
     Look! (taking K from desk to window to distract him)
    K. /ka/ (sees car)
     /mu/ (points out moon)
     /meh/ meh/ e meh/ (referring to both men and women)
    MOST FREQUENT UTTERANCES: /meh/ e meh/ ka/ e ka/ gah/ bu/
    MEAN LENGTH OF UTTERANCE: 1.38   17 months, 16 days

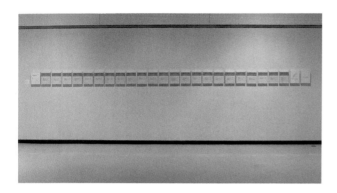

Mary Kelly (American/living and working in England, b. 1941)

Post-Partum Document, Part II 1974, 1975
Mixed media. 31 units, each 36.0 x 28.4; 26 units, each 25.8 x 20.7

Mary Kelly, sharing Conceptual Art's distaste for aesthetic objects, uses theoretical analyses to make works rooted in her involvement with feminist issues. Compiled during the first six years of her son's life, *Post-Partum Document* is a six-part, 135-piece record. Kelly comments: "I am trying to show the reciprocity of the process of socialization in the first few years of life. It is not only the infant whose future personality is formed at this crucial moment, but also the mother, whose 'feminine psychology' is sealed by sexual division of labour in child care." *Part I* (*Analysed Faecal Stains and Feeding Charts*) presents a series of soiled diaper liners, each with text that records feeding and diapering activities. *Part II* (*Analysed Utterances and Related Speech Events*) (detail shown on opposite page) comprises a series of transcribed, mother-child verbal exchanges, each combined with a rubber-stamp system that classifies the infant's speech development. Kelly uses pseudo-scientific method and psychoanalytical information to analyze how the intersubjective relationship between herself and her son is eroded. Through the process of weaning – from the breast, from programmatical communication – they are both displaced to roles fraught with trauma in the social order.

Gift from the Junior Committee Fund, 1987   87/46, 87/47

On Kawara (Japanese, b. 1933)

AUG. 5, 1981 "Wednesday" ("Today" Series No. 26) 1981
Acrylic on canvas, cardboard container. Canvas: 25.8 x 33.3; container: 27.0 x 34.5

Kawara began his series of *Date Paintings* in 1966. Each painting was done on the day specified in the work itself and accompanied by a box to fit, which also contained newspaper clippings read on that day. All the date paintings made in one year are recorded in a journal in the language of the country where Kawara spent the first day of the year, or in Esperanto. A calendar from the same country is used to enter the date and size of the paintings. Samples of the original colour used for each painting form another section of the journal. The subtitles of the date paintings – newspaper headlines until 1972, and, subsequently, the day of the week – are listed in the language of the place where they were made, or in Esperanto.

Kawara has begun several other similar series with such titles as *I Read, I Met, I Went, I Got Up*, and *One Million Years*. Any isolated element from this body of work may appear as one of those fleeting and ephemeral gestures that typified much of Conceptual Art. Within the whole, each single self-evident action, recorded in some commonly accepted system of articulation, marks a boundary – from unconscious to conscious, from private to public, from here to there, from past to future.

Purchase, 1982   82/3

MANY THINGS BROUGHT FROM ONE CLIMATE TO ANOTHER TO MAKE A GROUPING OF THINGS NOT RELATED TO THE CLIMATE AT HAND

Lawrence Weiner (American, b. 1940)

Many Things Brought from One Climate to Another to
Make a Grouping of Things Not Related to the Climate at Hand 1981
Language and the materials referred to

Weiner's medium is language – a concrete, precise medium that designates, according to the artist, "relationships of human beings to objects and objects to objects in relation to human beings." His sentences, based in the referential capacity of language, designate content only. Appended to all of his works is the statement "the artist may construct the work/ the work may be fabricated/ the work need not be built/ each being equal and consistent with the intent of the artist, the decision as to condition rests with the receiver upon the occasion of receivership." The provision makes clear that the work need not be executed in order for it to exist, since the words are sufficient to transmit visual form and meaning, and the work can assume unlimited forms, both physically and in the imagination of the viewer. Thus, works have appeared as statement only or as objects (buttons, posters, comics) realized by the artist, or by others, or surreptitiously chalked on sidewalks or in art museums.

 Many Things makes a specific statement of an action: "brought from one climate to another to make a grouping"; and contains a general description: "many things." Geography and a faint trace of the procedures of decontextualization are implied by "not related." The idea or image that occurs to the viewer will depend on the context in which the work is presented and on the personal references of the particular viewer. The form and content – the materiality of language – remain constant.

Purchase, 1981 81/3

Michelangelo Pistoletto (Italian, b. 1933)

The Orchestra of Rags: Il Grande Carro 1968
Rags, glass, electric hot plates, whistling kettles, stones

In addition to his famous mirror paintings, Pistoletto has produced works in performance, film, video and installation formats. His association with *Arte Povera* was a
natural extension of his liberation from the dogma of style and the hierarchy of media.
The Orchestra of Rags is considered to be a major work of that movement. Piles of
multicoloured rags support panes of glass under which kettles on hot plates whistle and
steam, sending up clouds of mist that condense on the underside of the glass. Seven of
these piles are arranged in the shape of the Big Dipper. Multiple sensations and layers of
illusion are aroused. The immediate experience of the smells and sounds of these
whimsical hearths, reminiscent of a domestic environment, opens out into the space
and eternal perspective evoked by the stellar configuration. An orchestra of sensations
and evocations join the immediate and the definite with the distant and the imaginary.

Gift of Vivian and David Campbell, 1988   88/99

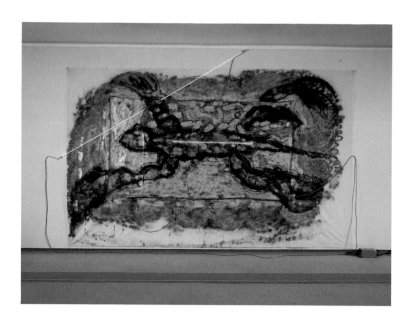

Mario Merz (Italian, b. 1925)

Crocodile in the Night 1979
Oil, metallic paint, and charcoal on fabric, neon lances,
electrical hardware. 274.0 x 435.0

In the mid-1960s Merz began to incorporate commonplace objects into his sculptural installations in an effort to free art from fixed and prescriptive programs. His view of art as a continuous process for transformation led him in 1968 to become associated with the *Arte Povera* movement. Neon, organic and found materials were used by Merz throughout the 1970s in increasingly complex installations that demonstrated the constant interaction between the natural and the cultural, between stability and flux. The ideas that underlie these works refer to proliferation and growth in spatial and temporal structures and to the unity of biological and creative processes.

Since 1979 Merz has returned to painting. His subjects are typically vegetal forms and primitive beasts. *Crocodile in the Night* is exemplary in its conjunction of antithetical materials and its improvisational look. The crocodile, archetype of ferocity and power and reminder of the vulnerability of human flesh, seems to be rendered helpless by the vaporous shaft of neon that traverses the axis of its body. It is as if the threat of nature were immobilized in the glow of packaged desire.

Purchase, 1982   82/22

394

Luciano Fabro (Italian, b. 1936)

Germany (La Germania) 1984
Steel, metal, glass, electrical elements, sandbags.
Installation: 285.0 x 975.0 x 177.0

In the early 1960s Fabro began exhibiting installations that used everyday objects and banal materials. These "occasions for experiences" were based on the premise that the viewer's interaction with the environment of a work are crucial elements to the work's realization. This attention to phenomenological experiences as the substance of a work, coupled with the effort to retrieve art from preconceived aesthetic categories, aligned Fabro with the *Arte Povera* movement since its inception in 1967.

In Fabro's best-known works, the *Italy* series, the country's silhouette is rendered in many different sensuous materials as a running commentary on Italy's rich cultural traditions and postwar boom. A homologous strategy is used in *La Germania*. A long iron pole slants upward from amid a pile of sandbags. Near the top two large steel slabs – the silhouettes of East and West Germany – are supported and loosely bolted together. From the top of the pole a streetlight casts a glaring light directly onto the slabs. History and political reality are intellectual and emotional subjects here, but the artist's position is equivocal: the sandbags can evoke both the idea of defence and the possibility of construction, as though to suggest that the conditions of existence within political conflict are both "normal" and inhumane.

Purchase, 1985   84/943

Jannis Kounellis (Greek, b. 1936)

Untitled 1982-85
Steel, wood, paint, plaster, wool, burlap. 487.0 x 964.0 x 45.0

Motivated by a heady form of social idealism that permeated intellectual culture in
Europe in the 1960s, Kounellis abandoned painting to begin making installations and
performances that incorporated natural elements (live animals, fire), abandoned bits of
everyday objects (bedframes, burlap sacks), music, and fragments of classical sculpture. Associated with the *Arte Povera* movement, such means and strategies were meant
to foster a re-integration of art and life.

    Untitled is made of stacked burlap sacks and steel shelves on which collected frag-
ments are placed. The decaying pieces of wood and the plaster-cast fragments of
classical sculptures embody the artist's feeling of the fragmentation of European life and
culture since the World Wars. Things wrapped in blankets are multilayered references
to blocked vision, the inability to see through history. The sacks signify both commerce and travel; it is in burlap bags that materials such as coffee beans are measured
and traded, and thus by which both goods and culture are diffused. Kounellis's use
of wood fragments also speaks to the need to put together again the fragments of
history and to build anew.

Purchase, 1985   83/230, 85/410

Helga Matura

Gerhard Richter (German, b. 1932)

Helga Matura 1966
Oil on canvas. 178.5 x 109.7

Helga Matura is a typical example of Richter's Photo-Paintings, a series of realistic, if out-of-focus, copies of photographs that the artist began shortly after his arrival in Düsseldorf from East Germany in 1961. Rejecting the personal expressionism of Art Informel and influenced by the Fluxus movement and Pop Art, Richter turned his attention to the non-art photography of journalism and amateur snapshots as the most reliable and detached record of visual reality.

But photographs, he found, were curiously inadequate. If they were supposed to capture objective reality with precision, examined closely they dissolved either into a seamless modulation of tones or an infinity of evenly spaced dispersions of grains. Richter's techniques of streaking, blurring or erasing became painting's counterparts for photography's technological shortcomings with the consequence that our experience of a Photo-Painting then becomes an analogy for our elusive hold on reality itself. On the one hand, *Helga Matura* seduces us by its claim to objective representativeness and on the other refuses us by its out-of-focus effect that disrupts expectations and frustrates both visual and intellectual possession. (*Helga Matura*, prettily posed here on a grassy bank, was a Frankfurt prostitute who made newspaper headlines in 1966, when she was brutally murdered.) So if art can never capture reality's substance, it can at least reconstruct our experience of its paradoxical resistance.

Gift from the Volunteer Committee Fund, 1986   86/127

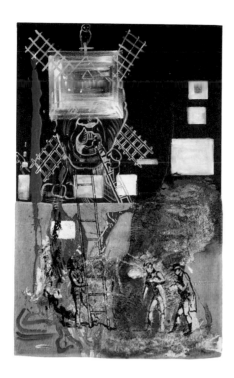

Sigmar Polke (German, b. 1941)

Sign: Measurement of the Stones in the Wolf's Belly and the Subsequent Grinding
of the Stones Into Cultural Rubble (Tafel: Vermessung der Steine im Bauch des Wolfes
und das anschliessende Zermalen der Steine zu Kulturschutt) 1980-81
Mixed media on fabric. 184.5 x 118.0

The work of Sigmar Polke is impossible to categorize. Since his earliest Pop-oriented
paintings of the 1960s, Polke has defied conventional techniques and debunked artistic
and social clichés. He has appropriated imagery from the banal forms of photography, comic books and wallpaper; he has employed such unusual grounds for his paintings as woollen blankets, furs, packaging foil and domestic fabric bought by the roll
in department stores. Polke's concern with the trivial and ornamental aspects of con-
sumer culture is then mixed up with the rhetoric of romantic mysticism and Pop trans-
cendentalism. The result is an art of provocation, irony, dissimulation and wit. These
features are all present in *Tafel*. The title, long-winded as it is, is full of conflicting
references both banal and profound and contains wordplay difficult to capture in the
translation. For example, the "stones in the wolf's belly" are from a traditional children's story and may also refer to a passage by Nietzsche that in turn refers to the
children's tale.

Purchase, 1984   84/767

A. R. Penck (German, b. 1939)

Standard 3 (Standart 3) 1974
Acrylic on canvas. 272.3 x 282.0

Born Ralf Winkler in Dresden, Penck adopted his pseudonym from the 19th-century scientist Albrecht Penck, who studied the geomorphology of the glacial epoch. Similar to his namesake, Penck analyzes the language of art for its potential to describe the morphology of everyday existence. In the mid-1960s he studied mathematics and cybernetics and refined his idea of pictorial language as a language of signs. These studies led to a systemization of his pictorial signs, which he called *Standart*. Flattened stick figures, hieroglyphs, objects, and abstract symbols of power and oppression are combined in endless permutations. *Standart* developed partly in response to the East German reality of severe limitations imposed on individuals and the processes of experimentation and growth. Conceived as a didactic model, *Standart* exhibitions often included exhortatory texts.

Penck emigrated to the West in 1980. In recent paintings he has begun to use volumetric forms and illusionistic space, alternating and combining these with his earlier mode.

Gift from the Volunteer Committee Fund, 1983   83/379

Georg Baselitz (German, b. 1938)

Group # 13, Nude and Tree (Gruppe # 13, Akt und Baum) 1979
Oil and egg tempera on plywood. Each panel: 250.0 x 170.0

Baselitz has developed a figurative style of painting in an attempt to retain content, cultural identity and history – all features absent in the formalist abstraction that had dominated the art of postwar Western Europe.

The most controversial feature of Baselitz's work is that his images, though still recognizable, are painted upside down in broad, expressionistic gestures, thus forcing the viewer to consider figurative subjects as abstract forms. Though the paintings are endowed with psychological and political relevance, the conflicting claims of abstraction and representation are the constant theme of Baselitz's work, and in this painting some of his most typical strategies are demonstrated. Nudes and landscape are among the most banal of subject matter and thus work against any serious reading of subjective or emotional content. The tree, with both roots and branches depicted, has no clear top or bottom. Numerous visual references to previous styles of Modern painting invert expressionistic claims, making clear that imagery is subservient to the materiality of paint.

Gift from the Volunteer Committee Fund, 1983   83/223

Jörg Immendorff (German, b. 1945)

Hü 1984
Acrylic on canvas. 285.0 x 400.0

In 1978 Immendorff began work on the *Café Deutschland* series of paintings, in response
to discussions with fellow artist A. R. Penck. Holding to the belief that art can and
must effect social change, he saw this series as a means to express his views on the cultural and political situation in Germany. In *Hü* we find his typical pastiche of ideo-
logical symbols, caricatures of personalities both historical and contemporary, and
frenzied, vertiginous space. Besides Hitler (left foreground, painting the destruction of
Europe) and Lenin (in the right foreground with Walter Ulbricht, East Germany's first
chancellor) are found Immendorff's friends, artists Georg Baselitz and A. R. Penck
(behind Lenin, second table, right). At the back of the café is Victory from atop the
Brandenburg Gate – the ultimate symbol of the partition between West and East
Germany and a potent reminder of continuing political aggression. Eagles peck at the
windows and floating above the scene, carved in ice (a reference to the Cold War), is the
title of the work, *Hü*, a German word, which provocatively means both stop and go.

Gift from the Volunteer Committee Fund, 1985   84/938

Mimmo Paladino (Italian, b. 1948)

Wayfarer (Viandante) 1983
Oil, wood, plaster with papier mâché on canvas mounted on wood. D. 320.0

Paladino belongs to that generation of young Italian artists called the *transavantguardia* by critic Achille Bonito Oliva. Along with such painters as Chia, Clemente and Cucchi, he has turned away from a political and social orientation to a more subjective approach that draws on diverse archeological and stylistic sources. His absorption in the physical act of painting acts as a channel for spontaneous psychological projection and leads to odd mixtures of emotion and decoration and to preoccupation with apocalyptic and Christian iconography. Recurrent motifs of death and disembodiment mingle with unspecified rituals and images of creation. Tondi and triptychs are frequent in his work, along with other material references to traditional religious art. In *Viandante* and other works since 1983, he attaches sculptural forms of carved or battered wood to the surface of the canvas, adding to its fetishistic qualities. The typical images of shrouded and cadaverous figures, floating heads, fish and serpents are caught in *Viandante* in a whirlpool of lurid red paint.

Gift from the Volunteer Committee Fund, 1984   84/66

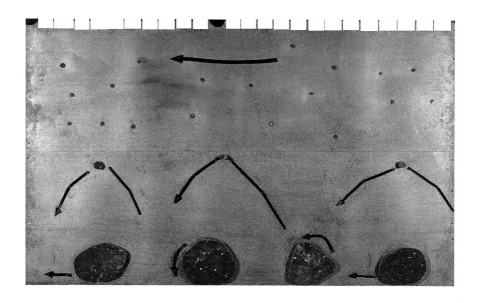

Paterson Ewen (Canadian, b. 1925)

Rocks Moving in the Current of a Stream 1971
Metal, engraved linoleum, plywood, acrylic paint. 153.3 x 245.3

In 1971, after he had already established a reputation for himself in Montreal, where he tried to find a path between the ways opened up by the Automatistes and the Plasticiens, Ewen abandoned painting as it is traditionally defined. *Rocks Moving in the Current of a Stream* hardly qualifies as a painting at all, with the support of canvas completely absent. Metal was the medium that replaced paint in mimicking certain qualities in the appearance of natural phenomena. "I needed something that looked and felt like water, but I didn't want to paint it on. I wanted to have something laid on and I thought of galvanized iron."

In turning to the natural world, Ewen did not want to merely reproduce the appearance of a landscape. He wanted the materials functionally to assume the look of a particular phenomenon. And so the imagery retains a rudimentary sign function, almost like a high school textbook: to the galvanized iron representing water, Ewen added shapes cut from plywood to stand for rocks, stones and pebbles moving in a current, their motion signified by the arrows and their location in water indicated by the standardized ripples at the top.

Purchase, 1983 83/27

404

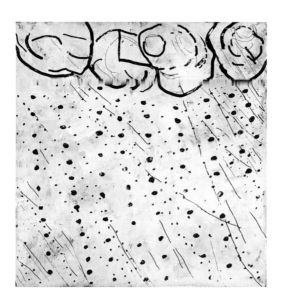

Paterson Ewen (Canadian, b. 1925)

Precipitation 1973
Acrylic on gouged plywood. 244.0 x 229.0

Ewen originally worked in wood, starting in 1971, as a means by which to produce a woodcut image drawn from its inked surface. But he soon realized that the gouged image on standard sheets of plywood was the work itself. The major break in Ewen's career was "to go from canvas and abstract painting to wood and imagery." But as important for the look of imagery was the substitution of an electric router for hand gouging. This change of tool in 1973 characterizes all his subsequent works, and the great series of paintings of 1973-74 to which *Precipitation* belongs, dealing with rain, clouds, hail and water, are given a bold graphic treatment, as Ewen wields the router with the skill of a draughtsman.

The images of these works are a consequence of the confrontation of tools and materials. And the forces Ewen reveals in drawing the image from the wood have more to do with phenomena than with landscapes: "phenomascapes," he called them. Like all the work of this period, *Precipitation* blends the schematic representation of a weather system with the painterly effects of the phenomena of light and space.

Purchase, 1988 88/5

Murray Favro (Canadian, b. 1940)

Van Gogh's Room 1973-74
35mm colour transparency, projector, painted wood.
Installation: 365.7 x 975.3 x 259.1

Van Gogh's Room is part of a series of projected reconstructions in which London,
Ontario artist Murray Favro explores the nature of human perception and cognition. Fascinated by the peculiar, distorted perspective of van Gogh's famous painting *Vincent's
Bedroom at Arles*, Favro has reconstructed a life-size, three-dimensional mock up of the
artist's room to correspond to a projected slide of van Gogh's painting. As the projected
image illuminates the constructed set, it not only enlivens and colours the objects, it
also triggers for the viewer a recognition of the identity of the scene.

    Favro is interested in the discrepancies between the two-dimensional projected
image and the three-dimensional space – for instance, the confusion between real
and projected shadows. The disjunction of constructed objects from their appearance
through the projection evokes a sense of mystery and functions as a complex metaphor
for the ways in which meaning is projected onto objects. The mechanical apparatus of
projection can be considered analogous to the ways in which reality is created by a
mental projection, not unlike the way in which paint creates an image on white canvas
or the way in which van Gogh's imagination produced the intensity of early Expressionism. Challenging the notion that images are true representations of reality, Favro's
work insists instead that everyone projects his or her conceptual models onto reality
and thereby constructs the coherence of the world.

Purchase, 1975   74/361

Eric Fischl (American, b. 1948)

White House 1975
Mixed media on fabric on wood panel.
H. 152.6 (width and depth irregular)

Fischl is well known for his large paintings depicting middle-class sexuality. His international reputation has grown phenomenally since his first figurative paintings of 1979. Prior to that Fischl was engaged in a struggle between the formalist painting that he had practised throughout his studies and a preoccupation with narrative and subjective meaning. His experimentation with figuration began when he cut two corners from one of his abstract works and made the association with the shape of a house. By turning it around it became a boat, a shield and so on. From 1975 on he exhibited the painted rectangular shapes accompanied by words and puns. Like the other identifiable objects that began to populate his paintings, houses are invested with personal history, projected values, and memory. Following the painting of *White House*, Fischl committed himself to a totally figurative style in which the house motif is transformed into the suburban American home, site of intrafamilial relationships, with ethical, erotic and social implications.

Purchase, 1982   82/16

Betty Roodish Goodwin (Canadian, b. 1923)

Moving Towards Fire 1983
Oil, pastel, oil wash, charcoal, graphite on paper. 294.0 x 325.5

Although Montreal artist Goodwin has always had a personal affection for drawing, it was not until the beginning of the 1980s, after working predominantly with found objects and in sculpture, that she began to make drawings as works in their own right. *Moving Towards Fire* is part of an ongoing series of works that not only realize the potential of drawing as a vehicle of expression, but also represent a significant contribution to the recent international revival of an emotionally charged figurative art.

"Drawing," Goodwin once wrote, "is the most unalienated medium. Private, it doesn't have an audience in mind, just the artist's expression." In this work the artist utilizes the specific material properties of drawing, such as its fragile and ephemeral qualities, to articulate her intimate explorations of emotional experiences and transformations. Three vertical, semitransparent sheets of paper are loosely draped from the wall, which underlines the depiction of a translucent aquatic space. The seemingly unfinished and transitory state of the drawing emphasizes the suspenseful moment in which the central figure of the swimmer is caught. No longer in control of its movement, the contracted body appears to be drawn, as if by burning desire, toward some unknown depth. The outline of a bridge and the figure of another swimmer surfacing above suggest a counterpoint; they imply the safety of passage and perhaps a more stable world beyond the horizon.

Purchase, 1985   85/296

Gathie Falk (Canadian, b. 1928)

All over Rose Trees and Light Bulbs 1984
Oil on canvas. 198.2 x 167.6

Falk's work typically deals with commonplace items that are arranged and combined in such a way as to demand a reassessment of their significance. Of her *Theatres in B/W and Colour* series, painted between 1983 and 1984, Falk states, "Theatre is a bit of life that is framed for the viewer to help him see things he has already seen but not observed, to extend his knowledge, and not least, to entertain him, take him out of himself." She also asserts that "seeing in detail around you makes you able to see large things better" and further explains, "You're never going to be able to see things in detail unless you can look at your kitchen table, see it and find significance in it – or the shadow that is cast by a cup." In this work, Falk has arranged the rose tree and the light bulb in repetitive, theatrical rows to create "something singular, if not exotic."

Full of cultural and mythic analogy and allusion, this canvas defies singular interpretation but may be viewed as an edifying, enthralling image of Falk's personal and sensitive view of everyday life.

Gift of Norcen Energy Resources Limited, 1986   86/53

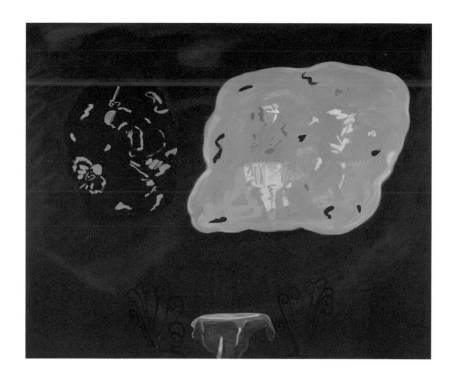

Shirley Wiitasalo (Canadian, b. 1949)

Beautiful Garden 1981
Oil on canvas. 152.2 x 183.0

By the mid-1970s Wiitasalo had chosen to paint from "personal attitudes," preferring to grapple with her own identity in relation to the contemporary world rather than with "painterly problems." The surfaces of her paintings become the sites of the viewer's consciousness, thus registering the play between an internal projection and an external construction. Within this area the real and the fictional confront each other and the perimeters of the inner and outer self are blurred.

    Beautiful Garden is a site of contentment and desire. As in many of Wiitasalo's paintings, this work includes other images on its surface. Contained in cartoonlike bubbles, they function as a disruption both of the visual imagery and of social desire. The schematic rendering of shapes creates ambiguous surface effects that dissimulate, at first glance, the scenes of violence depicted in the capsules. Here dissimulation cannot be dissociated from meaning and may be likened to the process of social experience. The disturbing occurrences depicted within a context of enjoyment spell out the irreconcilable contradictions of modern existence.

    Purchase, 1986   85/424

Renée Van Halm (Canadian, b. 1949)

Upon Awakening She Becomes Aware 1983
Acrylic on canvas mounted on wood, acrylic on wood, painted plaster.
249.0 x 318.0 x 201.0

Van Halm's *Upon Awakening She Becomes Aware* is part of a body of work that, in the late 1970s and early 1980s, marked a break with modernist formalism. Unlike the art of some of her contemporaries, however, Van Halm's work does not espouse the return to traditional forms and values of painting, such as the revival of Expressionism, with its privileges of artistic subjectivity and gesture. Instead, Van Halm reconstructs appropriated images from art history in a hybrid form of sculpture, architecture, painting and theatre to address issues of representation.

This particular work is based on a painting by Renaissance artist Pietro Lorenzetti entitled *Sobac's Dream*. Rather than presenting a faithful copy of the original, however, Van Halm's reconstruction purposely calls to attention the formal devices of figurative painting and subverts the proper laws of perspective in the visible play between illusionistic two-dimensional surfaces and three-dimensional theatrical construction. More importantly Van Halm has eliminated the explicit narrative portrayed by the figures in the original painting and instead has left fragments, such as three sculpted plaster hands, which now serve as signs for the subjective expression of a self. While the absence of the body emphasizes the viewer's active role in interpreting and supplying a subjective dimension, Van Halm's own activity may now be seen as an intervention in and re-interpretation of traditional representations of "subjecthood."

Purchase, 1983   83/35

Joanne Tod (Canadian, b. 1953)

Second in Command/First Church of Christ, Scientist 1984
Oil on canvas. Diptych, each panel: 168.5 x 198.3

Throughout the 1980s Tod has created critical images that address issues of power, identity and representation. Appropriating the highly illustrative style of advertising, she depicts situations with a conventional clarity and fluidity that endow her work deceptively with the authority of a final utterance.

When one views these two panels as emblems of power and devotion, a multiplicity of relationships is suggested. The images are engaging both in the pleasant disposition of the military figures on the left and in the lulling placidity of the classical temple on the right. The viewer is thus locked into representations that structure social identity.

Tod has expressed an interest in linguistics and imagery. The inclusion of text in the picture functions as a disruptive sign. The word *Sagittarius* has the effect of deconstructing accepted systems of authority, instigating the spectator to reflect upon his or her relationship to these systems. Thus the viewer stands on uneasy ground before the discriminatory hierarchy of the military figures, before the conflict between the astrological connotations of *Sagittarius* and the cool purposefulness of the military, and before a *Subject for Sunday* that affirms a set of beliefs hardly compatible with the beliefs commonly associated with such a temple.

Purchase, 1984   84/848

John Massey (Canadian, b. 1950)

A Directed View (the first two rooms) 1979
Fabric, transparency, projected image, spotlights, mirror, plaster.
Each room: 457.2 x 1463.0

While the conceptual artists of the 1960s and early 1970s were concerned with the way in which reality was mediated with language and conceptual constructs, artists in the later 1970s became interested in the subjective dimension of knowledge. Toronto artist Massey, for instance, began to explore the way in which desire figured in perception.

This work takes the form of a theatrical installation to rupture ordinary perception and to structure the relation between subject and object in terms of desire. Divided into two rooms, the first part of the installation involves a large man's hat suspended in front of a back-projected image of a stairwell. Not only does the unusual scale of the hat separate it from the existing context and radically alter the viewer's own sense of scale and presence, but, as Massey himself has said, the hat also represents an "object of desire," designed to create a psychological and perceptual proximity that puts the viewer into a relation of identity or communion with the object rather than one of intellectual comprehension through objective distance.

The second room is integrally linked to the first, as it explicates the myopic relation between subject and object in more abstract terms: a light has been set up to bounce off a mirror and then cast an ellipse of light onto a wall. Massey has filled in this ellipse with a roughly textured plaster surface that appears as though it were a section of the wall as seen through a magnifying glass. The beam of light may be seen as a representation of the "desirous eye," or as representative of a mode of enquiry that is capable of creating any kind of proportion for itself in the desire to know.

Purchase, with donation from Mr. and Mrs. Bram Appel,
and with assistance from Wintario, 1980   79/333

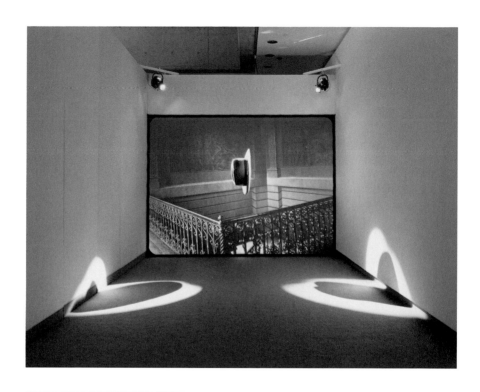

Jeff Wall (Canadian, b. 1946)

Double Self-portrait 1979
Cibachrome transparency, acrylic sheet, metal box, fluorescent tubes.
164.0 x 218.0

In his large-scale photographs, Wall seeks and creates effective relationships between the traditions of Modernism, cinematic processes, and the real conditions of contemporary society. The use of backlit transparencies, commonly used in advertising, is a means by which the traditional pictorial space of painting can regain its validity and relevance within current technology-based culture.

The portrait is a typology of representation based on art history traditions. In *Double Self-portrait* Wall addresses this mode of representation both historically and theoretically. Both the positioning of the figure in space and its relationship to the viewer are analyzed. The photograph is meticulously set up in a shallow space. The ordinariness of the components – couch, chair, blanket – combines with the almost human scale of the work and with the even luminosity that is emitted to absorb the spectator in the unequivocal authority of its subject matter.

Before this work the viewer is initially locked in the interplay of gaze. Yet the seam joining the two transparencies underlines the duality present in the slight differences in details in the temporally distinct images, which results in the spectator experiencing a distancing within the image as he or she becomes engaged in issues of authorship, displacement, and ordering of self and other.

Purchase, 1982   82/187

General Idea (Canadian, formed in 1968)

Colour Bar Lounge 1979
Mixed media. Floor piece: 101.3 x 380.0 x 24.0;
wall piece: 63.5 x 377.0

The trio of artists – A.A. Bronson, Jorge Zontal and Felix Partz – banded together under the name General Idea in 1968. Working as a collective in multimedia work allowed them to better assume the role of "cultural investigators" who mimicked the tactics of the mass media and appropriated a multitude of cultural vehicles. The scope of their activity and their commitment to ambiguity resist classification.

At the outset the prevalent framework of these activities was the *1984 Miss General Idea Pavillion*, an open-ended, easily manipulated concept within which works were realized. *Colour Bar Lounge* exists both independently of and within the context of the *Pavillion*. All six photographs and their accompanying captions are part of an ongoing iconography that has been disseminated in other formats. General Idea has commented: "We think of the *Colour Bar Lounge* as a sort of cultural laboratory where we can experiment with new cultural mixes and serve them up to our friends...." Any attempt, however, to correlate precisely image and text is fruitless. Rather, the viewer is exposed to a multiplicity of meanings and their ironical and paradoxical intent.

Purchase, 1981   81/72

Liz Magor (Canadian, b. 1948)

Four Boys and a Girl 1979
Fabric, metal, twigs and organic clippings, glue, wool, wood.
5 slabs, each 30.0 x 179.0 x 46.0; machine press: 81.0 x 183.0 x 83.9

Magor started using her art as a means of interrogating change in the world and determining the position of the artist therein. Her sculptures were static objects of common origin that existed in the world and interacted with ordinary things and sometimes disappeared among them. *Four Boys and a Girl* was one of these culminating works, which, by registering the process of change in the work itself, questioned how identity is maintained over time. As Magor states: "I am always looking for comfort in a world disturbingly subject to change. Sometimes I find it in work, as a recording of my activity. Sometimes I find it in objects, things that sit still for a while and slowly gather, then release, their history. I wanted to do work that would objectify some history of life, or at least the life of a body and the process of change that affects that body."

While five slabs are produced from the same machine, each takes on its own character and identity. The materials – old clothes and compost – are acted upon by the artist, constrained in certain ways to change their forms in decay. Given their own history, they now assume an identity beyond the control of the artist and "manifest *their* history, their own generation and transformation."

Purchase, 1985   85/297

Roland Poulin (Canadian, b. 1940)

Homage to Hung-Jen 1983
Steel-reinforced concrete. 50.7 x 396.0 x 81.5

In 1979 Poulin began using aluminous cement in his sculpture, which established an unequivocal sense of mass and accentuated the density of surface. A year later he began elevating his floor-bound elements and splitting them into two major components from the previous quadrangular configuration. Although the two L-shaped pieces that form this sculpture are minimalist in appearance, they initiate an entire range of discontinuities and shifts – slightly inclined planes, uneven lengths and distances, asymmetrical masses and mottled surfaces – that make for a constant tension and ambiguity of space. As Poulin states, "I am interested in sculpture that is complex but not complicated, [and] in producing difficult objects."

Fundamental to this work is the interplay of light and cast shadow. These areas of immateriality induce an intimate relationship between viewer and sculpture while the "problematic" of where the object begins and ends is raised. Because the viewer may assume numerous observation points, this sculpture can only be experienced in time, as his or her perception of it is continuously being revealed. *Homage to Hung-Jen* extends beyond purely formal considerations, and its significance lies in the investigation of the relationship between, as the artist explains, "physical and psychological phenomena."

Purchase, 1984   83/381

Ian Carr-Harris (Canadian, b. 1941)

Untitled 1984-85
Plywood, painted wood, electronic components, soundtrack.
Installation: 221.0 x 1000.3 x 208.0

In 1978, to the developing installational character of his sculpture, Carr-Harris added narrative soundtracks. As in his earlier sculpture, these installations were still confrontational, and the narrative demanded an outcome that was a decision.

This work, similarly, is a presentation and a demonstration. A short text repeated loudly every half minute exhorts: "This is a symbol. It is a symbol of fire. Fire is an old symbol. Never trust symbols." This voice speaks as a presence behind the presence of an imposing serried mass of black flames cut from plywood and glued together in vertical planes. Both the voice and the flames assume the amplified power of symbols, but because the voice is recorded and repeated its prescriptive effect is dissipated, in spite of its insistence; its own symbolic structure is included in this address and therefore contradicts and undercuts itself. Since this structure is circular, it must be broken by the participation of the viewer. The strength of the work is that it uses a presence to undermine a presence and a symbolic act to question the symbolic.

Purchase, 1985   85/302

Roland Brener (Canadian, b. 1942)

I am always thinking of you 1986
Multimedia construction. 245.0 x 119.6 x 123.0

In the early 1980s Brener realized that a sculptural practice based in the formalist tradition was no longer fulfilling his needs. He sought to make his work more accessible
by adopting technological materials whose references were to contemporary society
and industrial production rather than art history. This work exemplifies this process.
While retaining sculptural concerns that have their origins in Constructivism, Brener
clearly equates meaning with active involvement of the spectator. When in close proximity to the sculpture, the viewer activates a robot through a sonar device. As the robot
clumsily walks, it turns the metal hoop and at the same time intermittently completes
the electrical current to operate the radio in the base of the sculpture. Since a Mylar
sheet is placed before the robot, which is lit from behind, the viewer initially experiences it as a mysterious and distorted silhouette. However, the mechanisms are accessible as he or she moves around the piece and perception shifts to a more prosaic one.

    The spectator clearly identifies with the contemporary materials utilized. Yet
the diminutive robot, its hesitant gait, and the indistinguishable babble of the radio
subvert the ideals and positivity of the new order inherent in Constructivism.

Purchase, 1987   86/278

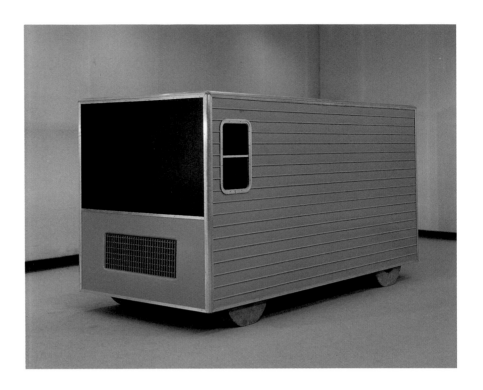

Robin Collyer (Canadian, b. 1949)

The Zulu (European Version) 1985
Vacuum-formed plastic, metal, concrete, acrylic sheet, Plasticine, wood.
205.0 x 371.8 x 170.5

Collyer's sculptures of the period of *The Zulu* are configurations of unaltered industrial materials that are combined and constructed to make certain referential associations. They play on the typology of forms found in the industrial and urban landscape. Although elegantly constructed, these sculptures have a put-together character that reminds the viewer, beyond the immediate associations of their appearance (and *Zulu* has the look of some strange vehicle), of a type of handyman adaptation that might be found in oddly transformed vehicles or storage sheds.

Like these vernacular constructions, which have a tendency to undermine the original values or source of the materials, Collyer's *Zulu* makes reference not necessarily to some particular van or motor home, but to a landscape and environment that have been transformed into a sign system. With its hollow structure, constructed from vacuum-formed plastic, *Zulu* is a nonfunctional object. With its substance evacuated, it takes on a sign function, but in a strange – or estranging – language, like the black Plexiglas windows, that rebuffs us.

Purchase, 1985   85/298

Jenny Holzer (American, b. 1950)

You create an incident... from *"Under a Rock"* 1986
Granite, LED sign, red and green diodes. Bench: 44.5 x 121.1 x 53.2;
sign: 24.0 x 285.0 x 14.0

Both the medium and the subject matter of Holzer's art are language. Composed of twisted aphorisms and quasi-clichés, her texts are presented in a variety of popular media formats and contain a multiplicity of points of view. The viewer of Holzer's work is brought to question how the power of language and media presentation can manipulate perception, and how authority is granted to language in its dominance of the social environment.

The *Under a Rock* series pairs LED signs and granite benches. The signs recite the same texts that have been engraved into the benches. *You create an incident...* details an episode of institutionalized abuse of power: "You create an incident to bring the fury down. Your fighters blow fingers and more in ten directions. Round crowds form, transfixed by the dead. Panic and belated love take all the space in brains, and the people left alive are glad to be full. No one ever knows what to do. You fire again, and people are grateful enough." Carved into the stone benches, these texts assume an aura of authority and endurance completely at odds with the relentless pace of the electronic messages. There is no time allowed to absorb and understand the flashing sign. The bench, on the other hand, invites one to sit and contemplate its message. The contradictions of everyday life are reflected in the contradictions between the medium and the message.

Gift from the Junior Committee Fund, 1987   87/134, 87/135

Lothar Baumgarten (German, b. 1944)

Monument for the Native People of Ontario 1984-85
Typeface: Perpetua (Eric Gill), tempera on painted concrete

The key to Baumgarten's thinking about art lies in his many extended stays among the
Indians of South America. His fundamental commitment to a renewal of cultural
thinking seeks to re-integrate man, culture and environment in an intuitive zone that
has been lost to Western civilization.

 Though styled as a monument for the native people of Ontario, the work is not
simply a program of romantic anthropology but addresses that fragile spiritual connection between man and environment. The decorative frieze in the Walker Court spells
out a catalogue of tribal names, which instantly evokes cultures and places that are
violently at odds with the classicism of the Walker Court and the graphic signs in
which they are rendered. Yet it is decoratively correct, harmonious with the architecture and the cultural forms in which it is framed. The viewer is inevitably reminded
that many of these people have been ruthlessly wiped out as a result of white men's
greed for land and power. Though grief is solicited, so is action against injustices and
inequities in the present context.

 Purchase, 1984   84/941

425

Inuit Art

Susan Ootnooyuk (Canadian, 1918-77)

Mother Wearing Necklace and Earrings c.1970
Grey stone, caribou teeth, beads, sinew. 22.0 x 7.6 x 6.3

Susan Ootnooyuk, working with the hard, dull grey stone of Arviat (Eskimo Point), has accented this sculptural figure in an unusual, feminine way. Necklaces and earrings were not traditionally worn by Inuit women, but over time they adapted new forms of personal adornment such as beads, earrings and rings, and integrated them with traditional ones such as caribou teeth ornamentation, facial tattooing, hair bindings and parka decoration. Although necklaces and earrings today have become more common attire, they have never been prevalent in sculptural or graphic representations.

In this carving the necklace is a focal point, framing the rough, high-cheekboned face, which is surmounted by the unusually elevated child behind. Attention is focused on the disproportionately large face, the jewellery and the child, rather than on the somewhat slablike body beneath with its rudimentary extremities and long parka flap.

Gift of the Klamer family, 1978   78/724

Lucy Tasseor Tutsweetok (Canadian, b. 1934)

Family c.1969
Dark grey stone. 16.4 x 17.0 x 4.6

Tasseor began carving in the mid-1960s and quickly established a reputation for being one of Arviat's most innovative artists. Due in part to the hard Arviat stone, she relies heavily on the initial shape of the material, never carving a complete figure but choosing instead to carve triangular arms and sharp-featured heads where outcroppings occur. Her early works, such as this one, emphasize the central role of the woman in Inuit life.

In later works, content is reduced to many small angular faces carved into the ridges of the stone. Because these visages are too numerous to represent a single family, there has been much speculation as to their significance. When asked, Tasseor suggests universality, saying "maybe they are your family too." In light of her fondness for "abstractions," it is likely that the heads are not meant to denote specific individuals, but rather function primarily as formal elements. This observation is supported by her response when asked about a carving by Pangnark: "I think that he was probably like myself, trying to represent something in a way, but I don't really copy. I don't really make it human but in some sort of abstract way."

Gift of Samuel and Esther Sarick, 1989   89/608

John Pangnark (Canadian, 1920-80)

Figure 1974
Grey stone. 21.5 x 22.3 x 18.3

The sculpture of one of Arviat's leading artists challenges many preconceptions about Inuit art. Pangnark's semirepresentational, non-narrative works indicate an intuitive preoccupation with the resolution of formal problems at the expense of easily identifiable subject matter. Several critics see, in the outward form of the work at least, similarities to modern European sculpture. The instinct for abstraction and a feeling for the sheer beauty of curves and hard-edged shapes – exhibited in this work – have led to Pangnark being referred to as the "Brancusi of the North."

However minimal the form employed, Pangnark's work always has some anthropomorphic reference. Typically, the only indications of humanness in his work are two nicks designating arms and the small incised face always found on an upward facing plane. Pangnark appears to know precisely how much relief an otherwise undifferentiated mass needs. *Figure* is an example of one of Pangnark's later pieces in which he imposed his will upon the stone less and less, choosing instead to refine the natural shape. Thus, even quite small works were transformed into monumental objects imbued with a spiritual quality common to all his work.

Gift of Samuel and Esther Sarick, 1989   89/552

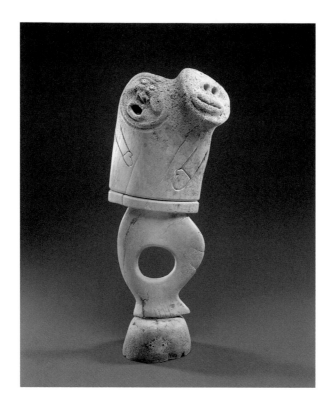

Karoo Ashevak (Canadian, 1940-74)

Two-Headed Figure 1971
Whalebone, stone, ivory. 65.3 x 31.5 x 16.5

Karoo Ashevak, Spence Bay's most noted artist, established himself as a leader in innovation and creativity despite a career that only lasted four short years. Working primarily in whalebone, but freely incorporating a variety of material for inlays and embellishment, Karoo produced lively, animated works charged with drama. Although his complex works often appear to be spontaneous and arbitrary creations, the artist generally had a particular subject in mind, which required an appropriate piece of bone be located before carving began.

Two-Headed Figure reveals Karoo to be a master at capitalizing on the unusual texture, shape and colour of whalebone. Eyes inset with several rings of contrasting materials, deeply drilled nostrils and open mouths are features common to his work. Details such as the small ivory pebbles in the open mouth, perhaps denoting a wish for food, impart a sense of the curious and exotic for which Karoo's art is noted and which did much to influence and define the nature of Spence Bay art.

Gift of the Klamer family, 1978   78/690

George Tataniq (Canadian, b. 1910)

Musk-ox c.1971
Greenish-black stone, horn. 24.5 x 32.5 x 14.0

Unique among Baker Lake sculpture is the work of Tataniq. The aesthetic general to this community could be described as one of a rhythmic interplay of broad expressive volumes that exaggerate the mass of the subject. Tataniq uses the hard black Baker Lake stone to produce his imposing sculpture, which is characterized by straight, sharp lines that clearly define the form as opposed to rounded flowing shapes. The dominance of line, of hard edges, gives his work a refined elegance that elevates his art beyond the descriptive.

Tataniq has addressed a wide number of themes since he began carving in the early 1960s. If there is a favoured subject, it is the musk-ox, a stout, shaggy member of the sheep family, which undergoes a particular transformation at the hands of this artist. Details, such as the broad head rendered in a series of flat planes, the finely incised eyes, nostrils, mouth and tail, and the delicate curving antlers, define the creature without detracting from its massiveness.

Gift of Samuel and Esther Sarick, 1989   89/568

Nancy Pukingrnak Aupaluktuq (Canadian, b. 1940)

Camp Scene c.1974
Graphite and coloured pencil on paper. 50.5 x 66.0

Pukingrnak's penchant for minute and informative detail is in contrast to much Baker Lake art, which features bold, simplified images. Highly animated and descriptive, her art can be seen as visual manifestations of the Inuit oral tradition, which recounts legends, adventures, and, as seen in this drawing, episodes from everyday life. The left side of this composition features graphic illustrations of the harsh realities of hunting and hostilities. In the upper scene bodies lie strewn around an imposing musk-ox holding the spear-wielding hunter at bay; a gored dog lies nearby dripping blood while another attacks. In an ambiguous scene below, a man and his dog are subjected to a barrage of arrows, which appear to pass through them or deliberately miss.

Oblivious to this exchange, the other participants in this complex and detailed scene are engaged in a variety of activities. One man smokes his pipe as another uses a telescope to gaze at caribou, whose small scale indicates their distance away. A girl has her hair dressed, an older woman with tattoo marks chants the traditional *ai-yai-yai* to a child held by its mother, and another woman prepares skins inside her tent. In the upper right, a stone fish weir may be seen, the speared fish carried to camp where the women clean and hang them up to dry.

Gift of the Klamer family, 1978   78/559

434

Jessie Oonark (Canadian, 1906-85)

Untitled c.1972
Stroud, felt, embroidery floss, thread. 212.0 x 144.0

A major retrospective organized by the Winnipeg Art Gallery in 1986 recognized the special talents of Jessie Oonark, a member of the Royal Canadian Academy of Art and an officer of the Order of Canada. From the hundreds of drawings she executed between 1959 and 1982, 105 were selected for inclusion in Baker Lake's annual print collections released from 1970 to 1985. Wall hangings had a special appeal for Oonark, who was a tireless seamstress. Her strong interest in parka designs led her to use their interlocking panels, trim and fringes as important elements for her stylized two-dimensional images.

This wall hanging – selected from the exhibition *The People Within*, which was organized by the AGO in 1976 – is considered to be one of Oonark's best and reveals her work to be a complex synthesis of observation and experience. Although untitled, this particular work undoubtedly reflects Christian beliefs. The upper rectangle containing white figures hearkens back to the Old Testament, when the word of God was delivered to mankind by Moses. Directly beneath could be the figure of Jesus holding loaves of bread, which are eagerly awaited by the surrounding people. Starvation was once a harsh reality for Oonark, and Jesus as the giver of bread was also the giver of life – an attractive proposition to the new converts. Such meaning was not corroborated by the artist who has never been noted for being overly concerned with a literal interpretation of her complex and multilayered works.

Purchased with assistance from Wintario, 1977   76/229

Luke Iksiktaaryuk (Canadian, 1909-77)

Drum Dance c.1974
Antler, wood, sinew, gut, metal. 16.4 x 32.6 x 40.7

Like many inland Inuit, Iksiktaaryuk settled in Baker Lake after his people experienced
starvation in the late 1950s. Although he began carving in the 1960s, he is most noted
for composite antler carvings that depict scenes such as the drum dance and for
his single-figure renderings of shamans, both produced over a five-year period from
1970 to 1975.

Iksiktaaryuk uses caribou antler as a material of choice, mastering it as a sculptural medium in its own right. This work demonstrates his manipulation of the natural
shape of the antler to suggest various shapes and forms. A longer portion of shaft with
limited protrusions serves to identify male figures whereas the spreading area where
the tip extends from the main trunk is often incorporated into the broader form of the
female. In *Drum Dance*, the tips not only depict parka hoods, but also serve to animate the audience, carved as they are to appear to sway and move as if in time to the
drum beat. The use of a sectioned antler as a base for the audience and a single piece
of antler for the drummer's arm and the beater it holds attests to an instinct for
economy of means.

Gift of the Klamer family, 1978   78/386

Kiawak Ashoona (Canadian, b. 1933)

Spirit Figure c.1961
Green stone. 37.0 x 21.6 x 13.6

Kiawak's predilection for the demonstrative leads naturally to a subject matter where exaggeration reinforces a particular idea or action. The shaman as subject allows him to be both descriptive and expressive, for the shaman is no ordinary being and has no particular appearance. Rather, he is able to undergo transformations and spirit flights in order to communicate with supernatural creatures. *Spirit Figure*'s dramatic rendering depicts the shaman having undergone two significant changes: one into the most powerful helping spirit, the bear, which is indicated by the clawed feet, and the second into the musk-ox, indicated by the horned head. An aggressive interaction with the surrounding space is achieved by the bent legs and the arms thrusting across the body in the opposite direction of the torso's tilt. An interesting feature is the removable head, in all likelihood necessitated through accident or a flaw in the material.

Kiawak comes from a family of noted Cape Dorset artists; his mother was Pitseolak and his brother, Kaka.

Gift of Samuel and Esther Sarick, 1989   89/598

Parr (Canadian, 1893–1969)

Seven Caribou 1964
Wax crayon on paper. 50.8 x 65.8

Parr, the old hunter, has given us immediate, basic and direct records of life as he lived
it. His creatures are not elaborately defined with markings or details; they are not even
well-proportioned and sometimes one type of four-legged animal cannot be distinguished from another, yet no viewer has any trouble in recognizing what is taking place
or understanding what is important. The caribou in this drawing look not unlike Parr's
bears and dogs, yet their antlers do distinguish them. And somehow what exact type
of animals they are seem secondary to the visual image in which the different shapes
and sizes are so effectively distributed and repeated with the accent of red horns.

Many of this Cape Dorset artist's works are concerned with the hunt and therefore with animals. Caribou, walruses, birds, bears, seals and dogs are gathered together
in unusual groupings with little regard for perspective. Overlapping is avoided; variations in size indicate not only larger and smaller animals, but also their distance away.
In this work, the small figure on the left has a large set of antlers and therefore is
a mature caribou whose relative size indicates that he is further off than others in
the herd.

Gift of the Klamer family, 1978   78/551

438

Kenojuak Ashevak (Canadian, b. 1927)

Owl 1970
Felt-tip pen on paper. 50.8 x 66.0

The release of the print *Enchanted Owl* established Kenojuak as one of the North's leading artists, recognized by the Order of Canada. Her magnificent, bold and flamboyant drawings, over 160 of which have been released as prints, have done much to define Cape Dorset's aesthetic.

Her early work with its emphasis on flatness, positive/negative space and interconnected images evolved into highly symmetrical, curvilinear designs in which the actual subject matter is less important than what is done with it; the subject functions as a means to an end. Birds may be the dominant subject, but appear to have no more significance than the fact that birds, unlike narrative or realistic scenes, lend themselves to graphic elaboration, as seen in this full-blown drawing. Reduced to shape and pattern, the bird is recognizable only by its eyes; even the nose is a decorative shape, and the body, which originally played a major role in the process of beautification, has all but disappeared.

Although in later works Kenojuak retreats from abstraction, she maintains that she is just trying to "make something beautiful, that's all."

Gift of the Klamer family, 1978   78/549

Aqjangajuk Shaa (Canadian, b. 1937)

Figure with Ulu c.1967
Green stone. 38.5 x 47.0 x 6.0

Figure with Ulu is Aqjangajuk at his best. The artist has taken the large rectangular, slightly flattish stone and has captured the expressive qualities of movement and energy through the piece's strong interaction with the surrounding space. The sense of strength and aggression is heightened by the tension established by the potential upward thrust of the massive bent legs and the reaching arms, one grasping toward the viewer, the other clenching a large *ulu* (woman's knife). The lack of bodily definition and masculine features enhance a sense of brute strength in apparent contradiction to the suggestion by the ulu that the figure is female. The flamboyance typical of much Cape Dorset art is overwhelmed by the directness and psychological impact of this intense image.

Gift of the Klamer family, 1978   78/199

Osuitok Ipeelee (Canadian, b. 1922)

Caribou Head c.1970
Green stone, antler. 54.7 x 45.6 x 31.5

In early 1951 when James and Alma Houston journeyed by dog team from Frobisher Bay to Cape Dorset, their requests for sculpture for export to the South were greeted with the information that the best carver on the south Baffin coast was Osuitok. First asked to carve in the 1940s by the Roman Catholic mission, Osuitok made small ivory models of such things as kayaks and fox traps – the latter completely functional on a miniature scale. When Osuitok turned to the green jadelike stone so readily identified with Cape Dorset sculpture, he demonstrated an ability to work with all materials and established himself as a leading artist in a community noted for artists of distinction.

Osuitok confidently pushes his material to its full potential, excavating freely to create works often precariously balanced but highly refined and elegant. The long, thin neck, narrow muzzle and real antler horns impart a sense of lightness to *Caribou Head*. Combining the expressive with the descriptive, Osuitok's work remains self-contained, independent of a particular context.

Gift of the Klamer family, 1978   78/244

Latcholassie Akesuk (Canadian, b. 1919)

Bird c.1973
White stone. 41.6 x 43.0 x 16.8

Concentrating on a limited number of subjects and employing little detail or surface
definition, Latcholassie's sculpture has always been distinctive. The minimal nature
of *Bird* stands out in contrast with the elaborate, unreserved works associated with
much of Cape Dorset art. Rather than conveying a sense of action or a particular story,
the artist appears deliberately to subordinate the content to formal concerns. In this
piece simple volume and flowing lines are given just the right amount of relief by protrusions and appendages, which also provide the only indication of the subject matter.
Although Latcholassie often carves transformation figures, sometimes part human,
part animal, the image of the bird provides the basis for the majority of his work.

   The subtle, suggestive nature of this artist's work is enhanced by the use of white
stone. This stone, quarried near Cape Dorset and at one time available in large pieces,
does not lend itself easily to details, thus making it an ideal and favoured material
for this artist.

   Gift of Samuel and Esther Sarick, 1989   89/553

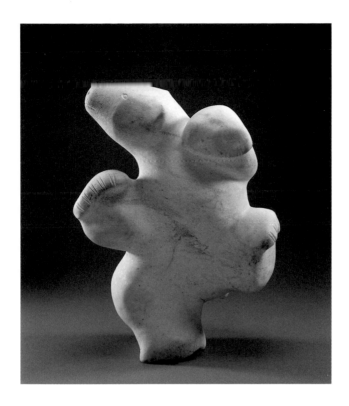

Pauta Saila (Canadian, b. 1916)

Dancing Bear c.1973
White stone. 47.9 x 36.5 x 19.6

Artists sometimes become noted for a particular aspect that dominates their oeuvre. One of Cape Dorset's best-known and oldest artists, Pauta, has such an apparent preference for the polar bear as his subject that it has become his trademark. In fact, the artist has said that he carves polar bears because he truly likes to carve them.

Dancing Bear demonstrates that Pauta's creatures are not naturalistic ones supported by four legs. Rather, a sense of movement created through flowing lines and rounded forms reveal the quintessential Pauta, who shares the penchant for flamboyance that has helped define the Cape Dorset aesthetic. Although a sense of humour is often in evidence, his work, even the relatively small pieces, always has a sense of the monumental. This work is of average size for this artist, who has created some of the largest pieces of Inuit art extant. The white stone was a feature of Cape Dorset art in the early 1970s.

Gift of Samuel and Esther Sarick, 1989   89/625

443

Qavaroak Tunnillie (Canadian, b. 1928)

Spirit
Green stone. 28.7 x 56.4 x 14.0

An exciting aspect of Inuit art is the appearance of unrecognizable creatures, commonly referred to as spirits, that are as much a function of the imagination as an interpretation of a specific animal or legend. The sharp claws, mane and body indicate that this is a lionlike creature, which has grown a dorsal fin and tail of a sea creature. Whatever its actual identity, the aspect most important is the unlimited freedom of expression inherent in the depiction of a subject matter that has few limitations. Like most Cape Dorset artists, Qavaroak is more interested in form, in creating vigorous sculpture rather than illustrations. The piece's aggression is enhanced by a gauntness imparted by clearly delineated ribs. The texture of the mane and the carefully incised face and tail fin contrast with the angular yet flowing legs and tail that further animate the piece. Qavaroak's predilection for suggesting a grand scale results in animation balanced with monumentality, with even relatively small works being imbued with authority and weight.

Gift of Samuel and Esther Sarick, 1989   89/622

444

Elijassiapik (Canadian, 1912-72)

Mother and Child with Kudlik 1950s
Light and dark green stone, black stone, ivory, bone, black pigment.
14.0 X 24.7 X 21.5

Scenes such as the one depicted in this carving are classic examples of the domestic and narrative nature of Inukjuak sculpture, which shows life as it was only a short time ago. Naturalistic renderings of the traditional lifestyle predominate in this community, which was one of the first to be visited by James Houston, the person most responsible for launching the contemporary period of Inuit art. Addition of complementary materials enabled Inukjuak sculptors to create a greater sense of verisimilitude and to embellish their stone surface. In this sculpture, the already rich and lustrous dark green stone is enhanced by the addition of the woman's inset face and attached ivory hands. The mother, with her child in her parka, prepares food in front of the *kudlik*, the oil lamp. The seated position of the woman and the way the large, flat base from which she is carved flows out around her emphasize her weight and width. The rounded shape of the lower body is echoed by the circle of the open hood, which forms a wide, flat area from which the neckless heads rise. The solidity and massiveness of the figure is thus accentuated, thereby creating a personification of earth mother/provider.

Gift of the Klamer family, 1978   78/433

Nuveeya Ipellie (Canadian, b. 1920)

Sea Goddess 1976
Dark green stone, ivory, baleen. 22.5 x 26.0 x 10.9

Goddesses are often thought of as beautiful creatures. The Taleelayo legend, however, has versions in which this powerful underwater being who controls the sea's creatures is described as ugly. The broad-featured, fishlike face of this work suggests that this may be the version that the artist believes. Even with this in mind, Nuveeya has given the work a sense of grace and delicacy consistent with his interest in the beauty of the form rather than in the physical beauty of the subject or the accuracy of the portrayal. The carefully inlaid ivory eyes, the sharp, clean lines of the face, the lustre of the highly polished stone, and the graceful curve of the upturned body, culminating in an arched sweep of the tail, impart a sense of elegance and finesse consistent with the artist's interest in jewellery-making.

    Born in Lake Harbour, Nuveeya lived in Pangnirtung and Cape Dorset before settling in Iqaluit in 1945. Taught carving by his father, Ennutsiak, he in turn has influenced his son Seepee.

    Gift of the Klamer family, 1978   78/644

Henry Evaluardjuk (Canadian, b. 1923)

Walking Bear c.1980
Dark green stone. 20.9 x 42.7 x 12.8

For the Inuit, survival often depended on close observation and a full understanding of animal life. Evaluardjuk's striding polar bear, rendered in the mottled green stone popular with Iqaluit artists, provides testimony to his skill in capturing the essence of this powerful creature, which knows no natural enemy. An undulating line runs the length of the body, defining a self-assured creature moving with padded tread. Although expressive, there is little exaggeration or distortion. The large feet, so ideal for swimming, the powerful legs and body, and the longish neck are accurately rendered without extensive detail, which would detract from the expressiveness of the whole.

Gift of Samuel and Esther Sarick, 1989   89/650

447

Matiusie Iyaituk (Canadian, b. 1950)

This Woman is Happy to See that Her Son is Becoming a Good Hunter 1980
Grey stone, antler, leather, black pigment. 21.4 x 24.6 x 22.9

Modern is how many Inuit refer to art that has moved away from technically refined naturalism in favour of more intuitive, formal explorations. For a younger artist like Ivujivik's Matiusie, a need to develop an expressive style distinctly his own reflects an awareness of new realities. Artists of his generation straddle traditional Inuit culture and that of the South, co-opting aspects of both freely and easily.

In this sculpture a traditional subject matter is interpreted in a novel way. The abstracted rhythmic forms are more expressive than descriptive. The antler-inlaid faces identify the subject as a mother who holds one child in her parka hood and embraces another, after he has successfully harpooned a seal that is still secured by the harpoon line. The inlaid faces and the one eye of the seal also provide contrast and animate what would otherwise become an undifferentiated mass. A series of carefully drilled holes depicting parka trim provides additional definition of the figures as well as a pleasing rhythm that emphasizes the flowing volumes.

Gift of Samuel and Esther Sarick, 1988   89/606

Shorty Killiktee (Canadian, b. 1949)

Spirit with Young c.1969
Green stone, ivory. 24.5 x 14.4 x 14.3

Balanced on one foot, a strange spirit creature holds its equally odd, small offspring. Carved in characteristic green Lake Harbour stone, the two figures are articulated with similar markings: incised almond-shaped eyes with circular pupils, hollowed-out nostrils and mouths, and unusual round or teardrop-shape cavities, which effectively represent, in reverse, their claws. Both creatures also have inset ivory tongues, while the adult has additional ivory horns and little spikes sprouting from its head. The small junior model is clasped to its parent's body indicating a tender bond not unlike that of the human child and its mother seen in so many carvings.

Gift of the Klamer family, 1978   78/686

Markosee Karpik (Canadian, b. 1935)

Shaman 1974
Whalebone. 48.3 x 100.4 x 43.1

Whalebone has a quality all its own. Its organic nature seems to leave it harbouring some inner spirit long after it has been divested of flesh. Suggestive features inherent in the shape and texture of the unworked material add to this feeling so that it comes as little surprise that much whalebone carving depicts transformations and spirit creatures. In *Shaman* the natural structure of the bone appears to have induced Karpik to carve a face onto the rounded central portion, utilizing the softer marrow to create a gaping mouth, which includes two long incisors often associated with the shaman undergoing trans-formation in order to communicate with the supernatural world. A minimum of judicious carving defines outstretched arms that heighten the sense of drama.

The opposite side reveals another face with detailed teeth, well-defined eyes, and the suggestion of hair. The double-faced motif appears frequently in Pangnirtung carving, as the vertebra is a favoured carving part of the whale skeletons left to bleach on the shores of Baffin Island by 19th-century whalers.

Gift of Samuel and Esther Sarick, 1988   88/377

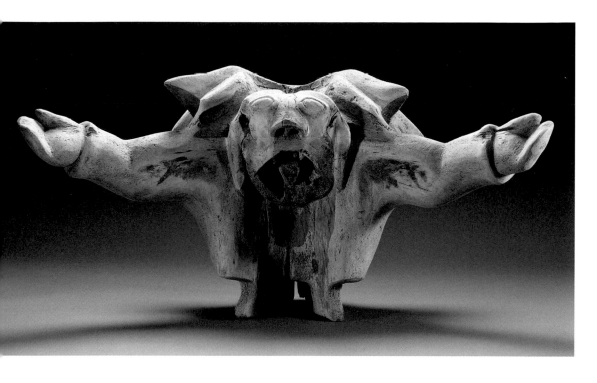

451

Joe Talirunili (Canadian, 1906-76)

Migration c.1976
Grey stone, wood, hide, string. 29.0 x 18.0 x 31.0

Throughout his long artistic career, Talirunili carved a great many migration boat scenes
showing the traditional *umiak* full of people. This subject was inspired by an early
childhood event, when several travelling Inuit were forced to use their sleds and the
skins they had with them to make a makeshift boat to get to the mainland after the
ice had broken up around them. Details of the scene changed, but the boat was always
overcrowded with people. The crude wooden paddles, simple square sail, blunt extremities of the figures, and rudimentary faces contribute to a sense of unity in *Migration*
that is compatible with the oneness of a communal experience.

   Also famous for standing owls and human figures, Talirunili has become one of
Povungnituk's most noted artists. His work has a rough quality, which adds to its
immediacy and vitality. As one of the first artists involved in Povungnituk printmaking,
Talirunili has had over 70 stonecuts based on his drawings released since 1962. The
works on paper are particularly descriptive and provide information about traditional
Inuit life in much detail, a strong characteristic of Povungnituk art.

   Gift of the Klamer family, 1978   78/185

Eli Salluala Qinuajua (Canadian, b. 1937)

Fantastic Figure
Grey stone. 54.2 x 47.4 x 14.3

In 1967 an open art competition was organized in Povungnituk, which stipulated that the carvings submitted were to be "things never seen before." It was an attempt to determine what the artists, many of whom were working in a tradition of realistic art referred to as "POV naturalism," would make if they gave free rein to their imagination and disregarded marketability. Among the most remarkable and innovative works were those of the competition's eventual winner, Eli Salluala.

This work is a full-blown example of the style now known as *fantastic*, which is characterized by fanciful renderings of dreams, fantasies and spirits. In this large work, the artist has typically carved out most of the stone, leaving a complex interplay of delicate serpentine form that defines an ambiguous creature featuring a broad tooth-filled mouth for its body. The sinuous form at one point evolves into a large eye staring aggressively upward. The overall rectangular format of this work is determined by the shape of the stone printing block from which the carving was made.

Gift of Samuel and Esther Sarick, 1989   89/657

John Tiktak (Canadian, 1916-81)

Mother and Child c.1973
Black stone. 23.2 x 14.8 x 7.5

The mother and child is a common theme in Inuit art and is indicative of a high regard
for the maternal bond, which can be seen as expressing a general concern for humanity
and its interdependence as well as the special relationship between a mother and child.
The death of Tiktak's own mother in 1962, to whom he was very close, was followed
by a period that featured work characterized by depictions of the mother as inseparable
from the child physically, emotionally and spiritually. In this piece, Tiktak has expressed
this bond in a tangible and most economic way. The large figure of the mother is the
supportive mass from which the child appears to emerge, physical separation being
limited to an excavation on each side.

Tiktak's works appear to be deeply personal statements combined with an innate
understanding of form. His elemental statements achieve such sophistication of form
that his work has been compared to that of Henry Moore. Tiktak enjoyed recognition
as one of the North's foremost artists, his work being eagerly sought by knowledgeable
collectors following a one-person exhibition in 1970.

Gift of Samuel and Esther Sarick, 1989   89/643

John Kavik (Canadian, b. 1897)

Mother and Child c.1973
Grey stone. 12.5 x 11.0 x 5.0

The intensity of the harsh but rewarding life Kavik experienced out on the land prior to settlement life is manifested in his art. His method is to energetically saw, drill and file front, back and sides. The intense works that result are most concerned with bold shapes with little detail. Hands and feet are barely defined, if not omitted outright. A file slash separates nose and mouth; eyes are roughly drilled. Except for some of the early works, Kavik's sculptures are not highly finished, resulting in a gaunt, stark quality responsible for much of the pieces' directness and poignancy. The mother, indicated by the extended hood of the woman's parka that Kavik is careful to define, holds her child in front of her. With great economy Kavik uses two parallel grooves to indicate the arms that envelop the child, binding him to the mother. It is a unique vision and one that Kavik continues to share into his nineties.

Gift of the Klamer family, 1978   78/413

Mark Tungilik (Canadian, 1913-86)

Scene c.1982
Grey-green stone, ivory, baleen, copper, black pigment.
18.1 x 33.6 x 10.3

Miniatures, particularly in ivory, have been a feature of Inuit art since prehistoric times.
More recently, this tradition has characterized the art of Repulse Bay and Pelly Bay,
the community where Tungilik was born and where, as a teenager, he first began to
carve elaborate composite pieces such as dog teams that featured ivory harnesses. An
eye operation late in life halted the deterioration of his eyesight and allowed him again
to produce small detailed works, some less than a centimetre in size.

This is a major piece for Tungilik and shows many features of his work – a preference for situating his carved figures in a setting, usually to enhance realism; the use of
stone as a supporting base for ivory figures; fully carved human figures complete with
well-defined facial features; and a reference to spiritual beliefs, in this case, a tableau
of low-relief animal carvings that can be read as an invocation for abundance of food. The
spiritual element is heightened by the images of a musk-ox and polar bear emerging from
the top of the stone arch to serve perhaps as illustrations of spirit helpers. Although
a Christian, like many Inuit, this artist does not disregard traditional beliefs.

Gift of Samuel and Esther Sarick, 1989   89/671

Index of Artists

Colophon

Editor: Catherine Van Baren
Design: Bruce Mau
Design Associates: Alison Hahn and
Nigel Smith
Production Manager: Alan Terakawa
Film and Print Coordinator: Guy Poulin
Typeset by Archetype in Perpetua,
Plantin and Alpha Gothic
Colour Separations: Quadraceps Ltd.
Printed in Canada by Bradbury
Tamblyn & Boorne Ltd. on Warren
Cameo Dull and Mohawk Superfine
Bookbinding: Beck Bindery
Service Ltd.
Photography: Art Gallery of Ontario,
Photographic Services

Front Cover: adaptation of Michael
Snow's *Atlantic*, 1967 (see page 381
for work in its entirety), reproduced
courtesy of the artist; inside front
cover: adaptation of Henry Moore's
*Working Model for Three Way
Piece No. 2: Archer*, 1964 (see page
228), reproduced by kind permission
of The Henry Moore Foundation;
inside back cover: adaptation of
Robert Rauschenberg's *Story*,
1964 (see page 320); and back cover:
adaptation of Eustache Le Sueur's
The Raising of Tabitha, c. 1640/45
(see page 99).